Thomas Alfred Walker

Manual of Public International Law

Thomas Alfred Walker

Manual of Public International Law

ISBN/EAN: 9783337233419

Printed in Europe, USA, Canada, Australia, Japan

Cover: Foto ©Suzi / pixelio.de

More available books at **www.hansebooks.com**

A MANUAL

OF

PUBLIC INTERNATIONAL LAW.

London: C. J. CLAY AND SONS,
CAMBRIDGE UNIVERSITY PRESS WAREHOUSE,
AVE MARIA LANE,

AND

STEVENS AND SONS, LIMITED,
119 AND 120, CHANCERY LANE,
LAW PUBLISHERS AND BOOKSELLERS.

Leipzig: F. A. BROCKHAUS.
New York: MACMILLAN AND CO.

A MANUAL

OF

PUBLIC INTERNATIONAL LAW

BY

THOMAS ALFRED WALKER, M.A., LL.D.

FELLOW AND LECTURER OF PETERHOUSE, CAMBRIDGE.

CAMBRIDGE:
AT THE UNIVERSITY PRESS.
1895

𝕮𝖆𝖒𝖇𝖗𝖎𝖉𝖌𝖊:

PRINTED BY J. & C. F. CLAY,

AT THE UNIVERSITY PRESS.

PREFACE.

IN the course of work as College Lecturer in Cambridge I have on many occasions been asked to recommend for the use of students commencing to read Public International Law some text-book which, whilst excluding unnecessary detail and mere theoretic discussion, might well serve as a fairly comprehensive general introduction to detailed study of the subject. No English treatise which has fallen into my hands fully satisfying the conditions which I should require in such a book, I have in this volume attempted to supply the need. I am moreover not without hope that its pages may be found not altogether devoid of interest by some few other readers who, lacking the time or the opportunity to pursue the subject into detail, would yet desire to have some definite knowledge on certain all-important rules by which the conduct of nations is practically guided.

The references, which are almost exclusively confined to reported cases actually decided in British and American Courts, will enable those so disposed to extend their reading into the wider field of original authority.

T. A. WALKER.

PETERHOUSE,
CAMBRIDGE, *February* 12, 1895.

CONTENTS.

PART I.

INTRODUCTION.

CHAPTER I.

DEFINITION OF INTERNATIONAL LAW.

PART II.

INTERNATIONAL LAW OF NORMAL RELATIONS (PEACE).

CHAPTER I.

EQUALITY OF STATES.

CHAPTER II.

THE RULE OF NON-INTERVENTION.

CHAPTER III.

THE DELIMITATION OF DOMINION.

CHAPTER IV.

MEANS OF INTERNATIONAL REDRESS.

PART III.

INTERNATIONAL LAW OF ABNORMAL RELATIONS.
(a) WAR.

CHAPTER I.

THE COMMENCEMENT OF WAR. THE TESTS OF BELLIGERENT CHARACTER.

CHAPTER II.

LEGAL EFFECTS OF THE OUTBREAK OF WAR.

CHAPTER III.

SANCTIONS OF THE LAWS OF WAR.

CHAPTER IV.

TERMINATION OF WAR.

PART IV.

INTERNATIONAL LAW OF ABNORMAL RELATIONS.
(β) NEUTRALITY.

CHAPTER I.

NEUTRALITY WITHIN THE SPHERE OF DIRECT STATE ACTION.

CHAPTER II.

NEUTRALITY WITHIN THE SPHERE OF STATE PREVENTION.

W. c

CHAPTER III.

NEUTRALITY WITHIN THE SPHERE OF INDIVIDUAL ACTION.

INDEX OF CASES.

SOME ABBREVIATIONS USED IN REFERENCE.

Acton	Acton's Reports
B. & A.	Barnewall and Alderson's Reports ... K. B. 1817–22
B. & C.	Barnewall and Creswell's Reports ... K. B. 1822–30
B. & P.	Bosanquet and Puller's Reports... C. P. 1796–1804
B. & S.	Best and Smith's Reports ... ... Q. B. 1861–70
Bell, C. C. ...	Bell's Crown Cases 1858–60
Black.	W. Blackstone's Reports ... ... C. P. 1746–79
Black	Black's Reports ... ... U. S., Supreme Court
Blatch. Pr. Ca.	Blatchford's Prize Cases ...U.S., District of N. York
Burr.	Burrow's Reports... ... ... K. B. 1756–72
C. & P.	{Carrington and Payne's Reports} ... K. B. & C. P. 1823–41
Camp.	Campbell's Reports ... ... K. B. & C. P. 1807–18
Cl. & F.	Clark and Finnelly's Reports ...H. of Lords 1831–46
Cl. & F., H. L. C.	{Clark and Finnelly's Reports, House of Lords Cases}
Cranch	Cranch's Reports ... U. S., Supreme Court, 1801–15
C. Rob.	Christopher Robinson's Admiralty Reports, 1798–1808
D. & B., C. C. R.	Dearsly and Bell, Crown Cases Reserved... 1856–58
Dall.	Dallas' Reports ...U. S., Supreme Court, –1800
Den.	Denison's Crown Cases Reserved 1844–52
Dods.	Dodson's Admiralty Reports 1811–22
D. & E.	Durnford and East's Reports ... K. B. 1785–1800
Dougl.	Douglas' Reports ... ... K. B. 1778–81
E. & B.	Ellis and Blackburn's Reports ... ... Q. B. 1852–58
Edwards... ...	Edwards' Admiralty Reports 1808–12
F. & F.	Foster and Finlason's Reports ... Nisi Prius 1856–67
Gall.	Gallison's Reports ... ... U. S., 1st Circuit
H. & M.	Hemming and Miller's Reports... Chancery 1862–65
How.	Howard's Reports... U. S., Supreme Court, 1843–54
John.	Johnson's Reports ...New York S. Court, 1806–23
John. & Hem.	{Johnson and Hemming's Reports} ... ... Chancery, 1859–62
Kelynge	Kelynge's Reports ... ... K. B. Temp. Chas. II.
L. & C.	Leigh and Cave's Crown Cases Reserved... 1861–65
L. J.	Law Journal Reports.
L. J. N. S. ...	„ „ „ New Series 1832–

Ld. Raym.	...	Lord Raymond's Reports ... K. B. & C. P. 1694–1732
L. R.	... ...	Law Reports.
	App. Ca.	Appellate Cases.
	A. & E....	Admiralty and Ecclesiastical.
	Chan. D.	Chancery Division.
	C. C. R.	Crown Cases Reserved.
	Exch. D.	Exchequer Division.
	P. C. ...	Privy Council Cases.
	Prob. D.	Probate Division.
	Q. B. ...	Queen's Bench.
Marsh.	... ...	Marshall's Reports ... ... C. P. 1813–16
Mass.	... ...	Massachusetts Reports.
M. & S.	... ...	Maule and Selwyn's Reports ... ... K. B. 1813–17
Mood. C. C.	...	Moody's Crown Cases 1824–44
Moore P. C. C.		Moore's Privy Council Cases.
Paine	... ...	Paine's Reports ... ... U. S., 2nd Circuit
Pet.	... ...	Peters' Reports ... U. S., Supreme Court, 1828–42
Q. B.	... ...	Queen's Bench Reports.
Rep.	... ...	Coke's Reports.
Russ. & Myl.	...	Russell and Mylne's Reports.
Snow	... ...	Snow's Cases and Opinions on Internat. Law, 1893
St. Tr.	... ...	State Trials.
T. Raym.	...	Sir T. Raymond's Reports ... ... {K. B., C. P. & Ex. / Temp. Chas. II.
Taunt.	... ...	Taunton's Reports ... ... C. P. 1807–19
U. S. R.	... ...	United States Reports.
Ves.	... ...	Vesey's Reports ... ... Chancery, 1746–55
Ves. Jr.	... ...	Vesey (Junior)'s Reports ... Chancery, 1789–1817
Wall.	... ...	Wallace's Reports... ... ... U. S., Supreme Court
Whart. Dig.	...	{Wharton's Digest of the International Law of the / United States.
Wheat.	... ...	Wheaton's Reports ... U. S., Supreme Court, 1816–27

ERRATA.

p. 13, in marginal references, *for* principles *read* principle.
p. 16, in marginal references, *for* Sparks *read* Spinks.
p. 31, line 11, *for* Brussels *read* Berlin.
p. 77, in marginal references, *to* The Charkieh, L. R. *add* 4 A. & E. 59.
p. 167, line 15, *for* Charlestown *read* Charleston.

A MANUAL
OF PUBLIC INTERNATIONAL LAW.

PART I.

CHAPTER I.

DEFINITION OF INTERNATIONAL LAW.

§ 1. **International Law consists in those rules of conduct** Definition. **which civilised States observe in their relations with one another and with one another's subjects.**

A State may be defined as the *union of a determinable* What is a *territory with a determinable people combined politically, that* State? *people enjoying independence from habitual external human control.* A community becomes entitled to the name of a State when it becomes possessed of certain clearly marked characteristics, when it becomes possessed of (1) a determinable territory, (2) a regular government, and (3) independence; it retains its state-character so long as these remain reasonably intact. State-being is, in a word, a simple historic fact. But while the possession or non-possession of state-character by a community is a mere matter of fact, and in strictness accordingly such possession is *per se* ₁ Wharton, *Dig.* 535. sufficient to establish the status of the community, and to bring it to the gates of the International Circle, without any formal act of acknowledgment on the part of previously established states, formal recognition by such states con- Hall, *Int. Law*, II. 1, stitutes the best evidence of the actual acquisition of the § 26. status.

W.   1

1 Wharton,
Dig. 531.

Recognition of this order, known as *Recognition of Independence*, may be accorded in various ways, by the negotiation of a treaty, by the interchange of ambassadors and the like. The method is of little moment. But recognition of independence in some form must necessarily precede, or be combined with, the admission of a new state into the International Circle, that is, into the regular society of civilised states.

Such re-
cognition
must not
be pre-
maturely
accorded.

A parent state may be trusted not to precipitate such a recognition. That there may be more necessity for the restraint of law in the case of recognition by a third Power was abundantly shown by the action of President Taylor in

President
Taylor's
First Annual
Message,
1849.
Wharton,
Dig. § 47.

1849 in investing an agent, despatched to Hungary for the purpose of making inquiries as to the progress of the insurrection there, with power to declare the willingness of the United States promptly to recognise the independence of the Hungarians in the event of their ability to sustain it.

Premature
recogni-
tion by
foreign
powers
is an
interna-
tional
offence
against
the parent
State.
1 Wharton,
Dig. 532.
Diaries and
Corresp. of
Lord
Malmes-
bury, ii.
pp. 36, 37.
Rush,
Residence at
the Court of
London, i.
chap. i.
Stapleton,
Life of
Canning,
ii. chap. viii.
1 Wharton,
Dig. 529.
Memoirs of
the Earl of
Liverpool,
p. 368.

Premature recognition by a third Power of the independence of insurgents can only be regarded as an illegitimate interference in the contest and an inimical act towards the mother-state which may well be resented by war. England was quick to resent anything in the nature of a recognition of the independence of the United States before the ratification of the definitive treaty of peace. She herself refused to recognise the independence of the revolted South American Colonies of Spain until 1825, though the rebellion broke out in 1810, the cause of Spain was almost from the outset hopeless, and all substantial struggle had long been over when Canning followed the example of the United States, and "called the New World into existence to redress the balance of the Old" by recognising the South American Republic as "independent of French Spain." There is a stage in such contests," wrote Mr J. Q. Adams in 1816, "when the party struggling for independence has, as I conceive, a right to demand its acknowledgment by neutral parties, and when the acknowledgment may be granted

without departure from the obligations of neutrality. It is
the stage when the independence is established as matter of
fact, so as to leave the chance of the opposite party to
recover their dominion utterly desperate. The neutral must,
of course, judge for itself when this period has arrived; and
as the belligerent nation has the same right to judge for
itself, it is very likely to judge differently from the neutral,
and to make it a cause or pretext for war, as Great Britain
did expressly against France in our Revolution, and substantially against Holland. If war thus results, in point of
fact, from the measure of recognising a contested independence, the moral right or wrong of the war depends upon the
justice and sincerity and prudence with which the recognising nation took the step."

Adopting the definition of a State before given, it is
possible to lay down certain simple propositions definitive of
the character of International Law.

(1) *International Law is the code of states and of communities to which has been accorded recognition of belligerency.*

With the proceedings of states *inter se* International
Law has alone to do. International Law takes no note of the
proceedings of gipsy peoples wandering through the world
without any settled home : it may look with friendly eyes on
nomadic tribes possessing a certain political cohesion and
roaming within fixed limits; but the least that it requires
of applicants for its protection is the combination of reasonably fixed territorial boundaries with a reasonably efficient and
responsible government and habitual freedom from external
human control. It is the code of nations acting by and
through their Governments, not of individuals uncontrolled :
the individual is restrained and protected by International
Law, but he is so restrained and protected, not as an individual, but as a member of a recognised state. International
Law depends for its effective operation on the solidarity of
peoples and the direct responsibility of their Governments.

Marginal notes:
Mr Adams to President Monroe, Aug. 24, 1816. 1 Wharton, Dig. 521.

(1) International Law is the code of States

1—2

With states may be classed communities to which has

and of recognised insurgent belligerent communities.

been granted recognition of belligerency. By recognition of belligerency a revolted community, struggling to attain by force of arms to actual independence, is accorded temporarily the treatment of a belligerent state. The grant of such recognition is founded on practical convenience and the call of humanity.

So long as insurrection is confined within reasonable limits and the forces of the Government are manifestly adequate for the purpose of its suppression, foreign Powers are able, and are entitled, to look to that Government for redress in respect of injuries to their subjects or property arising out of the struggle; and that Government in turn is entitled to proceed, and must proceed, against the rebels by municipal force. But when a rebellion has reached such proportions that it would be at once manifestly impracticable for the parent Government to treat all persons engaged in it as traitors or mere seditious rioters, and manifestly impossible to hold the parent Government responsible for the action of the insurgents, the parent Government may elect to recognise the belligerency of the revolters, whereby, while undertaking to treat those revolters as public enemies, it purges itself from all responsibility towards third Powers in

Effect of recognition of belligerency.

1 Wharton *Dig.* 519.

respect of their proceedings. Recognition of belligerency has thus a two-fold effect; (1) it confers certain rights and imposes certain corresponding obligations upon the insurgent community, (2) it releases the parent Government from certain prior obligations and confers upon it certain new rights. Even if the parent Government be unwilling to accord such recognition foreign Powers may under certain circumstances feel compelled to grant it. Their action will be justified

Circumstances justifying recognition of belligerency on the part of a foreign Power.

(a) If there be an actual armed struggle still continuing and likely to continue: that is, a real tangible revolt coupled with no manifest probability of its early suppression;

(b) If the insurgents be possessed of certain easily recognisable belligerent characteristics: if they command a determinable area of territory, obey an organised and responsible Government, and carry on the contest with regular armed forces which observed the ordinary laws of war; and, lastly,

(c) If, by local contiguity or otherwise, the interests of the recognising community are so involved in the proceedings of the insurgents as to compel it to take action. It is for each foreign State to consider in view of a civil war at what period these circumstances in its regard unite.

These principles find their best illustration in the circumstances of the recognition by Great Britain of the belligerency of the Confederate States. When that recognition was accorded, (1) six Southern States had, after declaring by formal Acts their secession from the United States, met in session by their representatives at Montgomery, and there declared the establishment of a new confederation, the union of "the Confederate States of North America," constituted a provisional Government with regularly organised executive, military and judicial departments, and elected Jefferson Davis provisional President; (2) measures had been taken by those States and others to raise an army of 100,000 men for the support of the cause of Secession, and plans laid and money voted for the creation of a navy to cruise against Northern commerce; (3) an army of 75,000 men had been called out in the North for the forcible reduction of the seceding States; (4) the struggle had actually begun by the bombardment of Fort Sumter by the Confederate forces, and President Lincoln's proclamation of the blockade of the whole Southern seaboard. Not only was there an armed struggle, but the greatest of civil wars in the history of the world had sprung forth from the parent brain, "a Minerva in the full panoply of war." Further, (5) the struggle so begun had reached the sea, thereby deeply affecting the interests of all maritime and trading communities, and (6) British interests were involved to a colossal extent in the industry and commerce of the Southern States.

The British recognition of the belligerency of the Confederate States (1861) was completely justified by the circumstances.

Mr Justice Grier in *Prize Cases*, 2 Black 665.

The British recognition was accorded by Her Majesty's Proclamation of Neutrality which appeared on May 14, 1861.

"This proclamation was published fourteen days after the receipt in London of the news that Fort Sumter had been reduced by bombardment, that the President of the United States had called out 75,000 men, and that Mr Jefferson Davis had taken measures for issuing letters of marque; twelve days after receipt of intelligence that President Lincoln had published a proclamation of blockade; nine days after a copy of that proclamation had been received from Her Britannic Majesty's consul at New York; and three days after the same proclamation had been officially communicated to Her Majesty's Secretary of State for Foreign Affairs by the U. S. Minister, Mr Dallas."

Papers relating to the Treaty of Washington, t. 218.

The United States Government complained, and continued to complain, in unmeasured terms of the action of Earl Russell, but that action was endorsed by other great civilised Powers, and received then, and has since received, the approval of general competent opinion. The course pursued by the British Government, says Mr Boyd, is "not only justified by having been followed by all the chief maritime states, but was under the circumstances the only proper course."

Wheaton's Elements, 1. 2 § 27 c.

Form of recognition unimportant. The form by which recognition is granted is a matter of little moment, if the fact of the grant be perfectly clear. The most approved method in the case of recognition by a foreign Power is by the issue of a Neutrality Proclamation, a method adopted by the European Powers who recognised the belligerency of the Confederate States.

When once granted, recognition cannot be withdrawn at will. Recognition once accorded cannot be withdrawn, without express agreement to that effect, so long as the condition of affairs remains unaltered, since the grant may have established legal relations with third parties which could not be permitted to depend on the arbitrary will of the recognising Power.

(2) *International Law is the code of civilised states.* The possession of a certain civilisation is not incompatible with exclusion from the inner pale of International Law.

Civilisation is a complex fact, the combination of advance with order, the condition, in brief, of a progressive society. The term is purely relative. The least progressive of peoples which have cast off barbarism possesses some spark of civilisation, and, when once such a people becomes possessed of the essential characteristics of a state, it must necessarily adopt some rules of international dealing; and those rules represent its international law. But in practice certain states, which have attained to a higher level of civilisation, are accustomed to regard themselves as constituting an exclusive International Circle, admission into which can only be obtained by some form of regular recognition, and the collection of the rules which these adopt in their mutual dealings is the International Law of the jurist. The moral and material regeneration of barbarous peoples is a matter to which civilised states might well address themselves, and to their duty in this respect, as recent events show, these states are fortunately not now entirely oblivious. But it is a duty which is in strictness *dehors* the dictates of International Law. International Law, if it is to be at once definite and reasonably progressive, must cut adrift from the practice of laggard nations. A community becomes a state when it becomes possessed of certain clearly marked characteristics : it becomes an international person when, possessing those characteristics, it makes known alike its ability and its intention to reasonably approximate its international conduct to the demands of the highest civilisation.

The possession of political independence and the recognition of that independence by foreign Powers may thus long precede the admission of the state within the International Circle. It was only when the Turkish Power had ceased to be a terror to Europe, and its very decay had become a standing source of international trouble, that in

(2) International Law is the code of civilised states.

What is Civilisation?

International Law is the law of an exclusive circle.

Parl. Papers, Africa. No. 4, 1835, p. 306.

Independence may long precede admission within the circle.

1856 the Porte was formally admitted within the European Concert. China and Japan have been for centuries independent states, but are only now knocking at the entrance gates of the International Circle.

(3) International Law is not "Positive Law" nor even "Proper Law" in the Austinian sense,

(3) *International Law, consisting in rules of conduct which regulate the conduct of independent states inter se, though true law, is not, as law, of the same order as ordinary municipal law.*

A law in the sense of the common lawyer is that which Austin terms a Positive Law, a command or rule imposed by a determinate sovereign to a subject or subjects, and enforceable by a determinate sanction in the case of non-compliance. International Law lacks alike determinate lawgiver, determinate sanction and determinate enforcing court; we have as yet neither regularly and permanently appointed international judge nor permanently appointed international police, and war, the exercise by an indeterminate power of that open force which it should be the prime object of the International lawyer to suppress, is in practice the ultimate sanction upon non-compliance with the dictates of the international code. John Austin and his followers, confining the term "law" to what they style "Proper Law," to rules emanating from and enforced by a determinate lawgiver, refuse the name of "law" altogether to the rules regulating

Clark, *Practical Jurisprudence,* Part I. Walker, *Science of International Law,* chap. I.

the international conduct of independent Governments. This narrow and arbitrary limitation of the term finds no support in history, in philology, or in customary usage, and lies open to the fatal practical objection that it must tend to popularise the notion that the rules of International Law are but of imperfect obligation, and so to encourage international law-

but is real law of an unique character.

lessness. But it remains, nevertheless, a fact that International Law, being the law of independent states, is law of an unique character: it derives its binding authority from the consent of its subjects, from regular observance and from its intrinsic excellence: its basis is not determinate and instant fear, but the voluntary consent of law-abiding and social sentiment, a consent evidenced by actual practice. ~~International Law is law observed, not law emanating from, and enforced by, determinate sanctioning authority.~~

(4) *International Law being based upon the consent of nations as set out in practice, its dictates must be sought in History, the record of practice.*

The authorities of International 'Law are the pages of the historian and his original sources in diplomatic correspondence, treaties and state-papers in general, the reports of international Courts of Arbitration and of municipal courts dealing with international questions, and all other documents which authoritatively set out the course of wars, negotiations, and other international incidents. The pages of the jurist are authoritative only in so far as they contain a true record and correct interpretation of the tendencies of actual historic facts, and express opinions which secure international adoption.

(5) *International Law being the code of modern civilised states, its fundamental notion is the conception of Territorial Sovereignty.*

The explanation of this fact is sufficiently evident. International Law consists in rules of conduct observed by independent states and by communities temporarily endowed with the qualities of independent states; and, just as the conduct of an individual, undirected by the teaching of compelling power, will be the compound result of the natural working of his native moral and physical endowment, and of the action of the external influences of his environment operating thereon, so the main guiding principles of the conduct of independent communities must necessarily be sought in, (1) the natural characteristics of those communities, and (2) the moral influences arising from their surroundings. And the essential characteristic of the modern state is territorial sovereignty. The ruler of antiquity was the head of a people, the chieftain of a tribe, or he preferred a claim to universal dominion, to world sovereignty, but the modern state is a society which possesses

(4) International Law consisting in rules practised, its authorities are the records of practice.

(5) The fundamental conception of modern International Law is that of Territorial Sovereignty.

Maine, *Ancient Law*, p. 103. Wharton, *Dig.* § 1.

sovereignty, that is, combines governing power with independence, within certain geographical limits. Territorial sovereignty is the one primary and all essential framework · of modern State-being. On the lines of territorial sovereignty, therefore, must be constructed any historically sound system of International Law.

The progress of International Law is assured by moral influences, working particularly through the interdependence of civilised states. But while territorial sovereignty must constitute the skeleton framework of International Law, the living and progressive element must be sought in living human influences. Modern states are indeed independent, but they are also interdependent. While nations recognise the conception of territorial sovereignty as containing the main general principles of their just mutual dealings, they are, as being composed of men, obnoxious to external moral influences: in a word, nations are moral entities, and enlightened self-interest playing its part in the field of international intercourse, by the needs of that intercourse, if not by the operation of the forces of pure benevolence, the strict principles of territorial sovereignty and its corollaries must be at times affected and relaxed. The progressive improvement of human nature necessarily involves the progressive development of International Law.

PART II.

INTERNATIONAL LAW OF NORMAL RELATIONS (PEACE).

CHAPTER I.

EQUALITY OF STATES.

§ 2. The international legal relations of States in the time of Peace are mainly regulated by three rules which are derived from the fundamental conception of Territorial Sovereignty.

From the conception of territorial sovereignty may be derived naturally and clearly three broad principles, viz. :—

I. All States are formally equal.

II. No State may legally interfere in the purely internal affairs of another State.

III. Territory and Jurisdiction are coextensive.

These principles constitute the three great general rules of the Public International Law of Peace.

The general principles of Public International Law derived from the idea of Territorial Sovereignty.

RULE I. ALL STATES ARE FORMALLY EQUAL.

§ 3. "All Sovereign States are equal in the eye of International Law, whatever may be their relative power."

The applicability of this doctrine to modern international relations has been lately challenged on the ground that it conflicts with the present general acknowledgment of the Primacy of certain Great Powers in the field of European politics. The Primacy of the Great Powers is indeed an accepted fact. The four Powers, Great Britain, Austria, Prussia and Russia, having been drawn into close alliance

All sovereign states are equal in status,

Wheaton, Elements, I. 2 § 33.

Lawrence, Essays on Modern International Law, Essay V.

though not equal in power.

The
Primacy
of the
Great
Powers

Hertslet,
*Map of
Europe*, 1.
564—574.

to resist the advances of Revolutionary France and the ambition of Napoleon, found it necessary, after the successful termination of the struggle, to admit their late adversary to their councils, and at the Congress of Aix-la-Chapelle in 1818, accordingly, were laid the hitherto abiding foundations of the Concert of Europe. By secret protocol signed on November 15, 1818, the Five Powers agreed to an union for " the maintenance of the treaties and the support of the rights established by them." "If," ran the terms of the agreement, " to attain these ends the Powers which have concurred in the present act should deem it necessary to establish different reunions, either among the sovereigns themselves or their ministers, to treat of subjects in which they have a common interest, the time and place of such assemblages shall be previously arranged by diplomatic communications; and in the event of such reunions having for their object the condition of other states in Europe, they shall not take place except in pursuance of a formal invitation to those by whom these states are directed, and under an express reservation of their right to participate directly or by their representatives."

Hertslet,
*Map of
Europe*,
1. 572.

This agreement has been singularly fertile of result. Congress after Congress has been held in Europe, and the map of the Continent has largely changed under the sanction of the Great Powers. Greece and Belgium, Servia and Roumania owe their present legal being to the European Concert, while the Turk himself has remained in Constantinople by force of the same influence. It may be that this Concert "is probably destined to become more and more effective as the desire for a peaceful settlement of their quarrels increases among the nations, and it may in some far distant time develope into that Supreme Court of International Appeal for which statesmen, philosophers and divines have longed throughout the last three centuries," but at present, although the various states of the world are notoriously unequal in point of actual force, and although

T. J.
Lawrence,
Essay I.

authority in the councils of the world is equally notoriously apt to be dependent on the force behind the counsellor, independent states are equal before the law. Independence, if it is independence, is freedom from external control. All true states are equally independent, and equally entitled to the respect and courtesy implied in territorial sovereignty. When the independence of the smaller state is so overshadowed by the power of a stronger neighbour, or of a body of stronger neighbours, that the action of the smaller is habitually controlled by the will of the stronger, the separate territorial sovereignty of the smaller is at an end, and with it the field of International Law. *will not seriously affect the principles, so long as the smaller states remain habitually independent.*

The formal equality of states is capable of simple illustrations:

(a) *International status resting on state-character is independent of historical origin.* *International status is independent of historical origin.*

States commonly come into being either by process of disruption or by process of union, that is either by the severance of an older state into smaller societies, as in the case of the movement which undid the work of the Congress of Vienna and created the modern Belgian Kingdom and the Kingdom of the Netherlands, or by the union of smaller communities into a larger whole, as in the case of the modern Kingdom of Italy. In rare instances, there have come into existence what may be considered original communities, for example, Liberia and the Congo Free State; but, when once it has been regularly admitted into the circle of States, the origin of the society is internationally of absolutely no legal importance. *See Parl. Papers, Africa. No. 4, 1835.*

(b) *International status resting on state-character is independent of constitutional form.* *International status is independent of constitutional form.*

The government of a state may be of any one of multifarious forms: it may be despotic, aristocratic or democratic. By such variations state-being is entirely unaffected. And so too international status. Crowned heads have been wont in time past to contest the *pas* among themselves and to

claim for their delegates a ceremonial preeminence over the
Wheaton,
I. 3.
representatives of republics, but republics have on their
part always jealously asserted their equality as independent
entities with monarchic communities, and to-day the equality
of all independent states with regard to their form of
government cannot be called in question. The international
· person is the community, not the temporary director of its
destinies. The being or identity of a state is accordingly in
no whit affected by internal constitutional changes. The
character of the government is a matter for the decision of
the nation : for the outside world it is legally sufficient that
there be *some* regular form of responsible government. "It
1 Wharton,
Dig. 521.
accords with our principles," wrote Jefferson in 1792, "to
acknowledge any Government to be rightful which is formed
by the will of the nation, substantially declared." If treaties
entered into by a Government are repudiated by a revolutionary Government by which it is overthrown, third Powers
may in self-defence hesitate to recognise the new rulers, but,
in the main, states are commonly content to adopt such
changes of government as accepted facts with reasonable
1 Wharton,
Dig. 537.
readiness. The France of Carnot and Casimir Périer takes
no lower place in the councils of Europe than did the France
of Napoleon III. or Louis Philippe.

Inter-
national
status is
indepen-
dent of
magnitude
of terri-
tory.
(c) *International status resting on state-character is
independent of magnitude of territory.*

The modern state is indeed essentially territorial : the
Maine,
*Ancient
Law,* p. 103,
Wharton,
Dig. § 1.
ruler of to-day is peculiarly and primarily the ruler of the
soil, and only secondarily of the people. But the reality of
sovereignty is independent of the extent of the domains of
· Hall,
Int. Law,
I. 1, § 2.
the sovereign. Monaco is as truly a state as is Russia or
Great Britain. The being and identity of a state is, accordingly, unaffected by annexation to or partial diminution of
its territory. When the entire territory of a community is
absorbed by another, the personal identity of the absorbed
society is merged into that of the absorbing state, and, when
a community is by some revolutionary event divided into

two or more, in such fashion that no one of the several
fragments can be fairly regarded as representing the former
whole, the original international engagements of that whole
are entirely at an end; but, under ordinary circumstances,
the mere transfer of territory from one community to
another, like the transfer of personal wealth, in no way affects
the national being of the interested bodies. It is sufficient
for the retention of a place within the International
Circle that there should be *some* determinate territory
over which a certain regular government continues to
exercise sway free from the direction of foreign control.

(*d*) *International status resting on state-character is
independent of treaty obligations, so long as independence be
preserved.*

A community may by treaty with another deprive itself
as regards that other of unfettered freedom of action, and
so by its own act deprive itself of one or more of the recognised privileges of the ordinary state. Russia agreed at
Paris in 1856 to refrain from establishing military and
maritime arsenals on her Black Sea shores, and Turkey has
by capitulation with various Powers declined in favour of
their own sovereigns jurisdiction over Frankish residents in
her dominions; in neither case was there the least abdication
of sovereign character.

Thus a weak state may by treaty place itself under the
protection of a stronger without yielding up its state-being.

The Ionian islands were placed under the protectorate of
Great Britain by treaty signed at Paris, between Great
Britain and Austria and Russia and Prussia, on November
5, 1815. They were thereby constituted "a single free and
independent state," by the name of "the United States of
the Ionian Islands," their government being vested in a
British Lord High-Commissioner and a Legislative Assembly,
who were entrusted by the treaty with the drafting of a
Constitutional Charter, subject to the ratification of the
King of Great Britain in Council. Great Britain was em-

Inter-
national
status is
indepen-
dent of
treaty
obliga-
tion,

provided
indepen-
dence be
preserved.
Wharton,
Dig. § 68 *a*.

(i) The
protected
State.

powered to occupy and garrison the fortresses of the islands, and the military force of the "United States" was placed under the orders of the British Commander-in-chief. The trading flag of the Islands was recognised by the contracting parties to the treaty as that of a free and independent state, but their ports and harbours were, with respect to honorary and military rights, declared within British jurisdiction, and none but commercial agents or consuls charged solely with the carrying on of commercial relations were to be accredited to the Islands by foreign Powers. Under the Constitutional Charter of the Islands passed by the Legislative Assembly on May 2, 1817, the British Consuls in all foreign ports were constituted the commercial agents of the Ionian Islands, and all applications necessary to be made by the "United States" to foreign Powers were ordered to be transmitted by the Senate to the Lord High-Commissioner, to be by him sent to the British minister at the Court of the foreign Power.

In spite of the closeness of the bond thus drawn between the Ionian Islands and Great Britain, the separate identity of the Ionian Republic was held to be maintained intact, and during the Crimean War the neutrality of that Republic was expressly acknowledged by the British Courts.

In 1864 the Ionian Islands were transferred to and absorbed into the Kingdom of Greece. Europe, however, still possesses examples of the protected state in the petty societies of Andorra and San Marino.

(ii) The State under suzerainty.

Somewhat different is the position of a state under suzerainty. "A member of a confederation or a protected state is *primâ facie* independent, and consequently possesses all rights which it has not expressly resigned; a state under the suzerainty of another, being confessedly part of another state, has those rights only which have been expressly granted to it, and the assumption of larger powers of external action than those which have been distinctly conceded to it is an act of rebellion against the sovereign."

L. Hertslet, *Treaties*, I. p. 45.

Ibid. I. p. 53.

The "Leucade." Sparks 237. SPINKS

• Hall, *Int. Law*, I. 1, § 4.

If a state enter into one or other of the forms of alliance (iii) The federal union. known as federal unions or confederations, the union will affect the being and international position of the state · exactly in so far as it goes in fact to affect its independence. Unions of this order are commonly half-way houses to closer unions, but may be mere temporary expedients to be brought to an end by new severance. The German Confederation was, for example, dissolved in 1866 by the events of ·the Seven Weeks' War, while, on the other hand, the events of 1870 set the seal of success on the statesmanship of Bismarck by placing the crown of a more closely united Germany on the brows of King William. By the nature of the federal bond must in each case be tested the fate of the state-being of the members of the alliance. Such an union as that existing between Hanover and Great Britain from the accession of George I. to the death of William IV. was a mere permanent alliance of two states under a common hereditary ruler, a *personal union*. The union between Austria and Hungary is of a closer character, a *real union :* while closest of all is such an union as that between England and Scotland since 1706, the state-being of each state being absorbed into that of the larger Great Britain.

(e) *International status resting on state-character is independent of merely transitory events.*

International status is independent of temporary events.

A nation may yield a chance or temporary obedience to the dictates of superior external force without forfeiting its state-character. The state-character of France, for example, remained unaffected by the foreign occupations of 1815 and · 1870. Independent state-being only ceases when obedience to foreign direction becomes a habit. State-character and therefore the place within the Circle remains if there be some regular form of government exercising sway in some determinable territory free from *habitual* external human control.

Import-
ance of
punc-
tiliousness
in inter-
national
courtesy.

§ 4. **Independence in fact, being the main foundation of international status and so the palladium of the state, any action on the part of a foreign Power which tends to impair or call in question that independence affords matter for just international resentment.**

It is this fact that lends importance to the seemingly trivial formalities of international etiquette, raises to the level of imperial questions the petty details of court ceremonial and the courtesies of the flag of war, and in a great degree condones the conduct of the parties to many historic scenes of disgraceful wrangling. No matter, it would appear from history, is too trivial to be created into a point of national honour, and to be made the occasion of fierce dispute.

Diplo-
matic pre-
cedence.

By an arrangement signed on March 19, 1815, by the representatives of the eight great states assembled in Congress at Vienna, diplomatic characters were for purposes of precedence arranged in three classes, and ranked in their respective classes according to the date of the official notification of their arrival. The three classes were (1) that of Ambassadors, Legates or Nuncios, (2) that of Envoys, Ministers or other persons accredited to Sovereigns, (3) that of Chargés d'affaires accredited only to the Ministers for Foreign Affairs. The plenipotentiaries at Aix-la-Chapelle on November 21, 1818, added the class of Resident Ministers accredited to Sovereigns, with rank superior to the class of Chargés d'affaires.

Hertslet,
*Map of
Europe*, I.
pp. 62, 3.

Hertslet,
*Map of
Europe*, I.
p. 575.

These conventions have, it is to be trusted, effectually removed one fertile source of ancient dispute. Want of care may, however, easily supply new material for national irritation.

CHAPTER II.

THE RULE OF NON-INTERVENTION.

RULE II. NO STATE MAY LEGALLY INTERFERE IN THE PURELY INTERNAL AFFAIRS OF ANOTHER STATE.

§ 5. "C'est une conséquence manifeste de la liberté et de l'indépendance des Nations, que toutes sont en droit de se gouverner comme elles le jugent à propos, et qu'aucune n'a le moindre droit de se mêler au gouvernement d'une autre." Intervention is *primâ facie* illegal, Vattel, I p. 286.

This doctrine, though of very recent growth, represents a well accepted principle of modern International Law. Various excuses have been and are, indeed, urged in justification of special acts of departure from the main rule. These can hardly be well considered apart from the circumstances of their particular application. But it is possible to lay down certain broad generalisations as possessing sufficient support in practice to be regarded as sound canons of legitimacy. but may be justified by special circumstances.

§ 6. (a.) The fulfilment of the duties of friendship, whether natural or supported by express treaty, may constitute a sound justification for intervention to protect against foreign force, but not for interference in merely internal affairs. The duty of friendship may justify intervention to protect against foreign force.

Any state may, it is clear, assist a neighbour in the preservation of its independence, and may enter into a treaty of alliance with it or with other states for the same lawful purpose. The strong may protect the weaker against unjust foreign force.

2—2

The British intervention in Portugal, 1826.

John IV. of Portugal died in March 1826, leaving as his heir his eldest son Don Pedro, then Emperor of Brazil. The Brazilians having provided by law that their crown should never be worn by the sovereign of their mother country, Don Pedro cast in his lot with his South American dominions, and resigned the Portuguese succession in favour of his infant daughter, Donna Maria. A Regency was accordingly established in Portugal in the name of the young Queen, and a representative Constitution was set up. Alarmed at the establishment of a liberal form of government in its neighbourhood, the Spanish Cabinet did not hesitate openly to countenance the designs of Don Miguel, the brother of Pedro, who had been disappointed in his claims on the Regency, and whose schemes were favoured by the Portuguese Queen Dowager. Portuguese deserters and rebels accordingly found a refuge on Spanish soil and there matured their plans for a revolution. The Portuguese ambassador appealed for aid to Great Britain. The request was at once acceded to. Canning, in a circular addressed to the representatives of foreign Powers at the Court of London, justified the sending of British troops to Portugal on the ground of the duties of friendship to an ancient ally, the faith of treaties[1], and the prevention of the outbreak of war in the Peninsula. "His Majesty," he said, "disclaims the right, and abjures the intention of interfering in the internal concerns of any nation. But His Majesty will not endure that foreign force or foreign intrigue shall introduce confusion and Civil War into a country with which Great Britain has been for centuries in relations of the strictest amity and alliance, and whose government has not given any just cause of offence, either to Spain or to any other Power." The British force despatched to Portugal, landing at Lisbon on Christmas day, 1826, was received with a

Memoirs of the Earl of Liverpool, p. 644.

Its justification by Canning considered :—

Hertslet, *Map of Europe,* 1. p. 760.

---

[1] Treaties between Great Britain and Portugal of 1661, 1703, 1714—5 and 1815; Hertslet, *Map of Europe,* 1. p. 760.

popular ovation, and the threatened danger was warded off Abdy's Kent, p. 53. without the firing of a shot.

This incident might be cited in illustration of the action of four distinct occasioning causes for the operation of international friendship, each of which has been more than once independently appealed to in justification of acts of interference.

(1) *The preservation of the rightful succession.* This constituted a constant pretext for intervention in the days of patrimonial principalities. But states can be no longer regarded as patrimonial, and, while against foreign attack a government may doubtless still legitimately assist a neighbouring sovereign, the pretext of the support of a rightfully entitled house will, if a dynasty be assailed or overthrown by purely internal forces, furnish *per se* no good ground for foreign interference. The international person is the nation, not the individual ruler, and to the nation naturally belongs the free choice of its constitution. So long as the disturbance is purely internal, and affects no foreign national interests, so long is intervention based on that disturbance alone internationally illegitimate. The intervention of Prussia in 1787 in support of the House of Orange in Holland, encouraged, if not entirely brought about, though it was by Great Britain, struggling to counteract French intrigues, involved a direct violation of the rights of an independent people. The justification of intervention begins with the needs of self-defence.

1. The preservation of the rightful succession.

Croker Correspondence, II. p. 296. Diaries and Correspondence of the Earl of Malmesbury, Vol. II.

(2) *The execution of a treaty of guarantee.* The same principles which govern acceptance or rejection of the plea of the preservation of the rightful succession must be applied to test the sufficiency of this second pretext.

2. The execution of treaties of guarantee.

One state may enter into a treaty guaranteeing another against foreign interference, such a treaty being in fact merely a special treaty of alliance, but a treaty of guarantee for the support of particular constitutional or other internal arrangements against the efforts of home reformers involves a covert attack on the independence of a free people. A treaty of guarantee against foreign interference is merely superfluous in the presence and in view of the general right possessed by a state to assist its neighbour in the preservation of its independence : a treaty of guarantee is in itself unjustifiable where such a general right cannot be referred to.

3. The restraint of wrongdoing.

(3) *The restraint of wrongdoing.* The dictates of humanity and the duty to protect the weak against oppression have always furnished ready pleas for intervening Powers, but the assumption of international police-powers is the assumption of a dangerous duty. If a state interfere to restrain the unlawful action of a third Power such interference may be well enough, but to justify intervention to protect subjects against the tyranny of their lawful rulers is to throw open a wide door to outrage. The proceedings of the Powers of the " Holy Alliance " demonstrate how numerous are the pitfalls in the path of the sovereign who would perform the duties of an international *custos morum.* Undertaking the functions of an " Areopagus of Europe," Alexander and his allies became at Troppau and Laybach in 1820–21 an alliance for the suppression by armed intervention of all constitutional reform, and under cover of "delivering Europe from the curse of Revolution," united with France, they trode under foot, and for the time utterly quenched, the flame of rising popular liberty in Naples, Piedmont and the Peninsula.

The Holy Alliance and its work.
Hertslet, *Map of Europe*, I. p. 317.
***Diary of Lord Colchester*, III. p. 213.**
Hertslet, *Map of Europe*, I. 658, 667.

The intervention of the Powers in Greece, 1827,

On the other hand, the cause of humanity was undoubtedly really served by that intervention of the Powers which led to the establishment of the modern kingdom of Greece. It was not until after several years of singularly bloody struggle and the enactment of a long series of frightful scenes of horror, when it became evident that the alternative offered to Europe was the independence or the annihilation of the Greeks, that Great Britain, France and Russia agreed to combine their efforts " for the object of reestablishing peace between the contending parties, by means of an arrangement called for, no less by sentiments of humanity, than by interests for the tranquillity of Europe," and the fierce blow struck at Navarino (Oct. 20, 1827) combined with the appearance of a French army in the Morea and the pressure of a Russian war to compel the Porte to agree to accept the conclusions of the Conference of London. The justification for this interposition alleged by the intervening Powers rested on, (1) the necessity of putting a stop to the effusion of blood in a struggle which, while it reduced the Greek provinces and islands to a state of anarchy, daily caused fresh impediments to the commerce of Europe, and gave opportunity for acts of piracy, which not only exposed the subjects of the Powers to grievous losses, but rendered necessary onerous measures of surveillance and suppression, and (2) the earnest invitation of the Greeks addressed to the sovereigns of France and Great Britain. The common sense of civilisation, contemporary and subsequent, approved the action of the three Governments.

Hertslet, Map of Europe, I. 769.

justified by its surrounding circumstances.

(4) *The invitation of the affected state.*

The actual invitation by a distressed government of foreign assistance to cope with internal disturbance does not deprive intervention in pursuance of that invitation of its character of an assault upon national freedom, but, unlike foreign intervention in general, such intervention is not *primâ facie* a hostile act, and is consequently naturally less provocative of general resentment.

4. The invitation of the interested state.

§ 7. (β.) **The requirements of self-defence furnish the only legally sufficient ground for foreign intervention.**

The action of the Powers at Troppau afforded to Lord Castlereagh the opportunity to address to British representatives abroad the famous Circular Despatch in which he laid down with peculiar clearness the general principle which underlies the best practice in the matter of intervention.

Self-defence forms the only sufficient ground for foreign intervention in internal affairs.

This
principle
indicated
by Castle-
reagh
"It should be clearly understood," wrote Castlereagh,
"that no Government can be more prepared than the British
Government is, to uphold the right of any state or states to
interfere, where their own immediate security or essential
interests are seriously endangered by the internal transactions of another state. But, as they regard the assumption of such right, as only to be justified by the strongest
necessity, and to be limited and regulated thereby, they
cannot admit that this right can receive a general and
indiscriminate application to all revolutionary movements,
without reference to their immediate bearing upon some
particular state or states, or be made prospectively the
basis of an alliance. They regard its exercise as an exception to general principles of the greatest value and importance, and as one that only properly grows out of the
circumstances of the special case; but they at the same time
consider that exceptions of this description never can, without the utmost danger, be so far reduced to rule, as to be
incorporated into the ordinary diplomacy of states, or into
the institutes of the Law of Nations."

Circular
Despatch to
British
Missions,
Jan. 19, 1821.
Hertslet,
Map of
Europe,
1. p. 666.

and
Chateau-
briand.
Stapleton's
Life of
Canning, 1.
pp. 268
et seqq.
It was on exactly similar principles that Chateaubriand
in 1823 defended the French intervention in Spain sanctioned by Austria, Prussia and Russia at Verona [1].

"No Government," said Chateaubriand, "has a right to
interfere in the affairs of another Government, except in the
case where the security and immediate interests of the first
Government are compromised."

Halleck,
4, § 7.
Self-defence is indeed to be distinguished from mere
selfishness, but the needs of self-defence constitute the overriding condition of all law.

Interven-
tion in
pursuance
To this rule interventions in pursuance of the decrees of
the European Concert constitute no real exception. No.

---

[1] M. de Villèle, however, in a moment of excitement made the singular
admission in the French Chamber that the French Government had stirred
up insurrection in Spain, "whenever and wherever it was possible."
Stapleton's Life of Canning, 1. p. 261.

special sanctity moral or legal attaches to the resolutions of such a combination: those resolutions are peculiarly valuable merely in so far as the common consent of many states affords convincing *primâ facie* proof of the intrinsic justice of the proceeding resolved upon. Powerful states whether acting alone or in combination are not incapable of injustice, and the number and power of the oppressors does not one whit alter the fact or palliate the oppression. Departures from legal principle are none the less breaches of law albeit the law-breakers may by reason of their colossal force be removed from fear of direct punishment. The partition of Poland was none the less iniquitous because Russia, Prussia and Austria shared in the guilt and divided the spoil, nor was the annexation of Cracow any the less an international crime because the perpetrator was one imperial ruler, and his powerful neighbours winked at the robbery. International Law, it is true, rests upon practice, and, accordingly, whatever rules *do* secure the general adhesion of civilised states must by the lawyer be classed as law. But moral injustice *cannot* secure such general adhesion. And accordingly, although interventions under sanction of the European Concert have been fairly frequent, they have been hitherto based, and must, it would seem, of necessity be based, on the common interest of civilised Powers, and particularly of the Powers of the Concert. Interventions of this order are indeed but measures of high international police.

of the decrees of the Concert of Europe is a special instance of intervention prompted by the needs of self-defence.

CHAPTER III.

THE DELIMITATION OF DOMINION.

RULE III. TERRITORY AND JURISDICTION ARE COEXTENSIVE.

How does territory become national?

§ 8. Any definite area of the solid surface of the earth may by the adoption of a certain procedure become the sole property of a single people.

Every state is, as territorially sovereign, necessarily possessed of a definite or definable extent of the earth's surface held by it in exclusive dominion, but, in order that that dominion may be universally respected, it is essential that each sovereign be prepared to justify his tenure by showing a duly recognised international title for every portion of his holding.

(a) By occupation.

§ 9. (a) Occupation, the formal taking of possession of lands previously uninhabited, or inhabited only by a barbarous or semi-civilised people, is by far the most important method of international territorial acquisition.

Concerning its character and operation it is possible to lay down certain propositions as expressing present generally recognised international law.

(1) Occupation to be valid must be effective.

(1) *Occupation to be valid must be effective.*

The necessity of arriving at a definite understanding as to the facts which must be held to establish original ownership in land, a necessity which had in ancient days made

Mallet, *Northern Antiquities,* pp. 287, 288.

itself felt amongst migrating tribes and individuals competing for settlements in the waste lands of Western

Europe, became of pressing international importance in the 15th and 16th centuries in consequence of the race in maritime discovery of the mariners of Spain, Holland, Portugal and Great Britain. The successful explorers of the period showed a general disposition to assert the sufficiency of mere discovery as establishing an absolute title in unoccupied or heathen lands for the state of the discoverer; while the shipmen of Spain and Portugal attempted to exclude foreign navigators from the seas of the New World and the East by virtue of the famous Bull of Pope Alexander VI., by which, drawing a line at a distance of one hundred leagues west of the Azores, he granted the exclusive dominion in all new discoveries westward and eastward to the Spanish and Portuguese respectively. The English and Dutch, however, made light of the Papal claims, and gradually, under the influence of the teaching of Grotius, it came to be generally admitted that, to constitute complete title by discovery, there must be more than a mere first finding: there must be a real occupation, that, in a word, occupation to be valid must be effective. "Discovery alone is not enough to give dominion and jurisdiction to the sovereign or government of the nation to which the discoverer belongs; such discovery must be followed by possession."

The earlier doctrine: per se constitutes title.

Johnson v. McIntosh, 8 Wheat. 533.

Selden, Mare Clausum, p. 139. Mare Liberum, c. 2 and 3. De Jure Belli ac Pacis, II. 3 § 11.

Mr Fish to Mr Preston, Dec. 31, 1872. Wharton, Dig. § 2.

But what constitutes effective occupation? As to this there is up to a certain point general agreement. In order that occupation may be deemed in law effective:—

(i) The occupation alleged must be a state measure. A good title may be acquired by virtue of the act of an official specially or generally commissioned for the work of taking possession, or by the ratification of the act of an uncommissioned *colonist*; but the operations of a mere private *discoverer* can found no national title.

i. Occupation to be effective must be a state act.

(ii) The occupation alleged must be reasonably continuous. The formal assumption of possession to continue legally effective must be followed by other acts of control or

ii. Occupation to be effective must be reasonably continuous.

by an actual settlement in the territory within a reasonable period. Territory having been once formally acquired, it can only be lost by voluntary or compulsory abandonment or by conveyance. But if land, of which possession has been formally taken, be suffered to lie untenanted or neglected for any considerable period, a presumption will arise that it has been abandoned, and another state may enter upon the territory as unoccupied. The principle finds apt illustration in the case of Santa Lucia.

"In 1639 Santa Lucia was occupied by an English colony, which was massacred by the Caribs in the course of 1640. No attempt was made to recolonise the island during the following ten years. In 1650 consequently the French took possession of it as unappropriated territory. In 1664 they were attacked by Lord Willoughby and driven into the mountains, where they remained until he retired three years later, when they came down and reoccupied their lands. Whether they died out does not appear, though probably this was the case, for at the Treaty of Utrecht Santa Lucia was viewed as a 'neutral island' in the possession of the Caribs. The French however seem to have considered their honour as being involved in the ultimate establishment of their claim. During the negotiations which led to the peace of 1763 they attached importance to the acquisition of the island, and by the terms of that peace it was ultimately assigned to them. There can be little doubt, considering the shortness of the time during which the English colony had existed, and the length of the period during which no attempt was made to reestablish it, that the French were justified in supposing England to have acquiesced in the results of the massacre, and that their occupation consequently was good in law."

Jenkinson, *Treaties*, III. 118, 157, 170.

Hall, II. 1, § 34.

An original formal title may, however, be kept alive by subsequent reasonably frequent acts of control, and a momentary interruption of possession is not sufficient to oust a title so established.

"From 1823 to 1875, when the matter was settled by arbitration, a dispute existed between England and Portugal as to some territory at Delagoa Bay, which was claimed by the former under a cession by native chiefs in the first mentioned year, and by the latter on the grounds, amongst others, of continuous occupation. It was admitted that Portuguese territory reached to the northern bank of the Rio de Espirito Santo or English river, which flows into the bay, and that a port and village had long been established there. The question was whether the sovereignty of Portugal extended south of the river, or whether the lands on that side had remained in the possession of their original owners. England relied upon the facts that the natives professed to be independent in 1823, that they acted as such, and that the commandant of the fort repudiated the possession of authority over them. In the memorials which were submitted on behalf of Portugal, amidst much which had no special reference to the territory in dispute, there was enough to show that posts had been maintained within it from time to time, and that authority had probably been exercised intermittently over the natives. The area of the territory being small, and all of it being within easy reach of a force in possession of the Portuguese settlement, there could be little difficulty in keeping up sufficient control to prevent a title by occupation from dying out. There was therefore a presumption in favour of the Portuguese claim. The French Government, which acted as arbitrator, took the view that the interruption of occupation, which undoubtedly took place in 1823, was not sufficient to oust a title supported by occasional acts of sovereignty done through nearly three centuries, and adjudged the territory in question to Portugal."

(iii)   The area affected must be reasonably proportionate to the occupying force.

If some formal act of possession, for example, the establishment of a post, be performed on an island of com-

Hall, II. 2, § 34.   *Parl. Papers,* XLII. 1875.

iii. The area claimed must be reasonably proportionate to the occupying force.

paratively small extent, its effects may well be taken to
extend to the whole: in the case of a large island or continent a limiting rule must evidently be sought. The
accepted rule has hitherto been that the crest of the water-
shed is the presumptive interior boundary, while the flank

Wharton,
Dig. § 2.
Snow, p. 12,
note.

boundaries are the limits of the land watered by the rivers
debouching at the point of coast occupied. In very recent

The "Hin-
terland
doctrine."

years, under the name of the "Hinterland doctrine," the
principle has been broached in certain quarters that the
possession of coast settlements establishes at least a *primâ
facie* claim on the unexplored interior, but for the present
it may be fairly said that the extent of territory deemed
claimable in respect of a coast settlement has hitherto
borne some reasonable ratio to the actual controlling
power of the occupier; that the dominion of the settler
has been held to cease with the cessation of his effective
influence.

A possible
departure
from the
doctrine of
effective
occupa-
tion:

Within the last few years the doctrine of effective occupation has been subjected to the operation of new influences.
Several of the greater Powers have adopted the habit of
distributing among themselves by mutual arrangement what
are termed "spheres of influence" in Africa and elsewhere.

the
" sphere
of in-
fluence."

Such arrangements have their obvious advantages: they
remove the causes of present dispute among the lions of the
earth. But it may be questioned whether this proceeding
is wholly fair to weaker Powers. Can a vast area of unexplored territory, in which there is no shadow of settlement
or control, be allotted to a great Power by means of an
amicable arrangement with another or a few other great
Powers, whose interest is similarly enlisted, in such a way as
to bar the intrusion of the settlers of a smaller Power, no
party to the sphere of influence treaty? It may be that
such an arrangement is full of promise for the future good of
the world. It may be that it points to the way of peace and
to the way to the suppression of the slave-trade and the
drink traffic with their concomitant horrors. But at least it

might be well that the "sphere of influence" and the "Hinterland doctrine" should be seen in their true light, as the natural tracings of a great police proceeding resting on the sound foundation of the personal interests of the possessors of power. And if the fact be as suggested, the older doctrine of effective occupation has gone by the board, and might indeed is right.

(2) *Occupation within the sphere of the Berlin Conference 1884–5 must be diplomatically announced.*

A Conference of representatives of the various interested Powers having been, in October 1884, invited to Brussels by Prince Bismarck to consider certain questions arising out of the African Colonisation fever which appeared to have seized upon all the chief states of Western and Central Europe, it was finally agreed under Articles 34 and 35 of the General Act adopted by the delegates that:

"Any Power which henceforth takes possession of a tract of land on the coasts of the African Continent outside of its present possessions, or which, being hitherto without such possessions, shall acquire them, as well as the Power which assumes a protectorate there, shall accompany the respective act with a notification thereof, addressed to the other Signatory Powers of the present Act, in order to enable them, if need be, to make good any claims of their own.

"The Signatory Powers of the present Act recognise the obligation to insure the establishment of authority in the regions occupied by them on the coasts of the African Continent sufficient to protect existing rights, and, as the case may be, freedom of trade and of transit under the conditions agreed upon."

This provision is in terms of only limited application, covering but the case of future occupations of places on the African coast, and indeed some of the Powers represented at the Conference were careful to guard themselves by express reservations against its wider extension. But the practical value of the arrangement has been promptly appreciated,

Marginal notes:
(2) Occupation within the sphere affected by the Berlin Conference must be diplomatically notified.

Parl. Papers, Africa, No. 4, 1885, p. 313.

An extension of the principle.

and not only have numerous notifications been made in pursuance of the agreement, but in some instances, where it was in no way obligatory on account of the area affected, the procedure has been adopted. Thus France notified her annexation of the Comino Islands and England her advance in Bechuanaland.

Hall, pp. 116—117 n.

(β) By cession.

§ 10. (β) Cession, the formal transfer of dominion by a previous lawful possessor, constitutes a second form of sound title to the ownership of territory.

The area of territory conveyed and the moment of the transfer of sovereignty are alike ruled by the express terms of the instrument of conveyance. Provided good faith be shown by the parties to the contract, the determination of the boundaries of the region conveyed must thus be a mere matter of textual interpretation and of the facts of the previous ownership.

U. S. v. Reynes, 9 How. 127. Davis v. Police Jury of Concordia, Ibid. 280. U. S. v. D'Auterive, 10 How. 609. Montault v. U. S., 12 How. 47. Treaties of cession, in general, date from signature.

The date of transfer, in default of express determination in the convention itself, must be taken to be that of the signature of the instrument.

"All treaties, as well those for cessions of territory as for other purposes, are binding upon the contracting parties, unless when otherwise provided in them, from the date they are signed. The ratification of them relates back to the time of signing."

Wayne, J. in Davis v. Police Jury of Concordia, 9 How. 289.

Louisiana was retroceded by Spain to France under the treaty of San Ildefonso of October 1, 1800. In 1803 it was conveyed to the United States under the Franco-American treaty of Paris. In the *United States v. Reynes*, where an attempt was made to set up a title to lands in Baton Rouge under a purchase from the Spanish Government made after the date of the treaty of Paris, the Supreme Court held that the rights and powers of sovereignty on the part of Spain over the territory ceased with the transfer of that sovereignty, and that must be referred to the date of the treaty of San Ildefonso. "The law of nations does not recognise in a nation ceding a territory the continuance of supreme

U. S. v. Reynes, 9 How. 127.

power over it after the treaty has been signed, or any other exercise of sovereignty than that which is necessary for social order and for commercial purposes, and to keep the cession in an unaltered value, until a delivery of it has been made."

Wayne, J.
in Davis v.
Police Jury
of Concordia, 9 How.
294.

§ 11. (γ) **Conquest constitutes** *per se* **a good international title.**

(γ) By
conquest.

" By the laws and usages of nations, conquest is a valid title, while the victor maintains the exclusive possession of the conquered country."

Taney, C. J.
in Fleming
v. Page,
9 How. 615.

If the original proprietor be not altogether subdued, the holding of territory seized by force of arms is, indeed, a mere military occupation, until the fate of the occupied land is finally determined by the terms of a treaty of peace. But that military occupation is during its continuance in itself sufficient to confer internationally the fullest rights of sovereignty, and, even though the original owner should stubbornly refuse to assent to a cession, long continued possession will finally establish the previous effective title.

American
Insurance
Co. v.
Canter,
1 Pet. 542.

U. S. v.
Rice,
4 Wheat.
246.
Fleming v.
Page,
9 How. 603.

With the territory pass alike its benefits and its burdens. " The conqueror who reduces a nation to his subjection receives it subject to all its engagements and duties towards others, the fulfilment of which then becomes his duty."

Mr Adams to
Mr Everett,
Aug. 10,
1818;
Wharton,
Dig. § 5.

§ 12. (δ) **The natural formation of new land by alluvial deposit may add by title of accretion new national territory to existing possessions.**

(δ) By
accretion.

In the case of the " Anna " in 1805, when it became a question whether a number of little mud islands composed of earth and trees drifted down by the Mississippi, and forming a kind of portico to the mainland, could be deemed American territory, so as to confer the protection of the neutral three mile zone against belligerent capture, Sir W. Scott ruled that the territorial protection must be reckoned from the islands. "They are," he said, "the natural ap-

The
" Anna."
5 C. Rob.
373.

pendages of the coast on which they border, and from which indeed they are formed. Their elements are derived immediately from the territory, and on the principle of alluvium and increment, on which so much is to be found in the books of law, *Quod vis fluminis de tuo praedio detraxerit, et vicino praedio attulerit palam tuum remanet,* even if it had been carried over to an adjoining territory."

In general, except in the case of sudden violent irruptions transforming the physical face of territory wholesale, accretions to natural boundaries, whether river banks or shore lines, advance the boundary mark, while accretions within territory delimited by fixed measurements make no international territorial change. Should land be cut off by the sudden violent alteration of the course of a river, or overwhelmed by a flood, its international ownership is unaffected.

§ 13. (ε) **Long continued and undisputed possession is accepted as conferring a sound international title by prescription, either as fairly raising a presumption of an original valid acquisition, or as unimpeachable evidence of the** *de facto* **determination in the territory affected of the sovereignty of the previous proprietor.**

§ 14. The methods of international territorial acquisition extend alike to land and water.

Certain waters are as naturally incident to or necessary to the protection of the land regarded as national territory.

§ 15. (1) **Landlocked waters, whether mere lakes or inland seas, if entirely surrounded by the territorial possessions of a single sovereign, are universally allowed to belong exclusively to the dominion of that sovereign.**

Thus the Sea of Aral is as entirely within the jurisdiction of Russia as is the Lake of Como within the jurisdiction of Italy.

§ 16. (2) Rivers, considered territorially, are naturally sub- jects of exclusive national jurisdiction.

(2) Rivers.

Where a stream divides the landed possessions of two states, the river is, in default of express evidence to the contrary, deemed to be, territorially speaking, the property of those states, the boundary line of the two dominions being the middle line of the *thalweg* or navigable channel. Where a stream runs between banks, both of which are possessed by the same sovereign, the property in the stream is in that sovereign, and that whether the river drains throughout its course the territory of one power only, or traverses the territories of two or more states.

Handly's Lessee v. Anthony, 5 Wheat. 379.

But navigable streams, while naturally subjects of national dominion, are equally naturally the great highway of international communication, and, accordingly, trading nations have, except in defence of their own exclusive privileges, shown a general desire to secure the international freedom of navigation of great rivers.

The doctrine of the freedom of river navigation.

The Powers at Vienna in 1815 declared for the principle of the freedom of navigation of streams separating or traversing two or more states, and engaged the governments interested in such waterways in an agreement to regulate by common accord of commissioners appointed for the purpose the amount and manner of collection of navigation dues and all kindred questions. And, in pursuance of these resolutions, the more important waterways of the world are being one by one thrown open to the unrestricted navigation of the flag of peace[1].

Act of the Congress of Vienna, Arts. cviii— cxvii. Ghillany, I. 301— 303.

Long disputes as to the navigation of the Rhine were settled by a convention of the riverain states signed at Mayence on March 31, 1831, and various supplementary

---

[1] An interesting historical résumé of the progress of the movement in this direction between 1815 and 1884 is found in the Report of the Commission, of which Baron Lambermont was the reporter, appointed by the Berlin Conference of 1885 to examine projects submitted to it of Acts of Navigation for the Congo and Niger ; *Parl. Papers, Africa*, No. 4, 1885, p. 138.

Hertslet,
*Map of
Europe,*
II. 848.
Ibid. II. 1095.
articles. The navigation of the Po was regulated by the Treaty of Milan of 1849. In 1853 by identical treaties with France, Great Britain and the United States, the Government of the Argentine Confederation conceded the free navigation of the rivers Paraná and Uruguay, wherever they might belong to it, to the merchant vessels of all nations, declared the freedom of its ports for the use of such vessels, and undertook to maintain beacons and marks to point out the channels of the rivers, and to establish a uniform system for the collection of custom-house duties, together with harbour, light, police and pilotage dues, along the whole course of the waters of the Confederation. Moreover (Art. 6) "If it should happen (which God forbid) that war should break out between any of the States, Republics, or Provinces of the river

Treaty of
San José de
Flores, July
10, 1853.
*Parl.
Papers,
Africa,*
No. 4, 1885,
p. 153.
Plate or its confluents, the navigation of the rivers Paraná and Uruguay shall remain free to the merchant flag of all nations, excepting in what may relate to munitions of war, such as arms of all kinds, gunpowder, lead and cannon-balls."

Austria and Russia had in 1840 agreed on a convention as to the navigation of the Danube. In 1856 the plenipotentiaries at Paris raised the navigation of that river to a position of unique importance by the creation of the Danube Commission. Resolving to apply to the stream the principles of river navigation established by the Act of the Congress of Vienna, they agreed to set up a temporary European Commission charged with the designation of the works necessary for the clearing away of obstructions and for the putting of the river in the best possible state for navigation, and with

*Parl.
Papers,
Africa,*
No. 4, 1885,
p. 154:
Hertslet,
*Map of
Europe,*
II. 1257,
II. 1016.
the preparation of the way for a permanent Navigation Commission of the riverain powers. Thanks to the necessities of political circumstances the European Commission has continued in the exercise of the functions originally designed to pass to the River Commission.

*Parl.
Papers,
Africa,*
No. 4, 1885.
Lastly the freedom of the navigation of the Congo and Niger was declared at the Conference of Berlin in 1885, the

Congo being placed under the care of an International River Commission, the Niger entrusted to the guardianship of the riverain powers, France and Great Britain.

In several instances the free navigation of waterways has been directly purchased from the possessors of prescriptive rights of control.   The Scheldt tolls were redeemed in 1863 by the Treaty of Brussels, while the Stade or Brunhausen toll in the Elbe was bought out in 1861 under the Treaty of Hanover.   The United States and Great Britain settled their long-standing differences as to the navigation of Lake Michigan, of the St Lawrence, the Yukon, Porcupine and Stikine by a mutual enfranchisement under the Treaty of Washington, 1871.

The free-dom of rivers to universal naviga-tion has been brought about by special treaty, Hertslet, *Map of Europe*, ii. 1550. *Ibid.* ii. 1478.

These various acts render clear the fact to which the remarks of the Russian, Austro-Hungarian and German representatives at the Conference of Berlin were calculated to draw attention, that, although the doctrine of the freedom of navigation of great rivers has advanced in general favour, the new order has arisen by virtue of particular treaty entered into by the interested nations, not by the outright recog-nition of a general law; and the right of riparian states to regulate the traffic has been, in each instance, formally acknowledged.   In no case have we witnessed the recognition of any *natural* right such as that which the United States, in harmony with her earlier Mississippi experiences, asserted in the navigation of the St Lawrence in 1824.

Parl. Papers, Africa, No. 4, 1885. pp. 128—130.

not by the recogni-tion of a general *natural* right.

Rush, *Residence at the Court of London*, ii. pp. 168—172.

§ 17.   (3) **The open sea washing the shores of states is to a distance of at least three miles from low-water mark the subject of territorial control.**

(3) The high sea within a limited distance of low-water mark.

"By a consensus of writers, without one single authority to the contrary, some portion of the coast-waters of a country is considered for some purposes to belong to the country the coasts of which they wash....This is established as solidly, as, by the very nature of the case, any proposition of inter-national law can be."

Manchester v. Massa-chusetts, 139 U. S. R. 240.   Stat. 41 and 42 Vict., c. 73. Coleridge, L. C. J. in R. v. Keyn.

In the Middle Ages claims were advanced by various

peoples to sovereignty over wide areas of open sea, and those claims were in many instances generally recognised, the weaker maritime peoples being well content to acknowledge a jurisdiction which involved the police of the ocean, no easy duty in the days of sailing vessels, when every sea swarmed with pirates and every coastman was on occasion a wrecker. Thus the Venetians were the acknowledged lords of the Adriatic, and the English maintained their dominion in the ocean between the North Cape and Cape Finisterre. But these high pretensions, assailed by Grotius and his followers on the ground of natural right, gradually shrunk to smaller proportions, and have, by the almost total disappearance of piracy before the advent of steam, been denuded of their ancient foundation. The view expressed by Vattel now commands general concurrence, that the dominion of a state in the neighbouring sea extends only so far as its safety renders necessary and its power can make effective.

Bynkershoek had suggested that the extent of national dominion in the case was naturally defined by the range of cannon shot from the shore. *Quare omnino videtur rectius, eo potestatem terrae extendi, quousque tormenta exploduntur, eatenus quippe cum imperare, tum possidere videmur. Loquor autem de his temporibus, quibus illis machinis utimur: alioquin generaliter dicendum esset, potestatem terrae finiri, ubi finitur armorum vis; etenim haec, ut diximus, possessionem tuetur. Neque alia sententia usi videntur.* The range of cannon shot was subsequently defined as being approximately a marine league, and, the principle having been almost universally adopted, the three mile zone of sea expanse beyond low water mark on the main shore may undoubtedly be validly claimed by any state as belonging to its exclusive international jurisdiction.

"There can be no possible doubt that the water below low water-mark is part of the high seas. But it is equally beyond question that for certain purposes every country may,

Margin notes:

Vattel, I. 23 § 289.
Cockburn, C. J. in R. v. Keyn, 2, Exch. Div. 63.
De Jure Belli ac Pacis, II. 2 §§ 2 and 3.
Mare Liberum, c. 5.

Occupation to be valid must be effective.
Vattel, I. 23 § 289.

Bynkershoek, *De Dominio Maris,* c. 2.

The marine league at least is territorial.
The "Anna," 5 C. Rob. 385 c.

by the common law of nations, legitimately exercise jurisdiction over that portion of the high seas which lies within
the distance of three miles from its shores. Whether this
limit was determined with reference to the supposed range
of cannon, on the principle that the jurisdiction is measured
by the power of enforcing it, is not material, for it is clear, at
any rate, that it extends to the distance of three miles, and
that many instances may be given of the exercise of such
jurisdiction by various nations." *(Vice Chancellor Sir P. Wood in General Iron Screw Collier Co. v. Schurmanns, 1 Johnson, and Hemming, 193.)*

It has been from time to time suggested that, in view of
the increased range of modern weapons, the territorial water
belt might well be extended, at least in respect of neutral
rights, and sundry untoward events have lent weight to the
suggestion. But, no generally accepted revision of the older
rule having yet taken place, the law is as laid down by
Blatchford, J. in *Manchester v. Massachusetts*: "As between
nations, the minimum limit of the territorial jurisdiction
of a nation over tide-waters is a marine league from its
coast." *(Suggested extension of the three mile belt. U.S. Dipl. Corresp., 1864, 704, 708. Wharton, Dig. § 32. Blatchford, J. in Manchester v. Massachusetts.)*

The principle of the marine league extends to straits and
narrow seas in general. The right of all nations to navigate
straits connecting free seas is now universally recognised,
but the right has in special instances, for example in the
case of the Sound, been obtained under treaty with the
territorial sovereign of the coasts, and for all the ordinary
purposes of government, the prevention of crime, the regulation of fishing and the like, the right of the sovereign of
the shore of a strait to dominion in its waters to the
distance of three miles from low water mark is regularly
admitted. When the width of the strait falls short of six
miles, the shores being held by different sovereigns, the
boundary between the two realms, in default of special
evidence to the contrary, follows, on the analogy of rivers,
the middle line of the navigable channel. *(The principle extends to straits, subject to the recognition of the general freedom of navigation. Hertslet, Map of Europe, II. 1301. Wharton, Dig. § 29.)*

(4) Inlets within a six mile headland line, and a territorial three mile belt from that line.

§ 18. (4) **If an inlet of the sea, whether port or harbour, estuary, gulf or bay, have a mouthline from headland to headland not exceeding six miles in width, the three mile territorial zone is by general practice measured from the mouthline, and the whole area of water within the inlet, whatever its extent, is held territorial.**

Claims of a more extensive character have been on occasion advanced, and indeed are in certain quarters still

Church v. Hubbard, 2 Cranch 187. Direct U. S. Cable Co. v. Anglo-American Telegraph Co., L. R., 2 App. Cases, 394. R. v. Cunningham, Bell C. C. 86. Wheaton 11. 4 § 179; Halleck 1. 6 § 16. Wharton, Dig. § 28.

maintained. Some powers have asserted a title to inlets bounded by ten mile headland lines, whilst others have claimed all waters within headlands, whatever the length of the joining lines. But these wider claims do not meet with much international sympathy, and, in general, it may be laid down as clear law that, while the foundation of marine dominion must be sought in the needs of self-defence, universal recognition cannot be claimed for any territorial dominion on the high seas not justified by the three mile rule. The fate of the last example of the assertion of an

Award of the Behring's Sea Arbitrators, Parl. Papers, United States, No. 10 (1893).

extensive high sea dominion, that advanced by the United States to prohibit the killing of fur-seals by any hunter within the eastern division of Behring's Sea, and disposed of by arbitration at Paris, was not such as to encourage general imitation.

International subjection is, in general, determined by national territorial bounds.

§ 19. International subjection is, in general, determined by national territorial bounds.

International subjection in the case of the individual is not synonymous with citizenship.

Citizens are (1) citizens by birth, or

Citizens are either citizens by birth or citizens by naturalisation. In the ascription of citizenship by birth states may follow one or other of two principles, that of locality or that of parentage: they may refer citizenship to birth within particular local limits[1], or they may ascribe it by reference to the

---

[1] "By the common law, a child born within the allegiance—the jurisdiction—of the United States, is born a subject or citizen thereof, without reference to the political *status* or condition of its parents"; Deady, J. in *Ex parte Chin King*, Snow 220. The same principle is followed in Great Britain; *Calvin's Case* 7 Rep. 1.

national character of one or both of the parents irrespective of the place of birth, the differing attitude of states in this respect being seemingly dictated by the relative leaning of their codes to a feudal or a Roman model. Citizenship by naturalisation arises by virtue of an express act of grace on the part of the naturalising state, an alien being admitted to full citizenship either in virtue of some special enactment or of some general naturalisation statute. In every case, to each state itself it exclusively belongs to determine what facts constitute a sound title to its citizenship.

(2) citizens by naturalisation.

It is no exception to this principle that a native state may decline to recognise, or recognise only subject to limitations, the operation within *its* jurisdiction of the naturalisation obtained by its citizens abroad. By certain powers, indeed, a disposition has been shown to assert, on behalf of their own powers of naturalisation, the doctrine of an absolute individual right of self-expatriation, and to deny the binding force of any limiting conditions imposed by a state on the expatriation of its subjects, even on the return of those subjects to their native land. The United States Government has displayed in this regard a peculiar fluctuation of opinion. Early in the present century that Government, in opposition to the opinion of Mr Justice Story, maintained against Great Britain its right to protect foreigners naturalised by it against the operation of regulations of their native state forbidding expatriation. But the opinion of Justice Story was approved by later American legal authorities, and in 1840 Mr Wheaton, then American Minister at Berlin, being applied to for protection against the requirement of compulsory service in the Prussian army by one, Johann Knocke, a Prussian, who, having been naturalised in the United States, had returned to his native land, declined to interfere, intimating to the applicant that, while he would have been protected in the enjoyment of his rights and privileges as a naturalised citizen of the United States in every country except Prussia, he having returned to the

Is there an individual right of self expatriation?

The attitude of the United States.
2 Wharton, *Dig.* § 171.

Case of Johann Knocke, 1840.

country of his birth, his native domicile and natural character must be deemed to revert, so long as he remained within the Prussian dominions, and he was bound in all respects to obey the Prussian laws exactly as if he had never emigrated. In subsequent similar transactions in 1852 and 1853 the same view was maintained. "If, as is understood to be the fact," said Mr Webster in the case of Victor B. Depierre, a French subject naturalised in the United States, "the government of France does not acknowledge the right of natives of that country to renounce their allegiance, it may lawfully claim their services when found within French jurisdiction." In 1859, however, the United States statesmen reverted to their older policy, and Mr Cass laid it down in the broadest fashion that "the moment a foreigner becomes naturalised his allegiance to his native country is severed for ever. He experiences a new political birth. A broad and impassable line separates him from his native country....Should he return to his native country he returns as an American citizen and in no other character."

Unable at first to obtain for their doctrine the approval of even their own jurists, the American politicians had recourse to the legislature and to negotiation. In 1868 an Act of Congress declared the right of expatriation to be a "natural and inherent right of all people, indispensable to the enjoyment of the rights of life, liberty, and the pursuit of happiness," denounced as inconsistent with the fundamental principles of the Republic "any declaration, instruction, opinion, order, or decision of any officer of this Government, which denies, restricts, impairs or questions the right of expatriation," and enacted that "all naturalised citizens of the United States, while in foreign countries, are entitled to, and shall receive from this Government, the same protection of persons and property that is accorded to native born citizens in like situations and circumstances."

In a treaty of the same year between the United States and the North German Confederation, it was agreed that

Case of
Ignacio
Tolen,
1852.

Case of
Victor B.
Depierre,
1852.

Halleck, I.
12 § 4.

Act of
July 27,
1868.

North German subjects naturalised in the United States should be capable of being tried on return to their native state in respect only of acts committed before emigration, they being thereby exempted from liability in respect of the act of emigration itself and its consequences. And in 1870, after the vindication by Great Britain of the contrary principle in the case of various Irish rebels arrested in Ireland after naturalisation in America, a convention was signed between the United States and Great Britain, whereby it was agreed that citizens of the one country naturalised within the dominions of the other should be taken to be in all respects citizens of the naturalising power.

Hall, II. 5 § 70.

Case of Warren and Costello, 1867. Lloyd's Wheaton, II. 2d § 1510. Ibid. § 151 N.

In default of such treaty arrangements, however, the main principle remains unimpaired, that each State, being sovereign within its own territory, may lawfully refuse to recognise within that territory the validity of the naturalisation obtained by its subject on foreign soil, or may in its discretion impose conditions limiting the operation within its borders of the effect of the naturalisation of a citizen by a foreign state. In practice some governments allow to their citizens complete freedom of self-expatriation, whilst others deny to their citizens the right to cast off their native allegiance without express permission[1]. If naturalisation be obtained without the consent of the native state, the naturalised individual is as between the naturalising power and all states, except only the native state, entitled to be regarded as a citizen of the naturalising power, but may be dealt with as a citizen by the native state, should he at any later time be found within its jurisdiction. The British Naturalisation

There is no right of self-expatriation irrespective of treaty stipulation.

In re Bourgoise, L. R. 41 Chan. D. 310.

---

[1] Great Britain after upholding for centuries the doctrine of indissoluble allegiance adopted in the Naturalisation Act 1870 a totally different policy, British citizenship being now *ipso facto* lost by naturalisation within a foreign country: Stat. 33 and 34 Vict. c. 14 s. 6; *Re Trufort*, L. R. 36, Ch. Div. 600. The same rule is followed by the law of France, provided the naturalisation procured abroad by a French citizen be absolute and unqualified; Case of *Alibert* 1842 and *Zeiter* 1869, Snow 218; *In re Bourgoise*, 41 Ch. Div. 310.

Aeneas Macdonald's Case, 1745.

Act of 1870, which expresses the adhesion of Great Britain to the principle of freedom of expatriation, itself furnishes an instance of the exercise of the limiting power of the native State, in the provision that a British subject taking advan-

Stat. 33 and 34 Vict. c. 14, s. 15. tage of the statute to naturalise himself abroad is not thereby discharged from liability in respect of any acts done before the date of his so becoming an alien.

The same individual may thus, it is clear, be claimed as a citizen by more than one sovereign in the pursuit of diverse legal systems. Internationally, however, the jurisdiction to which he is subject is, in general, determined by one simple consideration, to wit, his local situation. Internationally considered, subjection is, in general, a purely territorial question, state jurisdiction being within state territorial limits alike comprehensive and exclusive. This main principle is capable of clear demonstration.

(a) The jurisdiction of the state within its territorial limits is, in general, all comprehensive.
2 Wharton, Dig. 508.
(a) *The jurisdiction of the state within its territorial limits is, in general, all comprehensive.*

A state may, in general, exercise jurisdiction over all persons, whether natives or aliens, and all property, whether owned by natives or foreigners, within its territories, including as territories its territorial waters.

Mr Justice Story in the "Santissima Trinidad," 7 Wheat. 354.
"It may be laid down as a general proposition, that all persons and property within the territorial jurisdiction of a sovereign are amenable to the jurisdiction of himself or his courts; and that the exceptions to this rule are such only as by common usage and public policy have been allowed in order to preserve the peace and harmony of nations, and to regulate their intercourse in a manner best suited to their dignity and rights."

(1) All aliens on national soil are internationally subjects of the local ruler.
(1) All persons on national soil whether citizens or foreigners are, in general, internationally subjects of the territorial sovereign.

Sparenburgh v. Bannatyne, 1 B. and P. 163. 2 Wharton, Dig. 504.
The persons sojourning within the borders of a state at any moment fall into several classes: they may be (1) citizens, whether by birth or by naturalisation, enjoying the fullest

constitutional, legal and social privileges which the state laws can confer, (2) foreigners regularly resident, or (3) mere casual visitors. The classification of the individuals and the definition of the rights and responsibilities enjoyed by or imposed on each individual or each class of individuals belong to the local law. All sojourners whether citizens or aliens are in fact as between nation and nation subjects of the territorial ruler. When in the Old Bailey in 1664 a Quaker, brought up under the Conventicle Act, the operation of which was confined to " every person above the age of 16 years, being a subject of this realm," pleaded that he, being an alien born in France was no English subject, and therefore not within the statute, the Court unanimously overruled the plea, holding that any alien coming within the English Kingdom and living under the King's protection was during his stay a subject of the realm and punishable for transgressing its laws. Had the statute been limited in operation to *natural-born* subjects, said the Court, the plea would have availed, but otherwise where the obligation was upon subjects in general. Stat. 16 Car. 2, c. 4. Kelynge, 38.

The determination of the conditions on which it will admit, and the legal status which it will confer upon, the alien within its borders belongs to the territorial government. A state may impose conditions on alien immigration,

To exclude foreigners altogether from its soil, although within the strict legal right of every independent state, is practically to-day beyond the power of any civilised nation. A government well may, however, impose conditions on the admission and continuance of aliens within its borders. Every state possesses, and most of the states most advanced in civilisation freely exercise, the right to turn back over the frontier the immigrant alien who appears likely to become a charge upon the finances or a danger to the health or social order of the community, and to expel from its territory foreign vagabonds, criminals or other suspicious or objectionable strangers. Thus the United States Government under Passenger Cases, 7 How. 525. Holmes v. Jennison, 14 Pet. 615. *Parl. Miscell.* No. 1 (1887). 2 Wharton, *Dig.* 516.

Memoirs and Correspondence of Castlereagh, I. 375, 405.
powers conferred by Congress absolutely refused in 1798 to allow Irish rebels, released by the British ministry on condition of banishment, to be landed in America, and the legislature of the same great power has within recent years dealt in the most stringent fashion with foreign immigrants,

An Act to regulate immigration, ss. 2 and 4. *Parl. Papers, United States,* No. 3, 1887.
and prohibited under severe penalties the landing upon United States shores of "any convict, lunatic, idiot or any person unable to take care of himself or herself without becoming a public charge."

and regulate the legal status of aliens within its borders.
The policy of states in the treatment of the resident alien has been determined from time to time by the exigencies of national need. Some states have displayed an enlightened generosity, whilst others have adopted the attitude of the strictest conservatism. But, on the whole, the status of the alien in most civilised communities has improved with the passage of time. To-day, in virtue of the Naturalisation Act, 1870, the resident alien enjoys in the United Kingdom all the legal privileges which belong to a British citizen,

Stat. 33 and 34 Vict. c. 14.
except the right to office or to any municipal, parliamentary or other franchise, and the capacity to own a British ship. So too in the various states of the American Union the

Wharton, *Dig.* § 201.
resident alien commonly enjoys all the social and legal rights of the native-born subject[1].

The limit of the jurisdiction of the local sovereign over aliens:—
One limit upon the right of the territorial sovereign to deal with the foreigner resident within his dominions is, however, generally recognised.

a state cannot compel an alien to render purely political services.
The alien resident cannot be justly compelled to perform purely political or national duties for the benefit of the territorial sovereign.

The resident foreigner, who possesses the social and property rights of the ordinary citizen, is rightly regarded as incurring the corresponding liabilities in point of taxation

2 Wharton, *Dig.* 511.
and the like, and he may fairly be called upon to perform

---

[1] Several State Legislatures have of late prohibited the holding of real property within their territory by *non-resident* aliens or by alien corporations; *Parl. Papers,* Commercial, No. 17 (1887), Nos. 6 and 4 (1888), No. 13 (1890).

police duty in the maintenance of the peace by which he
benefits. But it is generally admitted that he cannot
equitably be compelled to enter the military or naval service
of the state, and adventure his life in defending the country
against foreign invasion, or in the suppression of civil strife.
The British Government declined during the American civil
struggle to protect against the call to military service any
British subject naturalised in America, so long as he remained
on American soil, or any British subject, who, though not
naturalised, had voted in elections, or otherwise exercised
the exclusive privileges of an American citizen; but Lord
Lyons addressed many effective remonstrances against the
compulsory enlistment of British citizens resident in the
United States who had in no way assumed such exclusive
rights.

((2), All persons within territorial waters, whether citizens
or aliens, and whether on board native or foreign vessels, are,
in general, subjects of the territorial sovereign.

All aliens, and *a fortiori* all citizens, found upon native
vessels in territorial waters are indisputably subjects of the
territorial ruler.

Further, all aliens, and *a fortiori* all citizens, found upon
foreign private vessels within territorial waters are subjects
of the territorial sovereign. Foreign merchantmen lying
within or passing through territorial waters are by universal
consent obnoxious to the operation of the local law, should
the local sovereign elect to exercise his powers, and by the
majority of states this jurisdiction is regularly exercised.

France adopts in this regard a distinct but thoroughly
reasonable practice. Distinguishing between acts affecting
only the internal discipline of the vessel and acts affecting
the external world, she declines jurisdiction over offences
committed on board foreign merchantmen in her ports unless
either (1) some person other than a member of the ship's
company is affected, (2) the intervention of the local police
is expressly invoked, or (3) the peace of the port is disturbed.

2 Wharton, *Dig.* 498.

U. S. Dipl. Corresp. 1864, II. 605, 611, 636, 645, 657.

(2) All persons on board native or foreign vessels in territorial waters are, in general, subjects of the territorial sovereign.

R. v. Lesley, Bell, C. C. 220.

Practice as to foreign merchantmen in territorial waters.

U. S. v. Dickelman, 92 U. S. 520. Case of Wildenhus, 120 U. S. Rep. 1. R. v. Keyn. R. v. Cunningham, Bell, C.C. 86. Wharton, *Dig.* § 35. Stat. 41 and 42 Vict. c. 73.

The "French" practice.

The "Sally" and the "Newton," Snow, 121. The "Tempest," *Ibid.* 122.

The
"Anemone,"
Snow, 124.
The case of
Wildenhus,
120 U. S.
Rep. 1,
Snow, 126.

Waite, C. J.
in the case
of Wilden-
hus, Snow,
123.

This practice has been adopted, seemingly, in Mexico and the United States.

"The principle which governs the whole matter is this: disorders which disturb only the peace of the ship or those on board are to be dealt with exclusively by the sovereignty of the home of the ship, but those which disturb the public peace may be suppressed, and, if need be, the offenders punished by the proper authorities of the local jurisdiction."

A limited
exception
is ad-
mitted in
the case of
vessels
entering
territorial
waters
en relâche
forcée.

The Brig
"Concord,"
9 Cranch,
387.
Wharton,
Dig. § 38.
The "New
York,"
3 Wheat. 59.
The "Mary
Barbour,"
Blatchford,
Pr. Cas.
167.
Livingston,
J. in the
"New
York,"
3 Wheat. 68.

A limited exception is fairly commonly admitted in the case of a vessel driven into a foreign port by *vis major* or stress of weather, such a ship being exempted from the local jurisdiction in respect of municipal penalties, customs duties and the like to which she would have been subject had she voluntarily come within territorial waters. The burden of proof of the existence of real stress is, however, on the vessel setting up the plea; that plea will be strictly examined and the exemption ceases if she seek to take advantage of it to violate during her stay the municipal law of the port.

"The necessity must be urgent, and proceed from such a state of things as may be supposed to produce on the mind of a skilful mariner a well-grounded apprehension of the loss of vessel and cargo, or of the lives of the crew. It is not every injury that may be received in a storm, as the splitting of a sail, the springing of a yard, or a trifling leak, which will excuse a violation of the laws of trade."

The "Carlo
Alberto,"
Cussy,
Phases et
Causes,
ii. 83.

In any case, the exemption is not generally recognised as extending to protect against the consequences of previous hostile acts directed against the sovereignty of the local government.

Extent of
the juris-
diction
commonly
exercised
in terri-
torial
waters.

Manchester
v. Massa-
chusetts,
139 U. S. R.
240.
R. v. Keyn,
2 Exch. Div.
63.

In general, the right of the local sovereign to exercise jurisdiction over all persons within his territorial waters is admitted and freely exercised not only for (1) the regulation and protection of the coast fisheries, (2) the enforcement of the local customs laws by the prevention of smuggling, (3) the maintenance of the neutrality of the local waters against the operations of belligerents, and (4) the protection of the territory against hostile attack, but for (5) the prevention of ordinary breaches of the peace.

In the case of *R. v. Keyn* in 1877 the Court of Crown Cases Reserved quashed a conviction on a charge of manslaughter preferred at the Central Criminal Court against the commander of the German steamer " Franconia," which ran down the " Strathclyde," a British vessel, within two and a half miles of Dover beach, the majority of the Court being of opinion that, whilst as between nation and nation the site of the collision was within British territory, it was in judicial language out of the realm, and any exercise of criminal jurisdiction over a foreign ship in such waters could only take place in virtue of previous express authorisation by Act of Parliament. All question in the matter was, however, set at rest in 1878 by the Territorial Waters Jurisdiction Act, which, expressly conferring power on British judges to try culprits for criminal offences committed on board foreign vessels within three miles of low water mark on a British shore[1], at the same time recites that " the rightful jurisdiction of Her Majesty, her heirs and successors, extends and has always extended over the open seas adjacent to the coasts of the United Kingdom, and of all other parts of Her Majesty's dominions to such a distance as is necessary for the defence and security of such dominions."

(3) All property within territorial limits, whether ashore or afloat, and whether owned by citizens or by aliens, by residents or by non-residents, is, in general, subject to the operation of the local law.

Real property within territorial limits, by whomsoever owned, is necessarily permanently within the control of the territorial sovereign, and must permanently bear its share of national as well as of ordinary territorial burdens. Movables may be only temporarily within the state. Civilised states in practice find it convenient alike in respect of immovable and

The case of the " Franconia."

R. v. Keyn, 2 Exch. Div. 63.

Stat. 41 and 42 Vict. c. 73.

(3) All property within territorial limits is, in general, subject to the operation of the local law.

---

[1] No proceeding may be taken against a foreigner under this Act without the consent of a Secretary of State or a Colonial Governor.

movable property to follow on occasion the rules of foreign law, to adopt foreign judgments assuming to affect the property, to give effect to foreign wills disposing thereof, or to enforce foreign contracts or other foreign proceedings in its regard, but in all such proceedings the jurisdiction of the local sovereign remains intact. In fine, when enforcing a principle of so-called private international law, the national court is merely applying to the question before it a solution prescribed by its own national law, and is declaring the principle of territorial sovereignty even when adopting the terms of a foreign code. So long as property remains within the territorial limits it is attachable under territorial law.

Westlake, Private Int. Law, p. 7. Dalrymple v. Dalrymple, Dodson's Report, p. 6.

(β) The jurisdiction of the state within its territorial limits is, in general, exclusive.

(β) *The jurisdiction of the state within its territorial limits is, in general, exclusive.*

No state may, in general, exercise jurisdiction over any person or property whatever within the territorial limits, including the territorial waters, of another state.

It is clear law that no sovereign may, except by consent of the local ruler expressly accorded, (i) exercise any military authority, either by the enlistment of troops or the direction of the passage of troops, within the territorial bounds of another state. Nor in like manner may he without such consent (ii) erect any court of justice or exercise any judicial or police authority within the territorial bounds of another state. So (iii) no state officer may, in general, arrest any criminal or make any seizure for a breach of municipal law within the dominions of a foreign sovereign. Two neighbouring powers may by treaty make special arrangements for dealing with fugitives at their common frontier. The United States and Mexico have, for example, found it convenient to stipulate by treaty for the reciprocal crossing of their common frontier by their respective forces in pursuit of Indian marauders. But, in general, the right of pursuit ceases when the criminal passes within the boundary of a foreign state.

Wharton, Dig. §§ 12 and 13.

Glass v. Sloop "Betsy," 3 Dall. 6.

The "Apollon," 9 Wheat. 362.

Wharton, Dig. § 18.

An American sergeant having in September 1862 pursued across the Canadian frontier a deserter from his regiment and arrested him at Bedford in the British province of Canada, his action was entirely disavowed by the U. S. Government, and the offender reprimanded. So when in March 1863 Captain Haddock of the U. S. army with three soldiers armed and in uniform arrested and forcibly carried off from Wolf Island in Canada another American deserter, his proceeding was disavowed by Mr Seward, and the over-zealous officer was dismissed from the U. S. service. In such cases the appropriate procedure is that of formal extradition. *U. S. Dipl. Corresp. 1863. p. 428.*

U. S. Dipl. Corresp. 1863, p. 468.

The surrender of fugitive criminals is, in view of the international interdependence of states, doubtless at least an international moral duty, but it is one which rests on courtesy and consideration of the general good, not on the universal recognition of an absolute right. *The extradition of fugitive criminals is a moral, but not a strictly legal duty.*

Every state possesses, in virtue of its territorial indepen-dence, a right to surrender a fugitive criminal taking refuge within its territorial jurisdiction, no state being rightly censurable if it declines to allow to continue within its society individuals of proved anti-social tendencies. On the other hand, it follows, as a consequence of the same inde-pendence, that no state has any absolute right to compel the surrender by another state of a fugitive criminal, except in virtue of express international convention. "The surrender of fugitives from justice is a matter of conventional arrange-ment between states, as no such obligation is imposed by the laws of nations." *East India Co. v. Campbell, 1 Ves. 247.*

U. S. v. Rauscher, 119 U. S. R. Snow, 151. Vogt's case, Boyd's Wheaton, II. 2. 116 d. McLean, J. in re Metzger, 5 How. 188.

Many states decline to entertain applications for the surrender of fugitive criminals, except in pursuance of express treaty stipulations. A state well may impose conditions upon such surrender. A state may, for example, adopt a limited list of strictly defined offences in respect of which extradition will be alone by it accorded: it may stipulate that, if surrendered, the fugitive shall not be tried in respect *A state may impose conditions on extra-dition.*

Wharton, Dig. § 268.

U. S. v. Rauscher, Snow, 154.

4—2

of any other offence than that in respect of which his
extradition is granted, until a reasonable opportunity has
been given him to return to the country from whose asylum
he has been removed[1]; or it may refuse to surrender fugitives
belonging to certain definite classes, for example, its own
subjects (*nationaux*) charged with the commission of offences
abroad, or foreign political refugees.   These and other conditions are, in practice, adopted by various states in pursuance
of their view of the dictates of sound policy.   Certain of
these conditions are from time to time productive of much
difficulty, and of not a few gross miscarriages of justice.
The refusal by Great Britain of the surrender of her
nationaux, for example, coupled with her repudiation of
jurisdiction over minor offences committed by such subjects
abroad, constitutes a grave blot on the British legal system,
while the sentimental attachment to the principle of the
protection of political refugees has enabled more than one
murderer to cheat the gallows.   But in the main, states do
in practice display a growing desire to respond in this
matter to the call of international comity, and do in
practice recognise the general international duty of extradition[2].

The determination of the conditions on which surrender
will be granted, and of the person or body in each state in
whom is vested the power of extradition must, however, alike
be left to the municipal law of that state.   In any case
extradition, it is clear, must be a national act : local officials,
unless expressly authorised by their Government, have no
power to surrender a fugitive criminal.

Side notes:
Trimble's case, Snow, 158. For the British refusal to surrender the slave assassins of the "Creole," see *Parl. Papers*, 1843, LXI.

R. v. Wilson, 3 Q. B. D. 42.

For the British definition of a political offence see in re Castioni, L. R. (1891), 1 Q. B. 149.

See the case of Arguelles, *U. S. Dipl. Corresp.* 1864, II. 60—74.

Extradition must be a national act.

U. S. Dipl. Corresp. 1863, 514, 559; 1864, II. 564, 603, 604.

---

[1] This condition is by some authorities held to be implied, without
express stipulation, in every grant of extradition ; Miller J. in *U. S. v.
Rauscher*, Snow 157.

[2] The British practice is set out in the Extradition Acts of 1870 and 1873,
33 and 34 Vict. c. 52 and 36 and 37 Vict. c. 60.   Its defects were clearly
pointed out in the Report of the Royal Commission of 1877.   For the earlier
British practice see the *Report from the Select Committee on Extradition*,
1868.

§ 20. It is no real exception to the principle that territory and jurisdiction are co-extensive that the jurisdiction of each state extends to all persons and property on board its vessels, whether men-of-war or merchantmen, on the high seas, or where no other civilised power exercises jurisdiction.

In the international common ground of the ocean or in the "No Man's Land" beyond the territorial limits of any Power the jurisdiction is naturally that of the flag. "It is clear," said Erle, C. J., in *R. v. Lesley*, "that an English ship on the high seas, out of any foreign territory, is subject to the laws of England; and persons, whether foreign or English, on board such ship, are as much amenable to English law as they would be on English soil." So when one Sattler, a foreigner, who having, after committing a theft at St Ives, been arrested at Hamburg, and placed on board an English steamer for transport to England, shot on board the vessel on the high seas the English detective who held him in custody, the Court for Crown Cases Reserved held him to have been at the Old Bailey rightly convicted of murder. And the conviction was similarly affirmed of one Anderson, an American citizen serving on board a British vessel, he having when on board the vessel in the Garonne caused the death of another American member of her crew under circumstances amounting in English law to manslaughter.

Conversely, no state may in general in time of peace exercise jurisdiction over any person or property whatsoever under a foreign flag on the high seas, except in the case of the suppression of piracy. "No principle of public law is better understood nor more universally recognised than that merchant vessels on the high seas are under the jurisdiction of the nation to which they belong, and that as to common crimes committed on such vessels while on the high seas, the competent tribunals of the vessel's nation have *exclusive* jurisdiction of the questions of trial and punishment of any person thus accused of the commission of a crime against its municipal laws: the

Side notes:

It is no exception to the main principle that the jurisdiction of the territorial sovereign extends to personal property under his flag on the high seas.

R. v. Anderson, L. R., 1 C. C. R. 161.
R. v. Lopez, 1 D. and B., C. C. R. 525.
R. v. Sattler, *Ibid.* 539.
R. v. Allen, 1 Mood. C. C. 494.
R. v. Lesley, Bell, C. C. 220.
R. v. Sauvajot, 1 Taunt. 32.   R. v. Prévot, *Ibid.*
R. v. Acow, *Ibid.*

R. v. Lesley, Bell, C. C. 234.
R. v. Sattler, 1 D. and B., C. C. R. 539.
R. v. Anderson, L. R., 1 C. C. R. 161.

No state may exercise jurisdiction over the foreign flag on the high seas in time of peace.

R. v. Lewis, 1 D. and B., C. C. R. 182.
R. v. Bjornsen, L. and C. 545.
R. v. Kohn, 4 F. and F. 68.

nationality of the accused can have no more to do with the question of jurisdiction than it would had he committed the same crime within the geographical territorial limits of the nation against whose municipal laws he offends. The merchant ship, while on the high seas, is, as the ship of war is everywhere, a part of the territory of the nation to which she belongs."

Mr Evarts to Mr Welsh, July 11, 1879. Wharton, Dig. § 33a.

John Lewis, a Frenchman naturalised in the United States, ill treated on board an American ship on the high seas a German shipmate. The victim dying in hospital at Liverpool shortly after the arrival of the vessel there, Lewis was indicted and convicted of manslaughter at Liverpool.

R. v. Lewis, 1 D. and B., C. C. R. 182.

The Court of Criminal Appeal quashed the conviction. So when foreigners rose upon and murdered on the high seas a

R. v. Serva and others, 1 Den. 104.

British prize crew unlawfully in possession of a Brazilian slaver it was held that they were not punishable under English law.

The Anglo-American dispute as to the asserted right of impress-ment of subjects on foreign vessels.

In the early days of the present century Great Britain maintained a supposed right, grounded in the inalienable character of British allegiance under British laws, to impress all British sailors found serving on board foreign merchant-men and to exercise a right of search for deserters from her fleet upon foreign vessels upon the high seas. The practical assertion of this claim culminated in 1807 in the forcible carrying off of certain deserters by H.M.S. "Leopard" from

Papers relating to the encounter between H.M.S. "Leopard" and the American frigate "Chesa-peake."

the U. S. frigate "Chesapeake," after an affray in which several of the crew of the American vessel were killed and wounded, than which high-handed proceeding history records no grosser outrage on national honour. This transaction was indeed repudiated by the British Government, and the author of the outrage, Admiral Berkeley, was recalled, but the British claim, as asserted by Canning himself, involved the right to search for deserters all foreign vessels on the

Mr Canning to Mr Monroe, Sept. 9, 1807.

high seas including, at any rate in special cases, foreign men-of-war. The supposed right must be pronounced to have been without the veriest shred of support in inter-national legal principle.

The claim of a belligerent to search for and seize on board neutral vessels on the high seas persons under his allegiance does not...rest on any belligerent right under the Law of Nations, but on a prerogative derived from Municipal Law; and involves the extravagant supposition that one nation has a right to execute, at all times and in all cases, its municipal laws and regulations on board the ships of another nation not being within its territorial limits." Mr Madison to G. H. Rose, March 1, 1808.

§ 21. An exception to the main rule is universally recognised in the case of proceedings directed to the suppression of piracy jure gentium. An exception in the case of piracy jure gentium.

" Pirates," says Chancellor Kent, " have been regarded by all civilised nations as the enemies of the human race, and the most atrocious violators of the universal law of society. They are everywhere pursued and punished with death." Abdy's Kent, p. 428.

Piracy is of two kinds : there is piracy jure gentium, and piracy under municipal law. Piracy jure gentium and piracy by municipal law.

Piracy jure gentium was defined by Justice Story in U. S. v. Smith in 1820 as "robbery upon the sea." It might be more precisely described as the offence of depredating upon the sea or by descent therefrom, without the sanction of any recognised public authority. The offence is commonly perpetrated animo furandi or lucri causa, but it is not essential for the commission of piracy that the act of aggression charged as piratical be done with a view to plunder. In re Tirnan, 5 B. and S. 645. Story, J. in U. S. v. Smith, 5 Wheaton, 161.

"A pirate," said Story, J. in the case of the Brig 'Malek Adhel,' "is deemed and properly deemed, hostis humani generis. But why is he so deemed? Because he commits hostilities upon the subjects and property of any or all nations without any regard to right or duty, or any pretence of public authority. If he wilfully sinks or destroys an innocent merchant ship, without any other object than to gratify his lawless appetite for mischief, it is just as much a piratical aggression, in the sense of the law of nations, and of the act of congress, as if he did it solely and exclusively for the sake of plunder, lucri causa." Wynne's Life of Jenkins, i. lxxxvi. Story, J. in U. S. v. Brig "Malek Adhel," 2 Howard, 232.

The principles governing the handling of the offence are fairly well recognised.

Essential elements of piracy.

(1) *The two essential elements of the offence are forcible aggression on or from the sea and the absence of the sanction of recognised responsible authority.*

Commission of unrecognised government is no defence.

(2) *The commission of an unrecognised Government is no defence on a charge of piracy*[1].

Thus in *U. S. v. Klintock* in 1820, where the prisoner, a citizen of the United States, had sailed as first lieutenant on the "Young Spartan," a privateer cruising under a commission from Aury, styling himself "Brigadier of the Mexican Republic," and "Generalissimo of the Floridas," which captured a Danish vessel under fraudulent circumstances, Marshall, C. J. laid it down that a commission granted by Aury, either as brigadier of the Mexican Republic, a republic of whose existence the court knew nothing, or as generalissimo of the

U. S. v. Klintock, 5 Wheaton 144.

Floridas, a province in the possession of Spain, would not avail in the Supreme Court to legitimatise the capture at sea of public or private vessels.

The Case of the "Huascar," 1877.

On the evening of May 6, 1877, in the absence of the captain and most of the officers, the crew of the Peruvian monitor "Huascar," lying in the harbour of Lima, revolted and declared for the insurrectionary leader, Don Nicholas Piérola. The vessel was immediately got under weigh and cleared out of the bay, steering for the south, no attempt to detain her being made by other Peruvian warships in the harbour. It was conjectured that her destination was Iquique, where she might hope to pick up Señor Piérola, and obtain coals and stores. After some hesitation the Government

---

[1] In the case of *U.S. v. the "Ambrose Light,"* it was held by District Court Judge Brown that an armed vessel found on the high seas in the hands of Colombian insurgents, who had not been recognised as belligerents by any independent power, was legally seized as piratical by an American gunboat; Snow 200. No act of forcible depredation on the high seas having however been exercised or threatened against any other than Colombian subjects, the decision in the case is more than questionable. Cf. the "Montezuma," Snow 206.

equipped and despatched a squadron in pursuit of the insurgents, but meanwhile on May 8th the Peruvian President issued a decree repudiating on behalf of the Government all responsibility for any acts of the rebels, authorising the capture of the "Huascar," and offering to recompense properly any person, not belonging to the crews of the vessels forming the squadron of operations, who should contribute to bring her under the authority of the Government. Exciting news of the "Huascar" soon reached Lima. Having on the high seas stopped two British steamers, including the Liverpool mail-packet, and made vain demands for the handing over of Peruvian official correspondence, she took out by force from a third British steamer two Peruvian Government officials, and finally crowned this series of acts of aggression by taking seven lighters of coal from a fourth British vessel without making any arrangements as to payment. Under these circumstances Rear-Admiral de Horsey, the British Commander-in-Chief on the station, deemed it his duty for the protection of British interests to put a stop to the proceedings of the rebel craft, and accordingly put to sea in pursuit. Coming up with the "Huascar" opposite Ilo with the "Shah" and the "Amethyst," he fought an action with her, and inflicted such damages upon her that, although she escaped under cover of darkness, she was compelled to surrender to the Peruvian squadron at Iquique on the following day.

This drastic action on the part of the British Admiral was keenly resented by the Peruvian populace, and, although he assured the Peruvian Government through the British representative at Lima that his proceedings were dictated solely by a sense of his duty to protect the interests of peaceable and law-abiding British subjects against the operations of a piratical craft, and in no way resulted from a desire to interfere in Peruvian internal movements, that Government deemed it necessary to join in the popular outcry, and to demand from the British Cabinet satisfaction for an outrage inflicted by the British commander "on the honour, sovereignty, and territorial immunity of a friendly state, without even a pretext to give an honest appearance to his action." "The 'Huascar,'" wrote the Peruvian Minister for Foreign Affairs to the Diplomatic Agents and Consuls of Peru abroad, "did not, on account of having refused to recognise the authority of Government, cease to belong to Peru. And, although the supreme decree of 8th May last was issued to bring about her apprehension, foreign ships of war were not thereby entitled to attack her, not only because International Law prohibits mixing in the internal affairs of other states, but also because the reward offered by that decree could not refer to the commanders of such ships without grossly offending their personal and national dignity."

Señor Rospigliosi to Mr Graham, June 25, 1877.

Parl. Papers, Peru, No. 1 (1877), p. 18.

The opinion of the British Law Officers having been asked by Lord Derby, they reported that, in their opinion, the papers submitted showed that the "Huascar" had been taken out of the hands of her lawful officers; that the Peruvian Government had disavowed any liability for her acts; and that she was consequently sailing under no national flag, and no redress could be obtained for any acts which she might commit; that, under these circumstances, she having been guilty of various acts of violence against British shipping and subjects on the high seas, Admiral de Horsey was bound to act decisively for the protection of British subjects and property, and his proceedings were in law justifiable. The action of the Admiral in putting a stop to the lawless proceedings of the "Huascar" was, in accordance with this opinion, formally approved by Earl Derby, with the reservation of a regret that he did not in the first instance endeavour to obtain redress by means of remonstrance, and the Peruvian claim for reparation was allowed to drop.

The action of the British admiral justified.

Parl. Papers, Peru, No. 1 (1877).

Commission

(3) *The possession of the regular commission of a recognised Government, whether of an independent state or of a*

belligerent community, at once removes a depredating vessel from the category of the pirate.

The Government granting a commission is responsible for acts done under its authorisation, and therefore endowed with exclusive jurisdiction over their perpetrators. The individual who levies war under the commission of a foreign Power may be punishable under his own municipal law, but internationally, except when treaty stipulations run to the contrary, he is a lawful belligerent. If, however, a foreigner depredate under commissions from two opposing belligerents, he may well be regarded as a pirate, his action being obviously actuated more by the *animus furandi*, the spirit of robbery, than by the *animus belligerandi*, the spirit of the honourable warrior.

(4) *The pirate jure gentium is justiciable in the courts of any nation, his conduct being an offence against every people.*

There may be pirates who are justiciable only in the courts of a single nation. These are pirates under municipal law. The relation between the two classes of offenders is capable of simple statement.

(i) Any state may by its municipal law announce the course which its courts are empowered to adopt with regard to the international outlaw who is guilty of piracy *jure gentium.* "The Constitution," said Marshall, C. J., "having conferred on Congress the power of defining and punishing piracy there can be no doubt of the right of the legislature to enact laws punishing pirates, although they may be foreigners, and may have committed no particular offence against the United States."

So an Act of Congress of 1819 declared that "if any person or persons whatsoever shall, upon the high seas, commit the crime of piracy, as defined by the law of nations, and such offender or offenders shall be brought into, or found in the United States, every such offender or offenders shall, upon conviction thereof, &c., be punishable with death."

(ii) A state may legislate for all persons on board its

Side notes:

of recognised government a complete defence.'

The "Divina Pastora,' 4 Wheat. 52. The "Neustra Señora de la Caridad," 4 Wheat. 497.

In re Tirnan, 5 B. and S. 680.

Wheaton, *Elements,* II. 2 § 123.

The pirate jure gentium is justiciable in the court of any nation.

The "Marianna Flora," 11 Wheat. 41.

Relation of piracy by municipal law to piracy jure gentium.

Marshall, C. J. in *U. S. v. Palmer,* 3 Wheaton, 630.

Piracy by

municipal law can be committed by a subject only.

vessels on the high seas or within its territorial waters, and for its citizens in any position whatever, and, in the exercise of this power, may declare any conduct on the part of such persons to be piratical. If the conduct so denounced does not fall within the definition of piracy *jure gentium*, the offenders are justiciable in the courts of the legislating power only, and the offence is merely piracy by *municipal law.* " Congress," said Mr Justice Johnson in *U. S. v. Palmer*, " can inflict punishment on offences committed on board the vessels of the United States, or by citizens of the United States anywhere, but Congress cannot make that piracy

Johnson, J. in *U. S. v. Palmer*, 3 Wheaton 642.

which is not piracy by the law of nations, in order to give jurisdiction to its own courts over such offences."

Slave-trading may be piracy by municipal law but is not piracy *jure gentium*.

It is now, in accordance with this doctrine, well settled law that, while one state may by its municipal law punish as piratical any slave-trading operations carried on by any persons under its flag, or by its citizens in any situation whatsoever, no state may enforce its anti-slavery policy against individuals covered by a foreign flag, except in virtue of express concession on the part of the sovereign of the flag.

Best, J. in *Madrazo v. Willes*, 3 B. and A. 358.

" The assertion of a right to control the subjects of other states in this respect, would be inconsistent with that independence which we acknowledge that every foreign government possesses."

The doctrine not at first recognised in Great Britain.

This view was not adopted by the British courts without some hesitation arising out of a keen desire to assist so far as possible in the suppression of the horrid traffic in human beings.

U. S. Statutes of Mar. 22, 1794: May 10, 1800; March 2, 1807; and April 20, 1818. Stats. 46 Geo. 3, c. 52; 47 Geo. 3. Sess. 1, c. 36; 51 Geo. 3, c. 22; 5 Geo. 4, cc. 17 and 113; 6 and 7 Vict. c. 98.

The United States and Great Britain had initiated the crusade against the trade by prohibiting by successive acts the engaging in it by their subjects, and had sought the support of other Governments.

In 1815 at Vienna and again in 1822 at Verona the representatives of the great Powers of Europe expressed the sincere desire of their sovereigns to concur in putting an end to " a scourge which has so long desolated Africa, degraded

Europe and afflicted humanity," and declared the universal Hertslet, Map of Europe, I. p. 60. abolition of the Slave Trade to be a measure particularly worthy of attention and conformable to the spirit of the Ibid. p. 695. times. The difficulty of the situation was, however, clearly brought out in the words with which the plenipotentiaries at the earlier Congress closed their general declaration.

"Too well acquainted…with the sentiments of their Sovereigns, not to perceive, that however honourable may be their views, they cannot be attained without due regard to the interests, the habits, and even the prejudices of their subjects ; the said plenipotentiaries at the same time acknowledge that this general Declaration cannot prejudice the period that each particular Power may consider as most advisable for the definitive abolition of the Slave Trade. Consequently, the determining the period when this trade is to cease universally must be a subject of negotiation between the Powers; it being understood, however, that no proper means of securing its attainment, and of accelerating its progress, are to be neglected; and that the engagement reciprocally contracted in the present Declaration, between the Sovereigns who are parties to it, cannot be considered as completely fulfilled, until the period when complete success shall have crowned their united efforts."

The difficulty thus pointed out was reflected in the decisions of the British courts.

In the cases of the "Amedie" in 1807 and the "Fortuna" The case of the "Amedie," 1807, and the "Fortuna," 1811. in 1811 the British courts displayed a strong inclination to treat the engaging in slave-trading operations as an international crime.

The "Amedie," an American vessel, was captured by an English cruiser, whilst employed in carrying slaves from the African coast to a Spanish colony, and condemned in a British West Indian Vice-Admiralty Court. The Court of Appeals in England affirmed the judgment, Sir William Grant laying it down that, whilst Great Britain had no right to control any foreign legislature which might see fit to recognise the legality of the incriminated traffic, she was entitled to regard the slave trade as *primâ facie* illegal, and to throw upon an individual reclaiming against the operation of the British edicts of suppression the onus of proving himself to have been dispossessed of some right to which he was entitled under his own law.

The authority of this decision was followed without examination by Sir W. Scott in 1811 in the case of the "Fortuna," an American vessel captured whilst sailing to the coast of Africa for slaves under the fraudulently assumed Portuguese flag. The principle laid down in the "Amedie" was taken by Sir W. Scott to be that "the slave trade carried on by a vessel belonging to a subject of the United States is a trade which, being unprotected by the domestic regulations of their legislature and Government, subjects the vessel engaged in it to a sentence of condemnation."

In 1813 the same great judge was, however, at pains carefully to limit the operation of this doctrine.

The "Diana," a Swedish vessel, being captured by a British cruiser whilst conveying a cargo of slaves from the African coast to the Swedish island of St Bartholomews, was condemned in the British Vice-Admiralty Court at Sierra Leone, the sentence of condemnation declaring that the slave trade from motives of humanity "hath been abolished by most civilised nations, and is not at the present time legally authorised by any." Sir W. Scott, on appeal, reversed the sentence. The court was, he said, disposed to go as far in discountenancing the odious traffic in question as the law of nations and the principles recognised by English tribunals would warrant, but beyond those principles it did not feel itself at liberty to travel; it could not proceed on a sweeping anathema of this kind against property belonging to the subjects of foreign independent states. The position laid down in the sentence of the court below that the slave trade was not authorised by any civilised state was, unfortunately, by no means correct, it being notoriously the fact that it was tolerated by some of them. This trade was at one time

The "Amedie," 1 Acton 240; 1 Dods. 34 n.

The "Fortuna," 1 Dods. 81.

Sir W. Scott in the "Fortuna," 1 Dods. 86.

The case of the "Diana," 1813.

universally allowed by the different nations of Europe, and
carried on by them to a greater or less extent, according to
their respective necessities. Sweden, having but small
colonial possessions, did not engage very deeply in the traffic,
but she entered into it so far as her convenience required
for the supply of her own colonies. The trade had been
abolished by some particular countries, but the court had
yet to learn that Sweden had prohibited her subjects from
engaging in it, or that she had abstained from it either in
act or declaration. Great Britain had taken a more correct
view and had decreed the abolition of the slave trade, as far
as British subjects were concerned; but she claimed no right
of enforcing her prohibition against the subjects of those
states which had not adopted the same opinion with respect
to the injustice and immorality of the traffic.

The
"Diana,"
1 Dods. 95.

Four years later the subject was reviewed by Sir W Scott,
and the doctrine enunciated, which has since held its ground.

The "Le Louis," a French vessel, was on March 11, 1816,
after a sharp struggle in which several men on either side
lost their lives, captured, whilst on a slave-trading expedition
from Martinique to the African coast, by the "Queen Charlotte," British cutter, and carried into Sierra Leone, where
she was condemned by the Vice-Admiralty Court. On
appeal, it was contended for the captors that the slave trade
was condemned by the law of France, and that the vessel
was therefore confiscable within the doctrine of the "Amedie."
Dr Lushington and Dr Dodson, for the appellants, while
denying that the slave trade was in fact condemned by any
French law in force at the time of the capture, took the
ground of the illegality of the exercise of any right of search
by a British vessel upon a foreign cruiser in time of peace,
except under special treaty or under general international
law. No special convention with France could, it was urged,
be cited to justify the exercise of the right of search over a
French vessel, and the engaging in the slave trade was not
piracy *jure gentium*.

The case
of the "Le
Louis,"
1816.

This contention was accepted by the court, and the
sentence of condemnation passed on the vessel reversed.
"To press forward," said Sir W. Scott, "to a great principle
by breaking through every other great principle that stands
in the way of its establishment; to force the way to the
liberation of Africa by trampling on the independence of
other states in Europe; in short, to procure an eminent good
by means that are unlawful; is as little consonant to private
morality as to public justice. Obtain the concurrence of
other nations, if you can, by application, by remonstrance, by
example, by every peaceable instrument which man can
employ to attract the consent of man. But a nation is not
justified in assuming rights that do not belong to her merely
because she means to apply them to a laudable purpose; nor
in setting out upon a moral crusade, of converting other
nations by acts of unlawful force."

The doctrine thus adopted was affirmed in subsequent
cases in the British courts, and was followed by the Supreme Court of the United States in the case of the
"Antelope" in 1825.

A mutual right of search for the suppression of the slave
trade within certain geographical limits was conceded by
treaties of 1831 and 1833 between France and Great Britain,
and the principle was extended by the Quintuple Treaty of
1841. By treaty of 1845, however, the joint cooperation of
British and French naval forces was substituted for the more
effective arrangement. By the Treaty of Washington of
1842 Great Britain and the United States agreed to co-
operate for the suppression of the slave trade by concerted
action of separate squadrons on the coast of Africa, but it
was not till 1862 that jealousy of British maritime claims
was so overcome that the Powers were able to agree upon a
mutual right of search of their merchantmen by men-of-war.
In recent years the activity of civilised states in the suppression of the traffic has been materially quickened by the
results of international deliberations at the West African

Conference of 1884 and the Brussels Conference of 1889–90 ; the blockade established on the African East Coast in 1888 by Germany, England, Italy and Portugal, with the assent of France, was a measure of high international police.   But by these proceedings the broad principle of law remains unaffected. The right of search for the suppression of slave-trading can be exercised by the cruiser of one Power against the shipping of another on the high seas only in pursuance of express treaty arrangement.

Revue de Droit Int. 1889, p. 207.

§ 22. The exercise by states of an extra-territorial jurisdiction constitutes no exception to the general principle that jurisdiction is co-extensive with territorial limits.

The exercise of an extra-territorial jurisdiction is no exception to the main rule.

Every state will, in general, exercise jurisdiction in respect of all offences against local law, whether by citizens or by foreigners, committed within its dominions, whether on land, or on a native or foreign private vessel within its territorial waters.   A state may in this way take cognizance of conduct within its borders which is directed against the peace or the laws of a foreign Power.

Stat. 24 and 25 Vict. c. 100, s. 4. R. v. Most, L. R. 7 Q. B. D. 244. R. v. Peltier, 28 St. Tr. 529.

A state may further take cognizance of the extra-territorial conduct of any of its citizens abroad on their return within its territorial bounds.   Many states do in fact deal with offences committed by their subjects abroad, whether on the high seas, within the territorial limits of other states, or in places beyond the bounds of any civilised country.   Great Britain, for example, regularly takes cognizance of the offences of British sailors in foreign ports, and of the crimes of treason, murder, manslaughter, piracy, and slave-trading, and of other misdemeanours committed by British citizens beyond her borders.   Thus, Joseph Azzopardi, a Maltese, having murdered a Dutchwoman in Smyrna, his conviction under Stat. 9 Geo. 4, c. 31, was held right by the Court for Crown Cases Reserved, whilst, on the other hand, jurisdiction was repudiated in the case of manslaughter committed upon a British sailor in Muscat by a Spaniard, one Mattos, late the interpreter of the victim's ship.

Stat. 17 and 18 Vict. c. 104, s. 267. Stat. 18 and 19 Vict. c. 19, s. 21. Stat. 35 Hen. 8, c. 2. Stat. 24 and 25 Vict. c. 100, s. 9. Stat. 33 and 34 Vict. c. 90. Stat. 5 Geo. 4, c. 113. R. v. Azzopardi, 2 Mood. C. C. 288. In re Tirnan, 5 B. and S. 679. R. v. Mattos, 7 C. and P. 458.

W.   5

Many states will even exercise jurisdiction over foreigners on their soil in respect of offences against foreign local law committed by them abroad. Thus the Mexican Courts in 1886 asserted a right to try a citizen of the United States arrested on Mexican soil for a libel on a Mexican subject published in Texas. The action of Mexico was strongly resented by the United States, but has a sufficiency of support alike in practice and in principle to establish its legality.

Cutting's case, Snow 172. 2 Wharton, Dig. 439. Holmes v. Jennison, 14 Pet. 569.

In every case the actual presence of the culprit or his property within territorial limits, or under the national flag on the high seas, is necessary for the effective exercise of jurisdiction.

Locality is necessary to found jurisdiction.

§ 23. It is no exception to the exclusive jurisdiction of the local sovereign within his own territories, landed or marine, that any state may in its discretion interfere to protect against ill-usage on the part of the territorial Government any person within foreign territory whom it regards as its citizen.

A state may interfere to protect a citizen abroad.
2 Wharton, Dig. 316.

The just principles which should direct the conduct of Governments in this regard were correctly stated by Canning in the case of Mr Bowring. Mr Bowring, an English subject travelling in France, being arrested on the nominal charge of illegally conveying letters, really on suspicion of entertaining sentiments opposed to the Bourbon Government, Canning instructed the British Ambassador in Paris to watch over the case, and take care that the prisoner received justice *according to the French law.* It appearing that Mr Bowring had by conveying letters actually justified his arrest, Canning deemed further interference impossible, intimating that "an individual who entered voluntarily into a foreign country, at the same time entered into a temporary and qualified allegiance to the laws of that country; that he confined himself to their observance; that he submitted to their operation; and that, however unwise the system of law might be in itself, however harsh, however little congruous to his notions of civil liberty, or to his happier experience of the jurisprudence of his own country, he had still no right to complain of the operation of those laws on himself, provided that operation was not partial, but was the same as it would be in the case of a natural-born subject of that state." *Stapleton's Life of Cunning, t. 364.*

In 1853 Captain Ingraham of the U. S. man-of-war " S. Louis " interfered to compel by a display of force the release by the Austrian man-of-war " Hussar " of Martin Koszta, a Hungarian rebel, who, after a residence of some two years in America, where he had made a formal declaration of his intention to become a citizen of the United States, had returned to Smyrna, where he was arrested by the Austrian consul under capitulation with Turkey and placed on the " Hussar " for removal to Austria. The circumstances of the case seem to suggest certain simple considerations :— *The case of Martin Koszta, 1853.*

(1) Koszta was not an American citizen even under U. S. laws. He was a citizen of Austria under Austrian law.

(2) Even had Koszta been a citizen of the United States under American law, he would have been, under the general principles of international law, in default of Austro-American treaty, or Austrian law rendering the assumption of American citizenship *per se* a complete renunciation of Austrian citizen character, nevertheless subject to the operation of Austrian laws as an Austrian citizen, wherever the Austrian laws could legally operate. *The action of the American commander was legally unjustifiable.*

(3) Citizens of Austria might under capitulation between Austria and the Porte be lawfully seized by the Austrian consul at Smyrna for offences committed within the Austrian dominions against Austrian law, and Martin Koszta was so seized.

(4) The possession of an American passport, a fact which was urged on his behalf, although it does not certainly appear that Koszta was actually in possession of such a document, could not protect an Austrian citizen in his situation against the operation of Austrian law. Martin Koszta was, therefore, in a word, lawfully arrested and held in custody by the

Austrians at Smyrna, and no sufficient legal ground appears for American intervention on his behalf.

Lastly (5) Turkey might well resent the conduct of Captain Ingraham in preparing for hostile action in Turkish territorial waters.

President Pierce, however, announced his complete approval of the action of the American officers at Smyrna, and the thanks of Congress with a medal were voted to Captain Ingraham for his "judicious and gallant conduct." Koszta himself was, by arrangement made on the intervention of the foreign consuls at Smyrna, who were anxious to prevent a conflict in the port, handed over to the French consul, and subsequently shipped back to America under convention between the two interested Governments. The Austrian Government, however, protested stoutly in a circular despatch against the conduct of Captain Ingraham, and it seems impossible to resist the conclusion that that protest was thoroughly well grounded. The American Government, which had displayed a rather too strong sympathy for the cause of the Hungarian rebels of 1848, may have been actuated by desire to save a human life, but their zeal for humanity outran their regard for law and the independence of foreign nations.

Cussy, Phases et Causes Célèbres, II. 12, § 12. Martens, N. Causes Célèbres, v. p. 583. 2 Wharton, Dig. 358.

The main rule is generally laid aside in certain special cases :—

§ 24. In certain special cases the necessities of international courtesy and the pressure of convenience have occasioned and licensed departure from the broad general rule that territory and jurisdiction are co-extensive.

The exceptions thus introduced are justifiable within the very compass of the rule. For "all exceptions to the full and complete power of a nation within its own territories must be traced up to the consent of the nation itself. They can flow from no other legitimate source."

Marshall, C. J. in the Schooner Exchange v. McFaddon.

(a) Foreign sovereigns and their suites.

§ 25. (a) Foreign Sovereigns travelling within a state in their proper character, together with their personal attendants, are held exempt from the local jurisdiction.

The extent

(1) The personal exemption of the foreign sovereign from

the process of the local law, whether criminal or civil, is of the exemption accorded; universally and clearly recognised, the sole exception being possibly when by personal service or by the facts of birth he possesses a dual character, and even this exception is of a dubious character. It is clear law that a foreign sovereign cannot within British dominions be made responsible for an act done in his sovereign character abroad, even though in Great Britain he be a British subject. And in respect of acts committed upon British soil itself the plea of foreign sovereign character would doubtless suffice to secure the culprit against personal chastisement, other than expulsion, by British municipal authority. The personal exemption of the sojourning foreign sovereign from the operation of the local law is, in fact, absolute and complete, so long, at any rate, as (i) the sovereign character is retained, and (ii) the exemption is compatible with the security of the territorial ruler.

1. Personal freedom from local process,
The Parlement Belge,
L. R. 5 Prob. D. 205.
Duke of Brunswick v. King of Hanover,
2 Cl. and F., H. L. C. 17.

The privilege further extends to protect (2) the residence (the *hôtel*) of the sovereign, (3) his personal belongings, provided these be owned by him in his sovereign capacity, and (4) his personal attendants. If an offence against local law be committed by a member of a foreign royal suite, application for redress must be made to his master, who may in his discretion remit the offender for punishment at home or surrender him to the local authorities.

2. Inviolability of the *Hôtel*,
3. Sanctity of property,
Vavasseur v. Krupp, L. R. 9 Ch. 351.
De Haber v. Queen of Portugal, 17 Q. B. 196.
4. Protection of the suite.

The privilege does not, however, operate to endow the foreign sovereign with any local jurisdiction. The travelling sovereign must whilst on foreign soil refrain from the exercise of any of the special functions of the ruler. Practice has gradually become more stringent in this regard. Richard I., on his way to the Crusades, hanged robbers outside his camp at Messina, dealing out equal justice to the stranger and the native. At a much later date sovereigns were accustomed, whilst sojourning abroad, to exercise a jurisdiction at once civil and criminal within the walls of their residences and over their own subjects. It is recorded that a certain thief,

The foreign sovereign may not exercise a local jurisdiction.
Richard of Devizes, s. 20.

Engelram de Nogent, being taken in a house at Paris wherein Edward I. of England was then resident, the question of the right of the English monarch to exercise jurisdiction over the criminal was discussed in the French Courts, and the claim admitted, the felon being accordingly hanged *in patibulo sancti Germani de pratis* (on the gibbet of St Germains in the Meadows), after conviction on trial before the Seneschal Robert Fitz-John in the *hôtel* of the English King. Engelram de Nogent was presumably a native Frenchman. Nearly four centuries later another English monarch exercised authority in similar fashion over one of his own suite, Charles II. having when in exile in Germany in 1655 caused to be shot, in a castle belonging to the Duke of Neuburg, one Manning, a member of his suite, whom he detected in treasonable correspondence with Secretary Thurloe.

In 1657 when staying at Fontainebleau Christina of Sweden, who had three years previously resigned her crown, caused to be put to death the Marquis Monaldeschi, an Italian, one of her chief attendants, whom she charged with having betrayed some important secret. This extraordinary incident gave rise to much discussion amongst the jurists of the period, three important questions connected with the personal rights of a sovereign being observed to be involved: viz. (1) Does a sovereign hospitably entertained within the territory of another retain the power to exact the death penalty for the crime of his domestic? (2) If so, can he put to death a criminal, his domestic, who is the subject of a foreign sovereign? (3) Does a prince who has abdicated retain the peculiar personal privileges of a reigning sovereign? Very various opinions were expressed on the points thus raised by the contemporaries of Christina, but the conduct of the mad Queen did not want able champions. In our day these questions are no longer open. The jurisdiction of a sojourning foreign sovereign is now held to be limited at least to the settlement of ordinary civil contentions amongst members of his suite: a member of that suite offending

4. Rep. 15 citing Fleta, Lib. 2, cap. 3, § 9.

even over a member of his suite. Martens, *Causes Célèbres*, i. 29 n.

Martens, *Causes Célèbres*, i. pp. 1—34.

against criminal law must, if not, as he may be, handed over to the local authorities, be sent for trial at home : he cannot be tried by his master on foreign soil. Such a proceeding as that of Christina would, according to present practice, be deemed incapable of justification, even though the sovereign exercising authority were a reigning monarch, and recourse were had to the regular judicial forms of the sovereign's own state.

In every case the local sovereign retains in the last resort the power of expulsion, and to this weapon he may well have recourse against any proceedings of a sojourning foreign ruler which tend to undermine his authority or that of the local law. *The privilege of the foreign sovereign does not justify an attack upon local authority.*

§ 26. (β) **Ambassadors and other diplomatic agents are granted a similar exemption from the local jurisdiction within the territorial limits of the state to which they are accredited.** *(β) Diplomatic agents and their suites.*

A state may, provided good reason be assigned, as on account of the known obnoxious character of the person proposed, or of the disagreeable purpose of his mission, refuse to receive a particular diplomatic agent, but, if once received, the agent is held entitled to be treated as the representative of national honour, his privilege being co-extensive with his mission. *Schooner Exchange v. McFaddon. The Parlement Belge, L. R., 5 Prob. D. 207. 1 Wharton, Dig. 596.*

(1) The privilege extends to the complete personal exemption of the ambassador from criminal prosecution at the hands of the local law, even for offences directly aimed at the sovereignty of the local ruler. This exemption has been repeatedly upheld under circumstances of the gravest provocation. *1. The personal exemption of the ambassador from criminal prosecution.*

Leslie, Bishop of Ross, who came to and was received in England in 1567 as the ambassador of Mary, Queen of Scots, then detained in an English prison, being detected in a conspiracy against Elizabeth, the civilians who were consulted by Elizabeth's ministers advised that (1) an ambassador procuring an insurrection against the sovereign to whom he is accredited ought not, *jure gentium et civili Romanorum*, to enjoy the privileges due to an ambassador; and that (2) an ambassador aiding and comforting a traitor against the prince to whom he is accredited is punishable at the hands of that prince. The Bishop, however, insisted stoutly on his privilege and was, though threatened with punishment, ultimately in 1573 merely banished from the country, whilst his fellow-conspirators suffered death.

Ward, Law of Nations, II. 486.

In 1584 Mendoza, the Spanish ambassador in England, was likewise detected in a plot for the dethronement of Elizabeth. The Council now took the opinion of Albericus Gentilis and Hottoman, who advised that the ambassador could not be punished with death under the English law, but must be referred for punishment to his sovereign. Mendoza was accordingly ordered to quit the realm, a special complaint against him being preferred to Philip.

Ward, II. 522.

When in 1587 L'Aubespine, the French ambassador in London, was detected in a plot for the assassination of the Queen, no attempt was made to try him.

Ward, II. 523.

Alphonso de la Cueva, Marquis de Bedmar, the Spanish ambassador to Venice in 1618, having engaged in a conspiracy for the overthrow of the Venetian Government and the firing of the city, the Senate, while putting to death his fellow-conspirators without mercy, not only respected the legatine character of the arch-conspirator, but conveyed him secretly out of the state, to save him from the fury of the incensed populace, a demand for his recall being made to the King of Spain.

Martens, Nouvelles C. C. II. App. iii. Causes Célèbres, I. 471.

In 1717 Count Gyllenborg, the Swedish ambassador in London, being detected in a great plot for the restoration of the Stuarts, was arrested, and papers, which demonstrated his guilt, were seized. In the following year the same procedure was followed with respect to the Prince de Cellamare, the Spanish ambassador in Paris, who had acted in France as the main agent in another ramification of the same plot directed to the overthrow of the Regent Orleans. In each case, however, although the obvious guilt of the parties

Martens, Causes Célèbres, I. 96.

Ibid. I. 149.

prevented stronger protest, the extraordinary character of the proceeding was freely admitted, and no attempt to punish the ambassadors was made, they being merely despatched to their own frontiers.

(2) The inviolability of the ambassador alike in person and goods as against local civil process is equally clearly recognised.

The Stat. 7 Anne, cap. 12, which, originating in the arrest for debt in London in 1708 of Mattueof, the ambassador of Peter the Great, was deemed declaratory of the Law of Nations, enacts that "all writs and processes that shall at any time hereafter be sued forth or prosecuted, whereby the person of any ambassador, or other publick minister of any foreign prince or state, authorised and received as such by Her Majesty, her heirs or successors, or the domestick, or domestick servant of any ambassador, or other public minister, may be arrested or imprisoned, or his or their goods or chattels may be distrained, seized or attached, shall be deemed and adjudged to be utterly null and void, to all intents, constructions, and purposes whatsoever[1]." The privilege extends, according to the British view, to protect "whatever is necessary to the convenience of an ambassador, as connected with his rank, his duties, and his religion." Real property owned by a foreign ambassador as a private individual, and even under certain circumstances chattels belonging to him, may in accordance with this rule be subject to obligations imposed by the local law.

"It is said,—and perhaps truly said,—" said Jervis, C. J. in *Taylor v. Best* in 1854, "that an ambassador or foreign minister is privileged from suit in the courts of the country to which he is accredited, or, at all events, from being proceeded against in a manner which may ultimately result in the coercion of his person, or the seizure of his personal effects necessary to his comfort and dignity; and that he

Margin notes:

2. The exemption of the ambassador from local civil process. Martens, *Causes Célèbres*, I. 73.

Stat. 7 Anne, c. 12, s. 3.

The exemption of the ambassador's goods not absolute. Abbott, C. J. in Novello v. Toogood, 1 B. and C. 562. Gladstone v. Musurus Bey, 1 H. and M. 495. 1 Wharton, *Dig.* 653.

---

[1] The statute does not protect the servant of an ambassador, who is a merchant or trader within any of the statutes against bankrupts, Sec. 5.

cannot be compelled, *in invitum*, or against his will, to engage in any litigation in the courts of the country to which he is sent. But all the foreign jurists hold that, if the suit can be founded without attacking the personal liberty of the ambassador, or interfering with his dignity or personal comfort, it may proceed. Various passages have been cited to show that, in countries where the Civil Law prevails, and where jurisdiction can be founded by a proceeding *in rem* in the first instance, where there are houses or lands, which are immovable, that may be taken to found the jurisdiction, the suit may proceed. Movable goods, too, which are unconnected with the personal comfort and dignity of the ambassador, may be taken for the same purpose."

Jervis, C. J. in Taylor v. Best, 14 C. B. 521.

An ambassador may submit himself to local process.

If a public minister chooses voluntarily to submit himself to the local jurisdiction, he is free to do so, and the local Courts are in no way called upon to protect him against his own act.

Taylor v. Best, 14 C. B. 407.

Ambassadors engaging in local commerce.

Practice is not uniform with respect to the treatment of an ambassador who actually engages in local mercantile pursuits, but even here his special privilege is admitted in Great Britain.

"If an ambassador or public minister, during his residence in this country, violates the character in which he is accredited to our court, by engaging in commercial transactions, that may raise a question between the government of this country and that of the country by which he is sent; but he does not thereby lose the general privilege which the law of nations has conferred upon persons filling that high character,—the proviso in the statute of Anne limiting the privilege in cases of trading applying only to the servants of the embassy."

Jervis, C. J. in Taylor v. Best, 14 C. B. 519.

3. Exemption of the ambassador from local municipal obligations.

(3) The diplomatic agent is exempted from the performance of any local municipal duties. Complaint may well be made should he fail to comply with police and administrative regulations as to sanitation and the like, but he is exempt from all local taxation in respect of property held by him as minister, including the payment of customs duties on

goods imported for his personal use, and from such obligations as jury service. He is not even compellable to give evidence as a witness in a court of law. The Venezuelan minister, who was an eye-witness of the assassination of President Garfield, gave as a mark of the sympathy of his Government with the United States evidence against Guiteau, but Mr Dubois, the Dutch minister in Washington in 1856, refused to give evidence in a case of murder except by sworn deposition.

Parkinson v. Potter, 16 Q. B. D. 152.
1 Wharton, Dig. 652.
The ambassador as a witness.
1 Wharton, Dig. 669.
Snow, p. 98.
1 Wharton, Dig. 668.

(4) A certain sanctity is accorded to the residence (the *hôtel*) of the ambassador, he being allowed a peculiar jurisdiction for religious and domestic purposes and the transaction of certain forms of business amongst subjects of his sovereign. But the walls of the embassy are not in general practice admitted to constitute a sanctuary for native criminals. When in 1726 the Duke of Ripperda was forcibly taken from the house of the English ambassador at Madrid, the Duke of Newcastle, whilst complaining of the proceeding in the special case, expressly guarded himself against the advance of any claim that foreign embassies could protect the persons of subjects of the territorial sovereign against the consequences of offences committed by them. In 1747 a similar incident occurred at Stockholm, and in 1760 Mr Mitchell, the British ambassador in Berlin, declared that he knew of no asylum conferred by an ambassador's house against crimes of state. An opposite practice would, however, appear to have been adopted in the Spanish South-American Republics, but this in consideration of exceptional local convenience. Mr Bassett, the representative of the United States in Hayti in 1875, having afforded asylum to some political refugees, his conduct was emphatically disapproved by his Government. "You are aware," wrote the Acting Secretary of State to Mr Preston, the Haytian minister, "that Mr Bassett, the minister resident of the United States at Port-au-Prince, has thought proper to receive into his official residence certain political refugees.

4. Sanctity of the ambassador's *hôtel*.
It cannot protect the native criminal.
1 Wharton, Dig. 678.

Duke of Newcastle to Marquis de Pozzo Bueno, June 26, 1726.
Martens, *Causes Célèbres*, i. 199.
Martens, *Ibid.* ii. 52.
Exceptional practice in Southern America.
1 Wharton, Dig. 693.
Snow, 142.

This act on his part has not been approved by this Depart-ment, as it is not sanctioned by public law, though it is inconformity with precedents in that quarter."

1 Wharton,
Dig. 681.

In 1867 a Russian subject committed, in the absence ofthe ambassador, a murderous assault within the walls of theRussian embassy at Paris upon one of the attachés of thelegation. The local police, being called in, arrested theculprit. The Russian ambassador, on being apprised of theoccurrence, demanded that the prisoner should be sent fortrial to Russia. The French Government however refusedto give up the criminal, arguing that the privilege enjoyedby the embassy did not cover the case of a stranger enteringand committing a crime within its walls, and that in anyevent the privilege had been in this case waived by thecalling in of the Parisian police. The Russian Governmentultimately yielded the point, and the prisoner was tried bythe French Courts.

Nitchencoff's
Case, Snow,
103 n.

Boyd's
Wheaton, II.
i. § 225.
Snow, 103 n.

5. Ex-
emption
from
local
process of
the am-
bassador's
family and
suite.

(5) The exemption extends to the family and suite ofthe ambassador, and, according to general practice, to thedomestics of the embassy, even though citizens of the terri-torial sovereign. British practice limits the immunity of thedomestic. "The privilege is conferred by the law of nations,"said Holroyd, J., in *Novello v. Toogood*, "in order that theambassador may not be prejudiced in his dignity or personalcomfort; it is not given for the benefit of the servant."Accordingly the immunity of the servant is lost, if he engagein local trading. The coachman of Mr Gallatin, the UnitedStates Minister in London in 1827, having committed anassault outside the embassy, the local police insisted onarresting the culprit, even within its walls. The Englishpractice is seemingly now exceptional, but was at one timenot without foreign support.

Taylor v.
Best, 14 C.
B. 487.
1 Wharton,
Dig. 644.

The
privilege
of the am-
bassador's
domestic
not abso-
lute.

Holroyd J.
in Novello v.
Toogood, 1
B. and C.
564.
1 Wharton,
Dig. 650.
U. S. v.
Jeffers,
Snow 140.
Hall, II. 4,
§ 51.
Martens,
Causes
Célèbres,
II. 22.

If an ambassador misuse his privilege, or otherwiserender himself obnoxious to the territorial sovereign, hisrecall may be demanded: in graver cases he may be sus-pended by the local sovereign from the exercise of his

Remedies
for misuse
of diplo-
matic
privilege.

1 Wharton,
Dig. § 84.

functions, or even dismissed.   His inviolability is in any case conterminous with his mission.   In respect of his offences he is otherwise punishable only at the hands of his own sovereign.   The inferior members of the mission offending against local law may be handed over for trial by the local authorities, or in the alternative sent home for trial, the right of the ambassador personally to correct the members of his suite or household for other than mere domestic offences being by no means generally established.

§ 27. (γ) **Foreign men-of-war are by the universal consensus of nations allowed when within territorial waters a tolerably complete exemption from the jurisdiction of the local sovereign.**

(1) The exemption of the vessel herself from all process of the local law is now universally admitted.

In December 1810 the "Exchange," owned by John McFaddon and William Greetham, citizens of Maryland, was captured by a French cruiser and taken into a French port. Subsequently she was at Bayonne provided with a French national commission, and in July 1811 as the "Balaon," French vessel of war, entered under stress of weather the port of Philadelphia.   Here she was seized and detained under process of the District Court issued on the libel of her original owners.   The District judge, after argument and the production of the commission of the French commander, dismissed the libel with costs on the ground that a public armed vessel of a foreign sovereign, in amity with the Government of the United States, was not subject to the ordinary judicial tribunals of the country, so far as regarded the question of title by which such sovereign claimed to hold the vessel.   This sentence having been reversed by the Circuit Court on appeal, the Supreme Court upheld the decision of the District Judge, Marshall, C. J., laying it down as a principle of public law, that national ships of war, entering the port of a friendly power open for their reception, are to be considered as exempted by the consent of that

(γ) Foreign war-vessels in territorial waters.
The Schooner Exchange v. McFaddon, 7 Cranch 116.
The Parlement Belge, L. R., 5 Prob. D. 197.
Briggs v. Light Boats, 11 Allen (Mass.) 157.
1. Exemption of the vessel herself from local process.
The "Charkieh," L. R.
The "Prince Frederick," 2 Dods. 451.
The Schooner Exchange v. McFaddon, 7 Cranch 116.
The "Constitution," 48 L. J., N. S., P. D. and A. 13.
The Parlement Belge, L. R., 5 Prob. D. 197.
The Schooner Exchange v McFaddon, 7 Cranch 116.

power from its jurisdiction. "The 'Exchange,' being a public armed ship in the service of a foreign sovereign, with whom the Government of the United States is at peace, and having entered an American port open for her reception, on the terms on which ships of war are generally permitted to enter the ports of a friendly power, must be considered as having come into the American territory, under an implied, promise that, while necessarily within it, and demeaning herself in a friendly manner, she should be exempt from the jurisdiction of the country."

The "Constitution,"
48 L. J.,
P. D. and A.
13.
Sir R. Phillimore in the "Constitution."

So in the case of the "Constitution" in 1879 the British Court of Admiralty refused a warrant to arrest an American man-of-war and her cargo on suit for salvage for services rendered by British tug-owners. "I have no doubt," said Sir R. Phillimore, "as to this general proposition—that ships of war belonging to another nation with whom we are at peace are exempt from the civil jurisdiction of the courts of this country; and I have listened in vain for any peculiar circumstances which would take this case out of that general proposition."

2. Exemption of the ship's company in mere matters of internal discipline.

(2) The privilege is clearly recognised on behalf of persons on board the foreign man-of-war in respect of all questions involving the internal discipline of the ship, and of all acts of the ship's company committed amongst themselves, when on shipboard. "It may be readily admitted," says Sir A. Cockburn, "that by the universal concurrence of all maritime nations, so far as the government and discipline of a man-of-war are concerned, those on board remain subject to the law alone which the ship carries everywhere with her, namely, the military law of the nation under whose flag she sails."

Report of the Royal Commission on Fugitive Slaves, p. xxx.

Case of G. Britain presented to the Tribunal of Arbitration at Geneva, App. Vol. 1. p. 112.

The senior officer of the Confederate steamer "Sumter," lying in the port of Gibraltar, having been murdered by his subordinate, Mr Hester, the culprit was sent out to Bermuda in a British man-of-war in order to be landed at a Confederate port for trial within the Confederate States.

(3) It may probably be further laid down that no process under local law will run to reach persons, being members of the ship's company, on board a foreign man-of-war within territorial waters in respect of acts extending beyond the ship's company, whether shore offences or offences committed on board.

3. Sanctity of the vessel against the service of local process.

This extension of the privilege of the national flag of war has not been adopted without considerable hesitation.

In May 1794 the General Assembly of Rhode Island having received information that several American seamen illegally impressed in the West Indies were being forcibly detained on board H.M.'s sloop-of-war " Nautilus " lying in the harbour of Newport, the commander of the " Nautilus," Captain Baynton, was detained on shore, whilst a deputation of five persons appointed by the Lower House visited the vessel and obtained the release of the men. The Attorney General of the United States, Mr Bradford, seems to have been inclined to regard the action of the Newport authorities as justifiable, and to have been of opinion that a writ of habeas corpus would run to compel the commander of a British man-of-war lying in American waters to bring up the body of a person on board claiming to be American and illegally detained.

Case of the " Nautilus," 1794.

Report of the Royal Commission on Fugitive Slaves, p. lxxii.

In the case of the " Chesterfield," too, in 1799, the U.S. Attorney General Lee advised that " it is lawful to serve civil or criminal process upon a person on board a British ship of war lying in the harbour of New York, adjacent to a wharf, and within the territory of the State of New York."

Case of the " Chesterfield," 1799.

Report of the Royal Commission on Fugitive Slaves, p. lxxv.

In the later case of the " Sitka," however, a British vessel of war which put into an American Western port, having on board a number of Russian prisoners of war, Attorney General Cushing unhesitatingly recognised the principle of the general exemption of the foreign man-of-war from the American local jurisdiction, and denied the right of the United States to try by issue of a writ of habeas corpus the

Case of the " Sitka."

question of the legality of the detention of a person as a prisoner of war on board such a vessel in American waters.

The general principles applicable to such cases are fairly clear.

Extent of the privilege.

(i) Every sovereign possesses a general, absolute and exclusive jurisdiction for all purposes whatsoever within his dominions, including his territorial waters. Any exception from this jurisdiction enjoyed by any person or property within those dominions must arise from the consent, tacit or express, of the territorial sovereign.

The Schooner Exchange v. McFaddon, 7 Cranch 136.

(ii) Every sovereign may, for reasons which seem sufficient to him, expressly interdict the entrance into his territorial waters of foreign men-of-war, may expressly impose any conditions upon the permission of such entrance which he may deem proper, and may warn off, or, if need be, forcibly expel an obnoxious visitor.

(iii) A vessel of war under national commission represents in a peculiar fashion by virtue of its special organisation the force, dignity and administrative power of the sovereign whose flag she bears. The acts of the vessel are *primâ facie* the acts of the sovereign: the responsibility of the sovereign is obvious and direct in respect of all which transpires on board.

(iv) Though a sovereign may voluntarily submit his person, his property, or any emblem of his dignity to the control and jurisdiction of another ruler, he cannot be fairly assumed to intend so to submit himself or his without some express formal declaration of his will to that effect.

(v) If, therefore, without any such declaration of willingness on the part of the commissioning sovereign to subject his vessel to the local ruler, and without any express imposition on the part of the local ruler of conditions on the admission of the vessel, a foreign man-of-war enter territorial waters, it may be fairly assumed that she so enters on a footing of reciprocal dignity, viz. on the understanding that, on the one hand, the local ruler will exercise no right of control which trenches upon the dignity of the commissioning sovereign, and, on the other, that the vessel shall comport herself with all due respect towards the local law. It may be fairly assumed that in sending his vessel into foreign waters the commissioning sovereign in no way resigns control over and responsibility for acts belonging to the government and discipline of the ship; it cannot be fairly assumed, in default of express declaration to that effect, that the local sovereign in allowing the entrance of the vessel consents to the introduction of privileged violators of the local law, or to the establishment of a floating sanctuary for the native criminal.

In accordance with these principles it is well settled law that :—

(a) *The foreign man-of-war within territorial waters cannot afford sanctuary for the local criminal, except in the cases of the political offender (semble) and the fugitive slave.*

In general, a fugitive taking refuge on board a foreign man-of-war within the territorial waters of any state after committing a crime ashore against the law of that state must, in default of express treaty to the contrary, be surrendered by the commander of the vessel on requisition by the local authorities, and that whether the fugitive be a native of the state, an ordinary subject of the sovereign under whose flag he takes refuge, or even a member of the ship's company.

In 1820 John Brown, a British subject, who had been captured by the Spaniards whilst in command of an insurgent vessel engaged in a revolt against Spanish authority, escaped from prison and took refuge on board H.M.S. "Tyne" in the port of Lima. The commander of the "Tyne" having refused his surrender and brought him in safety to England, Lord Castlereagh, adopting the advice of Sir William Scott that Captain Falcon's conduct was more to be commended for its humanity and spirit than for its strict legality, disavowed the action of that officer. To assume that the British flag

(a) No sanctuary on the foreign vessel for the local criminal,

Case of John Brown. Halleck, II. 7.

could protect Brown against the legal process of the territorial jurisdiction was, wrote Lord Castlereagh, "to maintain a principle which the British Government desire distinctly to disclaim as not consistent with their uniform practice, or with the Law of Nations.'

Report of the Royal Commission on Fugitive Slaves, p. lxxvii.

except for the political refugee (semble) and the fugitive slave.

Since the time of Lord Stowell a practice has, however, undoubtedly grown up in support of the protection of the political refugee who escapes on board a foreign man-of-war, and by Article 28 of the General Act of the Brussels Conference relative to the African Slave Trade signed at Brussels on July 2, 1890, and subsequently ratified by well-nigh all the leading civilised Powers[1], it was agreed that "Any slave who may have taken refuge on board a ship of war flying the flag of one of the Signatory Powers shall be immediately and definitively freed; such freedom, however, shall not withdraw him from the competent jurisdiction, if he has committed a crime or offence at common law[2]."

General Act of the Brussels Conference 1889—90, Art. xxviii. Parl. Papers, Africa, No. 7, 1890, p. 7.

(b) No exemption for the assailant of the local ruler.

(b) *The privilege of exterritoriality accorded to the foreign man-of-war within territorial waters does not extend to protect a vessel guilty of actual aggression against the security of the territorial ruler.*

The right of self-defence will in all cases justify the repelling of force by force, and a vessel guilty of a direct attack upon the sovereignty of the local ruler may thus be seized by way of prevention of further violence, or at the least expelled. In the spirit of this principle a foreign man-of-war, which refuses to respect harbour regulations as to sanitation, anchorage and the like, may be ordered out of port.

The "Virginius," Parl. Papers, Spain, No. 3 (1874).

---

[1] Germany, Belgium, Denmark, Spain, Great Britain, Italy, the Netherlands, Sweden and Norway, Austria, Russia, France, the United States, Portugal, Turkey, Persia, the Congo Free State and Zanzibar.

[2] For earlier practice and opinion see the Report of the Royal Commission on Fugitive Slaves 1876 and *Parl. Papers, Slave Trade, No. 1* (1876). For the present British practice see *Instructions for the Guidance of the Captains and Commanding Officers of H.M.'s ships of war employed in the suppression of the Slave Trade, 1892.*

(4)   The exemption ceases with the ship and its boats. Members of a man-of-war's company ashore in a foreign port are universally admitted to be subject to the local jurisdiction and as such triable for offences against the local law.

So, too, it is clear law that the inviolability accorded to a foreign man-of-war within territorial waters does not extend to protect from process at the hands of the local authorities prize goods put ashore or prizes brought into port after capture in violation of the territorial jurisdiction of the country into which they are brought. "We are of opinion," said Story, J., "that whatever may be the exemption of the public ship herself, and of her armament and munitions of war, the prize property which she brings into our ports is liable to the jurisdiction of our courts, for the purpose of examination and enquiry, and, if a proper case be made out, for restitution to those whose possession has been divested by violation of our neutrality; and if the goods are landed from the public ship in our ports by the express permission of our own Government, that does not vary the case, since it involves no pledge that, if illegally captured, they shall be exempted from the ordinary operation of our laws."

§ 28.   (8) "The grant of a free passage implies a waiver of all jurisdiction over the troops during their passage, and permits the foreign general to use that discipline and to inflict those punishments which the government of his army may require."

§ 29.   A state may further surrender or vary its general international rights in respect of any other state by special treaty stipulation, provided that the vested rights of a third Power be not thereby infringed.

Any two states may in the exercise of their independence determine for themselves the conditions of their mutual international dealings, so long as the equal rights of other Powers be not injuriously affected.   Thus in certain Oriental communities all subjects of Christian Powers are invested with peculiar privileges in virtue of express treaty with the local rulers.   The extent of these privileges is determined in

Margin notes:

(4) The exemption ceases with the vessel and her boats.

Prize goods landed from a foreign man-of-war are subject to local process, as well as prizes brought in after capture in violation of local territorial rights.

The "Santissima Trinidad," 7 Wheat. 352. Story, J. in the "Santissima Trinidad," 7 Wheat. 353.

(8) Foreign troops passing by permission through territory. Marshall, C. J. in the Schooner Exchange v. McFaddon 7 Cranch 140.

States may vary their mutual international rights by express treaty.

Exterritoriality of Western residents in the East.

each instance by the special capitulation. In general the Western residents are exempted from the process of the territorial courts, and the jurisdiction in matters affecting them is vested in Consular tribunals, the consul, who elsewhere is a mere commercial agent and enjoys no special exemption from local law, being for this purpose erected into a judicial officer, and endowed with peculiarly extensive protective powers.

Conditions of the international validity of a treaty.

§ 30. The conditions of the international validity of a treaty are in the main merely the conditions of validity of any ordinary contract.

These conditions are in fact chiefly four :—

1. Capacity of the parties,

(1) The parties to the treaty must be possessed of full contractual capacity, i.e. they must, in general, be independent states.

2. Authority of the contracting agents,

(2) The contracting agents must contract within the terms of their authority. The determination of the contractual authority of the contracting minister is originally in the sovereign employing him, and the limits of that authority are set out in the full powers with which the minister is furnished for communication to the agent of the other contracting Power. A minister may enter into an agreement beyond the limits of his authority *sub spe rati*, but such an agreement is in no way binding upon his principal until expressly ratified by him.

3. Consent of the parties,

(3) The contracting parties must freely consent to the terms of the treaty. The fact that a treaty has been brought about by the application of international force, as by reprisals or war, in no way affects the validity of the treaty, provided that the consent of each party has been actually freely given, but it is otherwise if the consent of one or other of the parties has been induced by fraud. Moreover the personal intimidation of the contracting agent may be good cause for refusing ratification of an agreement.

The presence of the full consent of a contracting Power is made clear by ratification. Ratification, tacit or express,

is essential to the validity of a treaty, and express ratification
is by usage required in all cases where the treaty is entered
into by negotiators accredited for the purpose. "Ratification," said M. Guizot in 1841, "is a real and substantive
right; no treaty is complete without being ratified; and if,
between the conclusion and the ratification, important facts
come into existence—new and evident facts—which change
the relations of the two powers and the circumstances
amidst which the treaty is concluded, a full right of refusal
exists."

decisively proved by ratification,

Hall, II. 10, § 110.

(4) The objects of the treaty must not contravene the
principles of international law.

4. Legality of object.

The terms of the treaty may be confirmatory of the
international rights of the parties to it, may stipulate for the
observance as between the parties of new practices not
enjoined by existing international law, or they may cover a
mere bargain of grant or surrender, whether unilateral or
mutual. But in any case the treaty binds as between the
contracting parties only, and no stipulation can be of general
international validity which contravenes the general vested
international right of a third Power.

§ 31. The definition of the effect of a treaty is a matter of
interpretation to be determined in accordance with certain well-
recognized canons.

*Rules for the inter-
pretation of the terms of a treaty.*

A treaty is to be interpreted generally :—

(a) In accordance with the plain and reasonable sense
of the words employed.

(b) Where the plain sense is wanting, in accordance
with the reasonable sense of the words, or, in default, in
accordance with the spirit of the agreement gathered from
the context.

(c) Where the terms employed vary in meaning in
different contracting states, in accordance with the meaning
attached in the state to which those terms apply.

(d) In accordance with the fundamental rights of
states.

(e) So as to effectuate the terms of the treaty by conferring that which is necessary to the enjoyment of things clearly granted.

Hall, ii. 10, §§ 111—112.

§ **32.** <u>Necessity constitutes a final overriding condition</u> of <u>all international law,</u> but, to justify a <u>violation</u> by one state of the general international rights of another, <u>the necessity alleged</u> <u>must be clear, instant and overwhelming.</u>

It is clear law that necessity will in certain cases condone a departure from general international principle. Thus <u>where the frontier line of any state is employed by marauders</u> <u>to cover operations against the peace of a neighbouring state,</u> and the territorial sovereign, whether in consequence of sheer weakness or of want of comity, fails to abate the nuisance, the injured state may, it seems sufficiently agreed, lawfully pursue the assailants across the border, and take such measures as may be necessary for the effectual suppression of their aggressions. Numerous precedents for the application of this principle were furnished by reason of the weakness of the administration of Spain in her American possessions during the first quarter of the present century. A fort held by outlaws on the Appalachicola River within Spanish territory, from which pillaging raids were made into the United States, was, in 1815, after demand upon and refusal by the Spanish Governor of Pensacola to suppress and punish the marauders, attacked and destroyed under orders from Mr Monroe by United States troops. Three years later General Jackson, operating against the savage Seminoles, on finding that the Indians were being encouraged and assisted by the Spanish commanders at Pensacola and S. Marks, took possession of these Spanish posts. Both operations were defended on the same ground. "This measure," wrote General Jackson to the Governor of S. Marks, "<u>is justifiable on the immutable principles of self-defence,</u> <u>and cannot but be satisfactory,</u> under existing circumstances, <u>to his Catholic Majesty the King of Spain.</u>"

Amelia Island at the mouth of the S. Mary's River

Necessity will justify departure from the well-recognised general principles of international law.

Wharton, Dig. 506.

The case of the Appalachicola River outlaws. 1815.

The case of Pensacola and S. Marks, 1818.

Wharton, Dig. 506.

having been seized in 1817 by a band of buccaneers, who carried on under cover of commissions from Buenos Ayres and Venezuela a predatory warfare alike on the commerce of Spain and the United States, and no effectual attempt to suppress the evil having been made by the Spanish authorities in Florida, President Monroe determined to break up the settlement, and ordered a man-of-war to the island to expel the marauders and destroy their works and vessels.

The case of Amelia Island.

Wharton, Dig. 550 a.

Similar action was about the same time taken by Great Britain in respect of Cuban pirates, who preyed on British commerce unchecked by the Spanish local officials.

The case of the Cuban pirates.

The plea of necessity in justification of proceedings *primâ facie* illegal will, however, be most rigidly scrutinised. In December 1837, after an ineffectual rising in Upper Canada which was suppressed by the local militia, a force " formed of all the reckless and mischievous people of the border," largely recruited from the State of New York, took possession of Navy Island in the Niagara River, and there proceeded to collect men and material for the prosecution of further revolutionary proceedings. The "Caroline," a small steamboat, being employed in conveying recruits and supplies to the island, the British officer engaged against the invaders directed a night attack against her, expecting to find her in British waters. When the attacking party approached Navy Island it was found that the vessel was moored to the American shore. The "Caroline" was nevertheless seized at her moorings, fired, and sent over Niagara Falls. The mutual irritation of the interested countries prevented an early dispassionate discussion of the occurrence. At a subsequent period Mr Webster stated the case of the United States with great fairness. "It is admitted," he said, "that a just right of self-defence attaches always to nations as well as to individuals, and is equally necessary for the preservation of both. But the extent of this right is a question to be judged of by the circumstances of each particular case; and when its

Stapleton's Life of Canning, i. 169—175. The necessity, however, must be real and imminent.

The case of the "Caroline." 1837.

alleged exercise has led to the commission of hostile acts

Mr Webster to Mr Fox, Apr. 24, 1841. *Papers relative to the special mission of Lord Ashburton in 1842,* p. 45. within the territory of a Power at peace, nothing less than a clear and absolute necessity can afford ground of justification." In pursuance of this doctrine he called upon the British Government to show in defence of the destruction of the vessel a necessity of self-defence "instant, overwhelming, leaving no choice of means, and no moment for deliberation."

Lord Ashburton, despatched on a special mission in 1842 to determine questions in dispute between Great Britain and the United States, while repudiating any intention on the part of the British officers or the British Government to show slight or disrespect to the sovereign authority of the United States and expressing regret that a frank explanation and apology had not been tendered at the time, had no difficulty in showing that the circumstances of the occurrence satisfied the test proposed by Mr Webster. The forces on Navy Island were formidable from their numbers and from their armament, remonstrances had been made with such small effect that an American militia regiment was looking on from a neighbouring island without any attempt at interference, the "Caroline" was the important instrument by which the numbers and arms of the invaders were hourly increasing, the necessity of making the attack within American bounds only arose in the moment of execution,

Lord Ashburton to Mr Webster, July 23, 1842. and the time and mode of assault were expressly chosen so as to ensure success with the least loss of life and property.

The justification begins and ceases strictly with the overwhelming need. The declarations of Lord Ashburton were accepted in a conciliatory spirit by the United States and the subject dropped. In point of principle there was no difference of opinion between the representatives of the two countries. A justification of international conduct based on mere necessity begins and ends, in fact, strictly with the absolute and overwhelming need.

The case of the "Cagliari," 1857. In June 1857 the "Cagliari," a Sardinian passenger steamer was seized, when on her voyage from Genoa to

Tunis, by some of her passengers, who assumed forcible control of the vessel, and made for the isle of Ponza, where they broke into the Neapolitan state-prison and released some hundreds of prisoners. With their numbers thus recruited they compelled the officers of the "Cagliari" to land them at Sapri, where they commenced a revolutionary movement, but were speedily cut to pieces by the Neapolitan troops. The captain of the "Cagliari" meanwhile steered for Naples to report, but when some twelve miles off Capri the vessel was captured by two Neapolitan cruisers and taken into Naples, where her crew, amongst whom were two English engineers, were flung into prison and there treated with great barbarity.

The Sardinian Government, considering that any assistance afforded to the Neapolitan rebels by the captain and crew of the "Cagliari" was the outcome of actual *vis major*, demanded the restitution of the vessel and the liberation of her crew on the broad ground of the illegality of the seizure of a foreign vessel on the high seas in time of peace except in the case of piracy. "The 'Cagliari,'" wrote Count Cavour, "was arrested on the high seas, that is to say, on that free sea which is not possessed by anyone, and over which no one has jurisdiction. The illegality of the capture, under this point of view, cannot be doubted; it could find no foundation in the law of nations, unless it were proved that the 'Cagliari' was a pirate-ship."

Count Cavour to Count Gropello, Jan. 16, 1858. *Correspondence respecting the "Cagliari,"* 1858, p. 95.

The Neapolitan Government, between whom and Piedmont relations were strained to the utmost, treated the demands of Cavour with studious contempt. The British Government, however, lending its support to Sardinia, the ministers of King Bomba yielded with peculiarly bad grace to the necessities of the situation. The two British engineers were granted £3000 by way of compensation for their sufferings, and the "Cagliari" and her crew were given up to the British consul and by him conducted to Genoa, but the direct claims of Sardinia were coolly ignored, and the

Neapolitan Superior Prize Court subsequently pronounced a judgment declaring the validity of the capture of the "Cagliari" on the high seas on the ground that she had been engaged in acts of combined hostility and piracy, and fixing her owners with responsibility in respect of the alleged culpable conduct of her commander and crew. In this unsatisfactory fashion the affair terminated. The British Law Officers, to whom the matter was referred by the British Government, took the just line that, while the principle of self-defence might perhaps fairly excuse the capture of the "Cagliari" and her bringing in for judicial examination before a proper court, the facts of the case were not such as to justify either the condemnation of the vessel or the ill-usage of her crew.

Correspondence respecting the "Cagliari," 1858.

On October 31, 1873, the "Virginius," a steamer under American colours, which had been previously employed in assisting insurrectionary movements in Cuba, was captured on the high seas by a Spanish man-of-war. She was at the time of her capture making for Cuba and carrying a number of passengers, who were proposing to join the forces of the Cuban insurgents, but she was unarmed and altogether unfitted for the exercise of acts of force. Being carried by her captors into Santiago de Cuba, fifty-three of her passengers and crew were, on November 4 and 7, after a hurried trial by court-martial, shot by the Spanish local authorities. Amongst the victims were sixteen British subjects, members of the crew of the "Virginius," who had shipped at Kingston in Jamaica, many of them doubtless in absolute ignorance of the character of the proposed voyage.

The case of the "Virginius," 1873.

Parl. Papers, Spain, No. 3 (1874).

Two distinct questions were raised by this affair : (1) Was the "Virginius," a vessel flying the American flag and possessed of regular American papers, lawfully seizable by a Spanish man-of-war on the high seas ? (2) If the capture were legitimate, were the subsequent proceedings of the Spaniards in the execution of the prisoners legally justifiable ?

The first question was raised in correspondence between Spain and the United States. It was argued by the Spanish authorities that the "Virginius" was a pirate, and further that she was not legally entitled to carry American colours, her American registry having been obtained by fraud, her real owners being Cubans. But the charge of piracy was utterly devoid of support: the "Virginius" had been at the time of her capture guilty of no such act of depredation as would constitute her a pirate *jure gentium*, and was in fact altogether unfitted for the exercise of any acts of force *on the sea*. And, however fraudulent might have been the conduct of her owners, she left Kingston as a duly documented American vessel, entitled as against all the world, save the United States, to fly the American flag. The plea of self-defence could then alone justify the seizure of the vessel.

In the end Spain agreed to restore the "Virginius" and the survivors of her passengers and crew to the United States, and to salute the flag of that Government, if it should not be shown that the "Virginius" was not rightfully entitled to carry the American flag. Satisfactory proof being forthcoming of the Spanish contention in this last respect, the United States Government was content, in substitution for the salute, to receive a disclaimer on the part of the Spaniards of any intention to offer an indignity to the American flag. The question of the legality of the seizure of a *bonâ fide* American vessel under circumstances similar to those attending the capture of the "Virginius" was thus not definitely decided.

The British Government took the simple ground that, even assuming the vessel to have been lawfully seized and the crew properly detained, there was no justification for the summary executions at Santiago. "Much," wrote Lord Granville, "may be excused in acts done under the expectation of instant damage in self-defence by a nation, as well as by an individual. But after the capture of the 'Virginius'

Earl
Granville to
Mr Layard,
Feb. 20,
1874.
*Parl.
Papers,
Spain,
No. 3, 1874,
p. 85.*

and the detention of the crew was effected, no pretence of imminent necessity of self-defence could be alleged; and it was the duty of the Spanish authorities to prosecute the offenders in proper form of law, and to have instituted proceedings on a definite charge before the execution of the prisoners."

CHAPTER IV.

MEANS OF INTERNATIONAL REDRESS.

§ 33. Negotiation, whether direct or through the good offices of third Powers, constitutes as yet the only regular mode for the peaceful determination of international difficulties.

In spite of well-meant and well-directed efforts the Powers of the Circle have not hitherto established a permanent Court or Board for the settlement of international disputes, although recent events seem fertile in promise. Special Tribunals of Arbitration for the settlement of special disputes have been from time to time successfully constructed, and special questions have been dealt with in special Congresses or Conferences of the interested states, or of the Great Powers of Europe and America, but these references and these assemblies have been hitherto temporary and particular only, and all alike the outcome of special negotiation. Negotiation, in fine, whether directly or mediatively undertaken, does as yet constitute the only peaceful means of redress which lies open to a state complaining of wrong, or seeking the recognition of a disputed right. When negotiation fails to secure redress, whether entire or in the way of compromise, and whether directly or as the result of arbitration, a dissatisfied state unwilling to yield the contested question can, in default of the interference of more influential neighbours, only appeal to measures of actual force.

Negotiation the ordinary peaceful path to international satisfaction.

Parl. Papers, United States, Nos. 9 and 12 (1893).

A dissatis-
fied state
may, on
the failure
of negotia-
tion, have
recourse
to forcible
measures.
The main
accepted
inter-
national
measures
of force.
(a) Repri-
sals,
3 Wharton,
Dig. § 318.

Hall, II. 2,
§ 120.

special
and
general.
3 Wharton,
Dig. 102.

Case of Don
Pacifico,
1850.
Snow, 246.

§ 34. Satisfaction being otherwise unprocurable, states may have recourse to forcible measures falling short of war, or, in the last resort, to war itself.

The measures of force which a state may employ against a neighbour are many and various. The main varieties are, however, capable of simple classification.

(a) The exercise of reprisals constitutes the simplest form of international forcible persuasion.

"Reprisals," says Hall, "are resorted to when a specific wrong has been committed; and they consist in the seizure and confiscation of property belonging to the offending state or its subjects by way of compensation in value for the wrong; or in seizure of property or acts of violence directed against individuals with the object of compelling the state to grant redress; or, finally, in the suspension of the operation of treaties."

A distinction was formerly drawn between Special and General Reprisals. Special Reprisals, consisting in the exercise under formal commission of hostile acts by an injured individual in order to indemnify himself against loss by the capture of property belonging to fellow-subjects of the wrongdoer, are entirely obsolete. General Reprisals, consisting in the exercise of acts of force by any individual choosing to apply for a commission to an offended state, are fast passing away, if they have not already become a thing of the past. General Reprisals confined to the officers and men of the military and naval force of the offended Power are still not unusual. Such General Reprisals approach very nearly to war: the grant of letters of General Reprisal being only differentiated from the grant of authority to levy war by the limited intent existing in the counsels of the responsible Government.

Retorsion, consisting in the retaliation of injustice or reference to an international *lex talionis*, is a special, and, in fact, the most primitive instance of the exercise of reprisals.

(β) Embargo constitutes a second well-accepted method for the procuring of international satisfaction by reference to force.

Embargo consists in the provisional sequestration under authority of a Government of property lying within its ports. Such a measure may be a purely municipal proceeding, the outcome of state policy, operating upon subjects of the state only, or, in case of state necessity, upon foreigners, although without any suggestion of a hostile purpose. Embargo of this order is Civil embargo. But embargo may be an international measure, the intent of the Government imposing it being to put stress upon the Government of the individuals whose property is thereby affected, albeit without having recourse to actual war. This is Hostile embargo. The distinction was pointed out by Sir W. Scott in the case of the "Boedes Lust" in 1804.

Property belonging to persons resident in Demerara was seized in May 1803, before the outbreak of hostilities between Great Britain and Holland, under embargo laid on Dutch property in English ports. "This property," said Sir W. Scott, "was seized provisionally, an act itself hostile enough in the mere execution, but equivocal as to the effect, and liable to be varied by subsequent events, and by the conduct of the Government of Holland. If that conduct had been such as to reestablish the relations of peace, then the seizure, although made with the character of a hostile seizure, would have proved in the event a mere *embargo*, or temporary sequestration. The property would have been restored, as it is usual, at the conclusion of embargoes; a process often resorted to in the practice of nations for various causes not immediately connected with any expectations of hostility.... This was the state of the first measure. It was at first equivocal, and, if the matter in dispute had terminated in reconciliation, the seizure would have been converted into a mere civil embargo, so terminated. That would have been the retroactive effect of that course of circumstances. On

(β) Embargo.

The "Boedes Lust," 5 C. Rob. 233.

Sir W. Scott in the "Boedes Lust," 5 C. Rob. 245. the contrary, if the transactions end in hostility, the retroactive effect is directly the other way. It impresses the direct hostile character upon the original seizure."

The distinction between Civil and Hostile embargo is thus purely a matter of the intent, and that intent will commonly be only made known by circumstances subsequent to the actual seizure.

(γ) Pacific blockade. (γ) Pacific blockade is a third favourite international measure of coercive force.

Pacific blockade consists in the cutting off by one state of communication with the ports or a particular portion of coast of another, otherwise than in the case of declared war, with the object of preventing commercial relations by sea.

M. Perels in the *Revue de Droit Int.*, 1887, p. 246.

Its recent introduction, Pacific blockade has only within very recent times asserted its title to a place amongst legitimate coercive measures falling short of war.

Prior to 1827 blockade was universally held to be 3 Wharton, *Dig.* 407. essentially a belligerent right. In that year the three Powers, Great Britain, France and Russia, having taken up the cause of the revolted Greeks, established a blockade upon the coasts of Greece, with a view to putting pressure on the Sultan, while yet peace was in name maintained. This example was followed by France in the blockade of the Tagus in 1831, by Great Britain in the blockade of New Grenada in 1836, by France in Mexico and La Plata in 1838, Hall, II. 11, § 121. Heffter, II. § 111. by Great Britain and France in La Plata in 1845 and by Great Britain in Greece in 1850.

The legality of the proceeding was however speedily questioned, and its dubious character freely admitted. "The and doubtful legitimacy. real truth is," said Palmerston writing to Lord Normanby on December 7, 1846, with reference to the La Plata blockade, "though we had better keep the fact to ourselves, that the French and English blockade has from the first to the last been illegal. Peel and Aberdeen have always declared that we have not been at war with Rosas, but blockade is a belligerent right, and, unless you are at war with a state, you have no right to prevent ships of other states from communication with the ports of that state, nay you cannot prevent your own merchant ships from doing so."

Very various views have been recently taken concerning the legitimacy of the measure.

(1) According to one view, blockade is purely a belligerent right, and Pacific Blockade is therefore unconditionally illegitimate. Pacific Blockade, according to the holders of this view, is, in fact, an outrageous expedient invented by France and England for coercing feeble states without assuming the responsibilities appropriate to a state of war.

" Le droit international accorde aux belligérants certains droits auxquels les neutres sont obligés de se soumettre, bien que l'exercice de ces droits sont préjudiciable à leurs intérêts. Pour jouir de ces droits, il faut que les belligérants acceptent la responsabilité de leur état ; quand il n'y a pas guerre, les neutres ne sont pas obligés de se soumettre aux restrictions de leur liberté d'action, que l'état de guerre seul autorise."

(2) Accepting the same premise that blockade is purely a belligerent right, other authorities are content to draw a different conclusion, and, recognising in the so-called Pacific Blockade a real *de facto* act of belligerency, to quarrel only with its maladroit designation.

(3) A third view, following on similar lines, adopts Pacific Blockade as legitimate within limits. It is as between disputing Powers as legitimate as any other measure of force falling short of war, and so long as it is confined to the subjects and property of those Powers it is accordingly internationally unexceptionable. But *third* Powers are entitled to decline to recognise the extension to their property and subjects of the operation of a measure not based upon recognised belligerent maritime right.

(4) A fourth body of international jurists seem disposed

w.   7

Side notes:

Various views as to its legitimacy.
i. It is illegitimate.

Professor Geffcken in the *Revue de Droit Int.* 1885, p. 146.

ii. It is legitimate but wrongly styled. Opinion of MM. Bulmerincq and A. Rolin, *Revue de Droit Int.* 1875, p. 611.

iii. It is legitimate within limits.

M. Perels in the *Revue de Droit Int.* 1885, p. 251.

iv. It is

justifiable on moral grounds. Heffter, II. § III.
to welcome Pacific Blockade on moral grounds, justifying it as a means of redress falling short of war, a lesser being substituted for a greater evil.

v. Its legitimacy is a question of history.
(5) According to a fifth view, the test of the legitimacy of Pacific Blockade is the sufficiency of practice. Pacific Blockade is, at any rate as against third Powers, an improper extension of forcible belligerent rights into the sphere of Peace, unless its legitimacy has been established by the general recognition of neutral Powers. The legality of the measure must arise from the present consent of third Powers

Opinion of Woolsey, Revue de Droit. Int. 1875, p. 611.
or from the sanction of the general practice of nations; and as yet the practice has been mainly that of two Powers and has been by no means generally acquiesced in.

Conclusions as to its position.
From the great mass of contending opinion and by no means consistent practice it is perhaps possible to claim general, if not universal, assent for several simple propositions.

(a) *As between disputing Powers Pacific Blockade is in principle as legitimate as any other of the recognised measures of coercion falling short of war.*

The fact that Pacific Blockade is a modern invention does not establish its illegality, and there is nothing in the nature of the case which renders any more or less illegal as between the disputants the seizure of a vessel at the entrance of a port than the seizure of that same vessel on the high seas. The plea of Reprisals would be held sufficient to justify the latter. In each case the state assailed has it in its power either to grant the redress demanded, or to resent the proceeding as an act of hostility.

(b) *As between the imposer of the blockade and third Powers, Pacific Blockade is in principle as legitimate as any other of the recognised measures of coercion falling short of war, provided that the proceeding be generally acquiesced in in practice by such third Powers.*

International Law resting upon practice, third Powers *may* expressly consent to or tacitly acquiesce in the adoption of the measure in a special case, or the measure may be established as unquestionably and without limitation legitimate by the general practice of nations.

(c) *Whether Pacific Blockade in any form has established its title to international recognition as a legal measure of coercion falling short of war is a question of historic fact.*

At present, in view of the paucity of instances, the divergence in the character of the actual operations in those instances and the disputes which arose thereon, we must be content to say that the title is not yet practically established.

(d) *The intrinsic humanity of Pacific Blockade as against a declaration of war may well affect the question of the policy of neutral Powers in granting or withholding recognition of the proceeding, but scarcely touches the point of its legality.*

Two comparatively recent events did much to throw clear light upon the disputed institution.

In October 1884 the French Government announced the establishment of a blockade upon the northern and western coasts of the island of Formosa, and intimated on inquiry that this measure would be considered to confer the right of driving back or capturing all ships which might attempt to force the lines. The rights so to be exercised were, contended M. Waddington in correspondence with Earl Granville, rights which England as well as France had exercised in previous similar circumstances, and of which the courts of the two countries had sanctioned the legitimacy. The British Government declined to recognise in the French any right to visit and capture British ships except in the exercise of rights applicable to a state of war. "The contention of the French Government," wrote Earl Granville, "that a 'pacific blockade' confers on the blockading Power the right to capture and condemn the ships of third nations for breach of such a blockade, is opposed to the opinions of the most eminent statesmen and jurists of France, and to the decisions of its tribunals, and it is in conflict with well-established

The case of the Formosa blockade, 1884.

M. Waddington to Earl Granville, Nov. 5, 1884.

Earl Granville to M. Waddington, Nov. 11, 1884.

principles of international law." The French Government maintaining its position, the British Cabinet proceeded to order the Foreign Enlistment Act to be enforced at Hong-Kong and other British Eastern ports, the effect being that the French cruisers were unable to refit in those ports or to employ them as a market for the purchase of necessary supplies of coal and other stores, and the French Government was involved in the vast trouble and expense of a regular provisioning service. Under these circumstances, the French denuded their blockade entirely of its pacific character by claiming the strict and full rights of belligerents, including the right to search neutral vessels on the high seas for contraband of war.

Parl. Papers, France, No. 1 (1885).

The blockade of the Greek ports, 1886.
In May 1886 the Governments of Great Britain, Germany, Austria, Russia and Italy, determined at all hazards to prevent new complications and bloodshed in the East arising out of the mad desire of the bellicose Greek demos to rush headlong into an unequal struggle with Turkey, established a blockade upon the Greek ports. The operation was, however, confined to the stopping of ships attempting to communicate with those ports under the Greek flag, and these were merely temporarily detained, and were released and assisted in their return to port when the pressure thus exercised resulted in the disarmament of the Greeks and the withdrawal of their forces from the Turkish frontier. Special care was even taken to prevent the stopping of cargoes belonging to third Powers and laden under the Greek flag before the notification of the blockade.

Parl. Papers, Greece, No. 4 (1886).

The Resolutions of the Institut de Droit International, 1887.
In the light of these proceedings the Institut de Droit International sitting at Heidelberg in 1887 arrived at the following resolutions:—

"L'établissement d'un blocus en dehors de l'état de guerre ne doit être considéré comme permis par le droit des gens que sous les conditions suivantes :

(1) "Les navires de pavillon étranger peuvent entrer librement malgré le blocus;

(2) "Le blocus pacifique doit être déclaré et notifié officiellement, et maintenu par une force suffisante ;

(3) "Les navires de la puissance bloquée qui ne respectent pas un pareil blocus peuvent être séquestrés. Le blocus ayant cessé ils doivent être restitués avec leurs cargaisons à leurs propriétaires, mais sans dédommagement à aucun titre."

Revue de Droit Int. 1887, p. 361.

PART III.

INTERNATIONAL LAW OF ABNORMAL RELATIONS.
(a) WAR.

CHAPTER I.

THE COMMENCEMENT OF WAR. THE TESTS OF BELLIGERENT CHARACTER.

Effect on states of the outbreak of war.

§ 35. The outbreak of war between two states calls into operation the International Law of Abnormal Relations.

An outbreak of war between two states operates primarily to distinguish between belligerent and neutral Governments; it introduces (1) as between the belligerents a *régime* of open force limited by certain well-recognised rules, which are comprised under the name of the Laws of War, and it establishes (2) as between each of the belligerents and third Powers a condition of things governed by principles which are set out as the Laws of Neutrality. (3) As between third Power and third Power the International Law of Peace continues to bear sway.

What is war?

§ 36. War may be sufficiently well defined in the words of Albericus Gentilis, as a public contest by arms carried on in proper or regular fashion. *Bellum est publicorum armorum justa contentio.*

Gentilis *De Jure Belli*, Lib. 1. cap. 2.

A war is a contest of recognized Governments.

This definition involves two propositions :—

(1) *War to be jural must be carried on under proper authority.*

Wars were variously classified by ancient authorities[1], but the sole classification of Wars which is of practical consequence in the present day is that of Wars International and Wars Civil; and with civil strife as such International Law has only in a limited degree to do. The International Law of Peace Relations watches over and guards foreign interests affected by internecine contests as by other municipal events, but with such contests the International Law of War is only concerned when, in consequence of the proportions of the struggle or of other peculiar circumstances connected therewith, occasion arises for the recognition of the belligerency of a section of a nation which is engaged in resisting by force the authority of its former Government. The authority of International Law, for example, will prevent the hanging of an ordinary prisoner taken in a war between civilised Powers; it has no call to interfere to prevent the execution of a defeated rebel leader by the victors in a South American revolutionary struggle. The Laws of War deal with hostilities carried on between and under the authority of regularly recognised Governments. "Public War is a state of armed hostility between sovereign nations or Governments." *Instructions for the government of U.S. Armies in the Field, Art. 20.*

(2) *War to be jural must be carried on in regular fashion.* War must be carried on in regular fashion.

The principles which determine the manner in and the extent to which force may properly be exercised by belligerents form the subject-matter of the *Laws of War*.

§ 37. The state of War commences with the first overt act of hostility. When does war begin?

[1] Wars were, for example, classified as being Public, Private and Mixed, or as being Perfect and Imperfect. A *Public* war was distinguished as a contest of independent Governments, a *Private* war being a contest of mere individuals, while a *Mixed* war was a contest between a Government and individuals. A *Perfect* war was a struggle wherein all members of the one belligerent state were authorised to commit hostilities against all members of the other belligerent state; an *Imperfect* war was a struggle limited as to persons, places and things. The progress of civilisation has rendered all such distinctions obsolete. Bas. v. Tingy, 4 Dall. 40. 3 Wharton, *Dig.* § 333.

104 *See declaration of London.* WAR. Part III.

Formal declarations of war unnecessary. The issue of a formal declaration addressed by the one belligerent to his enemy is no longer a necessary condition of the regular commencement of war. "Formal declarations of war," said Lord Ellenborough, C. J., in *Oom v. Bruce,* "only make the state of war more notorious; but, though more convenient in that respect, are not necessary to constitute such a state."

Oom v. Bruce, 12 East 226.

History of practice. The history of international practice in this regard shows several clearly marked stages in the progress of opinion.

(i) The Ancient World recognised the necessity of formal declarations of war, the Greek and the Roman being alike wont to declare war in solemn form after demand and refusal of satisfaction by the opponent, the declaration being publicly conveyed by inviolate herald from the offended to the offending state. The determination of the formalities proper to such declarations was a main function of the Roman Fetial College, and the principles followed were enshrined in the Jus Fetiale.

(ii) The Roman war-practice in this matter lingered on after the break-up of the Roman Empire, the Roman Church, whose faith subdued the barbarian conquerors, lending its sanction to the custom of formal challenge to the foe, which well harmonised with the proud temper of the warriors of the North. So long, accordingly, as the ideas of Chivalry held sway among men, public declarations in some form were regularly issued to the enemy by sovereigns about to commence war. As late as in 1657 a Swedish herald brought a declaration of war to the Court of Copenhagen.

(iii) During the seventeenth century, however, a wide divergence began more and more to show itself between the statements of legal authority and the facts of practice, Grotius and his fellows asserting under the Law of Nations, if not under the Law of Nature, the necessity of formal notice to the enemy before making an attack, while belligerents habitually neglected to issue such notice, although commonly excusing the omission on special grounds.

De Jure Belli ac Pacis, III. 3, 6.

Gustavus Adolphus declared formal notice to the enemy to be unnecessary in the case of a defensive war, and this convenient distinction commended itself alike to belligerents and writers in certain quarters. The practice of issuing such notices had in the early days of the 18th century become almost entirely disused.

(iv)　Vattel marks the transition to a new stage, he practically surrendering the doctrine of the necessity of a formal declaration of war *as between belligerent and belligerent*, and contenting himself with commending the practice, which had in his day become usual among belligerents, of issuing manifestoes, these having a twofold object, over and above notice to the enemy, the absolute need for which in all cases was no longer recognised, viz. (1) to warn subjects and neutrals of the outbreak of hostilities, and (2) to justify the war in the opinion of neutral Powers.

Manifestoes were very usually issued by belligerents after the day of Vattel, but these not unfrequently *after* the actual commencement of hostilities. In but a remarkably small proportion of the numerous cases in which hostilities were begun by civilised Powers between 1700 and 1870 was any form of public declaration *previously* issued[1].

(v)　In 1870 preliminary to the Franco-Prussian and in 1877 to the Russo-Turkish War recourse was again had to ancient practice in the issue of formal declarations. And such chivalry is doubtless highly commendable. But in England and the United States, at any rate, it is now clearly decided that war may legally exist without a formal declaration on either side.

"No one," said Betts, J. in the "Hiawatha," "can claim, as a right, that a public declaration of war shall be promulgated, unless it be the nation by whose Government it is made, and then it serves only as a notice to their own citizens and subjects. The declaration by manifestoes, heralds or nuncios, does not constitute war, and the omission

Hosack,
p. 329.

Molloy, I. 1,
§ 14.

Vattel,
Lib. II.
Chap. iv.

The
"Nayade."
4 C. Rob.
253.
The "Eliza
Ann,"
1 Dod. 247.
The "Hia-
watha,"
Blatchford,
Pr. Ca. I.

---

[1] J. F. Maurice, *Hostilities without Declaration of War.*

of the declaration can in no way impair its justness or efficacy, especially in a case of defensive war."

The
"Teutonia,"
4 P. C. R.
171.
The Prize
Cases,
2 Black 665.

Where, however, no formal declaration issues there must to constitute war be an actual commencement of hostilities. A civil war must well-nigh necessarily commence without declaration.

The legal
effects of
war ex-
tend to
individual
subjects.

§ 38. Though war is a contest of Governments, its legal effects are not confined to those Governments, but extend to the relations of their individual subjects.

The
Schooner
"Rapid,"
and cargo,
1 Gall. 303.

The advance of civilisation as set out in International Law has indeed limited very materially the operation of war upon the private individual, but has not yet been able to dissever completely the subject from the ruler. The subjects, whose force and whose wealth constitute the armoury of the state, are compromised internationally by the acts of its Government. "It is a law and requisite of civilised existence that men live in political, continuous societies, forming organised units, called states or nations, whose constituents bear, enjoy, and suffer, advance and retrograde together, in

Instructions
for the
government
of U. S.
Armies in
the Field,
Arts. 20, 21.

peace and in war. The citizen of a hostile country is thus an enemy, as one of the constituents of the hostile state or nation, and as such is subjected to the hardships of war[1]."

Citizen-
ship is not
a sufficient
test of
subject
character.

§ 39. The fact of hostile citizenship is not by any means a certain or sufficient test of subject character under the International Law of Abnormal Relations.

Wells v.
Williams,
1 Ld. Raym.
282.
Caseres v.
Bell, 8 D.
and E. 166.

Primâ facie, indeed, all natural born and naturalised subjects of the one belligerent would seem to be the natural and legal enemies of all the natural born and naturalised subjects of the opposing belligerent. But, though it is primarily to the arms and resources of her natural born and

[1] Portalis in the days of the French Revolution laid down another doctrine: "La guerre est une relation d'État à État, et non d'individu à individu. Entre deux ou plusieurs nations belligérantes, les particuliers dont ces nations se composent ne sont ennemis que par accident; ils ne le sont point comme hommes, ils ne le sont même pas comme citoyens; ils le sont uniquement comme soldats." To this elegant passage covering a doctrine historically false we are indebted for many lengthy and in some sort practically mischievous dissertations. See Hall, *Int. L.* 1. 3 § 18.

naturalised citizens that the belligerent state must look for support, her effective combatant force is not derived purely from these, but from the strength and the wealth of those individuals, whether citizens or foreigners, who actually lend their assistance, by their personal presence or by their property, in the operations of the contest.

The resident alien may lend active assistance to the Government of the land of his sojourn, whilst, on the other hand, that assistance may not be forthcoming from the native citizen resident abroad, who may even enlist amongst the active enemies of his native state, subject to the risk of punishment under the native law, should he be taken in the treason. The ultimate proof of hostility, amity or neutrality is to be found in actual hostile, friendly or neutral conduct.

§ **40.** **Domicil not Citizenship, is the primary test of subject character under the Laws of War and Neutrality.**

Domicil is the legal conception of residence or settlement, or in the language of Lord Loughborough, the place where the person would be, no particular occasion taking him elsewhere. Domicil in relation to belligerent or neutral rights and duties is ascribed by reference to (1) actual local position, coupled with (2) a freely formed intention of permanent stay. The main test is that of the *animus manendi*. An actual residence for the briefest period will constitute domicil where the *animus manendi* is clearly established. Mr Whitehill had arrived in the Dutch island of St Eustatius but a day or two before the capture of the place by the British forces under Rodney in Feb. 1781, but, it being proved that he landed in the island with the intent to establish himself there, he was held to be bound by the consequences of Dutch domicil. On the other hand, a foreign stay of many years' duration will not found a domicil where there is a clear continuing intention of speedy return. "The intention which gives a domicile is an unconditional intention 'to stay always'." This intention may be clearly expressed or be matter of inference. In this last case, that

Domicil, not citizenship, is the primary test of national character.

The "Venus," 8 Cranch 253.
The "Harmony," 2 C. Rob. 322.
The "Indian Chief," 3 C. Rob. 20.
The "Herman," 4 C. Rob. 228.
Definition of domicil.
Lord Loughborough in Bempde v. Johnstone, 3 Ves. Jr. 202.
The "Diana," 5 C. Rob. 60.
The "Venus," 8 Cranch, 279.
Sir W. Scott in the "Diana," 5 C. Rob. 60.
Marshall, C. J. in the "Venus," 8 Cranch 290.

is, where the intention must be gathered from the attendant circumstances, duration of residence must be the chief ingredient in raising a presumption of intent to settle or the reverse.

The "Harmony," 2 C. Rob. 324.

G. W. Murray, a partner in an American trading firm, came to France from New York in 1794 as supercargo, with the intention of remaining not more than six months in Europe, and left his wife and child in America. He nevertheless remained for a prolonged period, receiving and disposing of other cargoes, and had, after several journeys backwards and forwards from France, resided for over four years in France directing mercantile operations there, when property belonging to himself and his partners was captured by the British. Sir William Scott held that on the facts G. W. Murray was debarred from asserting a neutral American domicile, and must be held bound to the character of a domiciled French subject.

The "Harmony," 2 C. Rob. 322.
(i) All persons domiciled in hostile territory are hostile.
McConnell v. Hector, 3 B. and P. 113.
The "Citto," 3 C. Rob. 33.
The "Indian Chief," Ibid. 22.
The "Anna Catharina," 4 C. Rob. 112.
O'Mealey v Wilson, 1 Camp. 482.
Tabbs v. Bendelack, 3 B and P. 207 n.
McConnell v. Hector, 3 B. and P. 113.
The "Citto," 3 C. R. 38.
The "Venus," 8 Cranch 280.
The "Mary and Susan," 1 Wheaton 46.

Domicil being so defined, the proposition that domicil constitutes the primary test of subject character under the laws of war and neutrality is capable of simple establishment.

(i) *All persons, whether natives or foreigners, who are domiciled in belligerent territory, or in places under belligerent military occupation, may be treated as hostile by the opposing belligerent.*

This rule comprehends alike the citizen of a neutral Power and the resident citizen of the hostile state. The citizen of the neutral Power who is domiciled and remains within belligerent territory thereby assumes a belligerent character, and the citizen of a belligerent Power domiciled and remaining within the territory of an opposing belligerent reverses his subject character, is held the friend of the state of his sojourn and an enemy of his native state.

The national character which a person acquires by residence may be thrown off at pleasure by a return to his native country, or by turning his back on the country in which he has resided on his way to another, but, so long as he maintains his position and makes no sign, he will be held concluded by the fact of his residence.

The alien resident cannot indeed by the hostile belligerent be fairly fixed instantaneously on the outbreak of war with the consequences of his belligerent domicil, but must be allowed a reasonable period within which to make arrangements for the withdrawal for which he may elect.

Thus in the case of the "Ocean" in 1804 a claim was preferred on behalf of a British-born subject, who had been settled as a merchant in Flushing, but who had on the appearance of approaching hostilities dissolved his partnership and prepared to return to England, being, however, unable to effect his escape for some time in consequence of the unwarrantable detention of Englishmen in the territories under the control of France. Sir William Scott admitted the claim to restitution, holding it inequitable to deprive the claimant of his property either in respect of his former occupation or of his constrained residence in France, he having taken all the means in his power to remove from hostile soil. Moreover, in favour of an alien sought to be fixed with the consequences of a belligerent domicil, the principle is freely admitted that the native character easily reverts.

Mr Johnson, an American by birth, came to England in 1771, and resided for some years as a merchant in London. On the breaking out of the War of American Independence he quitted England and took up his residence in France. In 1783 he returned to England, but in 1785 he was recognised as an American subject under a British statute, and from 1790 onwards he acted as American Consul in England. He remained in England until September 1797, when he returned finally to America. Meanwhile in 1795 a vessel belonging to him was sent out on a voyage to the East as an American vessel with American papers. Having taken on board a cargo at Batavia for Hamburg, she put into Cowes,

Mr Justice Washington in the "Venus," 8 Cranch. 221.

United States v. Guillem, 11 Howard 47.

The alien resident in belligerent territory must be allowed a reasonable period to withdraw on the outbreak of war.

Marshall, C. J. in the "Venus," 8 Cranch. 288.

The "Diana," 5 C. Rob. 60. The "Ocean," 5 C. Rob. 90. The "St Lawrence," 9 Cranch. 120.

Native character easily reverts.

Sir W. Scott in the "La Virginie," 5 C. Rob. 93.

where she was seized in November 1797, and her condemnation sought on the ground that she, being the property of a British subject, had been engaged in trading with the enemy of Great Britain. Sir W. Scott held that, if Mr Johnson had remained in England until the time of the capture of his vessel, his venture would have been clearly a British transaction and as such illegal, but that the situation was altered by the fact of his having left the country, and that in pursuance of an intention previously formed. The national character of Mr Johnson as a British merchant was acquired by and founded in residence only, and the moment he turned his back on the country of his residence on his way to his own country he was in the act of resuming his original character, and was to be considered as an American. "The character that is gained by residence ceases by residence: it is an adventitious character which no longer adheres to him from the moment that he puts himself in motion *bonâ fide* to quit the country *sine animo revertendi*[1]."

The mere *intention* to quit belligerent territory will not, however, in default of some overt act of removal, save the resident foreigner from the consequences of his connection with a belligerent domicil.

Mr Elmslie, a British-born subject, settled in the Cape when it was under British military possession, and continued to reside there as American Consul after its restoration to the Dutch. A vessel owned by him having been captured by the British after the renewal of hostilities between Great Britain and the Dutch, he claimed restitution on the ground that he was an American neutral subject, and offered in support of his claim, amongst other matters, evidence in the shape of a letter showing his intention to remove from the

Side notes:
The "Indian Chief," 3 C. Rob. 20.
The "Snelle Zeylder," *Ibid.* 21 n.

The intention to withdraw must be displayed in overt act.
The "Venus," 8 Cranch. 281.
The "Frances," *Ibid.* 335.

[1] The cargo of the vessel which was claimed on behalf of Mr Miller, the American Consul at Calcutta, was condemned on the ground that by his residence under the protection of British arms and British laws under a British administration, he must be deemed a British subject, and his property taken in trade with the enemy as liable to condemnation. The "Indian Chief," 3 c. Rob. 22.

Cape to America. Sir W. Scott rejected the claim and condemned the property as Dutch, declaring that something more than mere verbal declaration, some solid fact, showing that the party was in the act of withdrawing, had always been held necessary to prevent condemnation in such cases.

In one particular the position of the resident neutral differs from that of the citizen of a hostile power domiciled within the same belligerent territory. The domiciled neutral merely puts on the garb of a belligerent.

The citizen of a belligerent Power, however, who is domiciled and remains within the territory of an opposing belligerent, whilst entitled to be treated as an ordinary subject of the land of his sojourn so long as he takes no active part in the struggle, may render himself liable to the punishment of a traitor under the laws of his native state, should he be found in arms against that native state.

(ii) *Citizens of a belligerent state domiciled in neutral territory are, in so far as their trade and interests are connected with that territory, regarded as neutrals.*

Thus in 1804, England and Holland being at war, Sir William Scott decreed restitution of the "Liesbet van der Toll," on the strength of the seven years' domicil of her owner in neutral Prussia, although the claimant was a Dutchman by birth, and the vessel, a fishing smack, had been purchased by him from her original Dutch owners but a few months before in Embden, and had been since employed in fishing on the Dutch coasts, resort being had for bait to Dutch ports.

Citizens of a belligerent State cannot, however, claim the privileges of the neutral on the strength of a neutral domicil acquired *flagrante bello.*

§ 41. The final touchstone distinguishing belligerent from neutral is willing subjection to belligerent or to neutral control.

While the main test of the international subject character of the individual is under the Laws of War and Neutrality the test of domicil, there may be occasions on which, without

Margin notes:

The "President," 5 C. Rob. 277.

The belligerent citizen adhering to the enemy is a traitor. The "Mary and Susan," 1 Wheaton, 57.

(ii) Citizens of the enemy domiciled in neutral territory are neutral, Marryat v. Wilson, 1 B. and P. 430. Bell v. Reid, 1 M. and S. 726. The "Herman," 4 C. Rob. 228. The "Danous," 4 C. Rob. 255 n. The "Venus," 8 Cranch. 280. The "Liesbet van der Toll," 5 C. Rob. 283.

but cannot claim the benefit of a neutral domicil acquired during the war. The "Dos Hermanos," 2 Wheat. 76.

The ultimate test of subject character is willing subjection.

The "Vigilantia," 1 C. Rob. 13. The "Phoenix," 5 C. Rob. 20.

The "Friendship," 6 C. Rob. 420. The "Atalanta," 6 C. Rob. 440.

the acquisition of a foreign domicil, a person may yet be affected by a foreign subject character. The stranger who voluntarily casts in his lot with a particular Power, whether belligerent or neutral, must, with the advantages so obtained, assume the corresponding liabilities.

(a) The neutral enlisting in a belligerent public service adopts the belligerent character.

Stat. 33 and 34 Vict. c.'90 s. 4.

§ 42. (a) **The citizen of the neutral Power, who enlists in the military, naval or civil service of a belligerent, may be fairly treated as a subject of that belligerent by the agents of the hostile Power.**

Under the legislation of some civilised states such foreign enlistment on the part of a subject is severely penalised as tending to call in question the real neutrality of his Government, but as between himself and the hostile belligerent the neutral citizen so enlisting merely deposits his neutral character and assumes the liabilities of the belligerent condition.

The Executive Directory by Decree of Oct. 29, 1798, threatened with the death of a pirate any citizen of a neutral state captured whilst acting under a commission granted Arrêté of Oct. 29, 1798; Martens, Recueil, VI. 775. by, or serving on board the vessel of, an enemy of France, but this order is unique in its savagery. Combatants of very varied races served on either side without demur alike in the American War of Independence and in the Civil War of 1861—65.

(β) All property is belligerent which is directly subjected to belligerent control.

§ 43. (β) **The property of the individual may be affected with a particular belligerent taint by reason of its subjection to particular belligerent control.**

A belligerent may well be permitted to regard as the property of his enemy all property which is so subjected to the control of that enemy as to be capable of lawful utilisation by him in the prosecution of his warlike operations. The international character of property must indeed be gauged in the first instance by the international character of the owner, but this test is by no means certain and all comprehensive. Property may assume a belligerent tinge by its situation, entirely irrespective of the settlement of its proprietor. A person may, in fact, in respect of his property,

rights, support a dual character. "A man may have mercantile concerns in two countries, and, if he acts as a
merchant of both, he must be liable to be considered as
a subject of both, with regard to the transactions originating
respectively in those countries."

Sir W. Scott in the "Jonge Klassina," 5 C. Rob. 302.

(i) *Property connected with houses of trade in belligerent
territory, although owned by citizens of neutral Powers domiciled on neutral soil, is subject to capture under the war rights
of the hostile belligerent.*

It would seem to follow as the converse of this proposition
that property connected with a house of trade upon neutral
soil, although owned by a belligerent proprietor, should be
exempt from condemnation at the hands of the hostile Power,
but this is not the case, such property being held contami-
nated by the belligerent personal character of its owner.

(i) Property connected with a belligerent house of trade is belligerent.
The "Vigilantia," 1 C. Rob. 1.
The "Portland," 3 C. Rob. 41.
The "Harmony," 2 C. Rob. 322

(ii) *The produce of all estates within belligerent territory,
or in places under belligerent military occupation, whatever
the international character of the proprietor, is possessed of
the belligerent character.*

In the case of the "Phoenix" in 1803 a claim was
preferred before the British Court of Admiralty on behalf
of certain persons in neutral Germany for property taken
on a voyage from Surinam, a Dutch colony, to Holland, and
described as being the produce of their estates in Surinam.
Sir William Scott condemned the cargo as Dutch property,
in spite of the neutral domicil of the owners. "Certainly
nothing," said he, "can be more decided and fixed as the
principle of this Court and the Supreme Court upon very
solemn argument there, that (sic) the possession of the soil
does impress upon the owner the character of the country, as
far as the produce of that plantation is concerned, in its
transportation to any other country, whatever the local
residence of the owner may be. This has been so repeatedly
decided both in this and the Superior Court, that it is no
longer open to discussion. No question can be made upon
the point of law at this day."

The "Jonge Klassina," 5 C. Rob. 297.
The "Anna Catharina," 4 C. Rob. 110.
Cremidi v. Powell, 11 Moore 88.
The "Friendschaft," 4 Wheaton 105.
Marshall, C. J. in the "Venus," 8 Cranch 299.

(ii) The produce of belligerent estates is belligerent.

The "Phoenix," 5 C. Rob. 20.
The "Vrow Anna Catharina," *Ibid.* 167.
Bentzon v. Boyle, 9 Cranch 191.

Sir W. Scott in the "Phoenix," 5 C. Rob. 20.

W.   8

Peculiarly strong in support of this principle was the famous American leading case of *Bentzon v. Boyle*, "the Thirty Hogsheads of Sugar" (1815). Adrian Benjamin Bentzon, a lieutenant in the Danish navy, was the owner of a plantation in the Danish island of Santa Cruz. On the capture of the island by Great Britain, he personally withdrew from it, but retained his estates there. Thirty hogsheads of sugar consigned to the London market on board a British ship by his factor in Santa Cruz, being the produce of the plantation, were, with the vessel, captured by an American privateer, and condemned in the United States Prize Court at Baltimore as hostile property. The Circuit Court affirming the condemnation, Lieutenant Bentzon appealed to the Supreme Court. It was suggested on his behalf that Santa Cruz could not, whilst merely in British military possession, be considered a British island, and that Mr Bentzon, having acquired his property in Santa Cruz whilst it was a Danish colony and having withdrawn from the island when it became British, could not be said to have "incorporated himself with the permanent interests of" the British nation within the doctrine laid down by Sir W. Scott in the "Vrow Anna Catharina" and the "Phoenix." The Supreme Court upheld the decision of the lower Courts. Marshall, C. J., delivering the opinion of the Court, ruled that for the first suggestion made on behalf of the claimant there could be no foundation. "Although," said he, "acquisitions made during war are not considered as permanent until confirmed by treaty, yet to every commercial and belligerent purpose, they are considered as a part of the domain of the conqueror, so long as he retains the possession and government of them. The island of Santa Cruz, after its capitulation, remained a British island until it was restored to Denmark." As to the second point, the case was well within the rule laid down by the British Courts. "The identification of the national character of the owner with that of the soil, in the particular transaction, is not placed on the dispositions with which he acquires the soil, or on his general character. The acquisition of land in Santa Cruz binds him, so far as respects that land, to the fate of Santa Cruz, whatever its destiny may be. While that island belonged to Denmark, the produce of the soil, while unsold, was, according to this rule, Danish property, whatever might be the general character of the particular proprietor. When the island became British, the soil and its produce, while that produce remained unsold, were British. The general commercial or political character of Mr Bentzon could not, according to this rule, affect this particular transaction. Although incorporated, so far as respects his general character, with the permanent interests of Denmark, he was incorporated, so far as respected his plantation in Santa Cruz, with the permanent interests of Santa Cruz, which was, at that time, British ; and though, as a Dane, he was at war with Great Britain, and an enemy, yet, as a proprietor of land in Santa Cruz, he was no enemy : he could ship his produce to Great Britain in perfect safety."

(iii) *Property, by whomsoever owned, which is incorporated into belligerent commerce, assumes a belligerent character.*

With regard to this principle there is general agreement. With respect to occasions for its application opinions are less harmonious.

(a) The vessel, which sails under a particular belligerent flag, pass or licence, be its owner who he may, can hardly be otherwise regarded by the hostile belligerent than as incorporated into the commerce and fleet of his enemy.

"The produce," said Sir W. Scott in the "Vrow Anna Catharina," "of a person's own plantation in the colony of the enemy, though shipped in time of peace, is liable to be considered as the property of the enemy by reason that the proprietor has incorporated himself with the permanent interests of the nation, as a holder of the soil, and is to be taken as a part of that country, in that particular trans-

9 Cranch 197.

(iii) Property incorporated into belligerent commerce is belligerent.
The "Vigilantia," 1 C. Rob. 1.
The "Embden," *Ibid.* 16.
The "Endraught," *Ibid.* 19.

(a) Neutral vessels sailing under the belligerent flag, pass or licence.
The "Vigilantia," 1 C. Rob. 13.
The "Success," 1 Dods. 132.
The "Vrow Elizabeth," 5 C. Rob. 2.
The "Ariadne," 2 Wheaton 143.
Sir W. Scott in the "Vrow Anna Catharina," 5 C. Rob. 167.
The "Julia," 8 Cranch 181.

8—2

The
"Aurora,"
8 Cranch
203.
The
"Hiram,"
Ibid. 444;
1 Wheaton
440.

action, independent of his own personal residence and occupation. So the flag and pass of a nation, taken up in war or peace, binds the vessel almost without exception."

This principle is adopted alike by the British and American Courts.

(*b*) Neutral
vessels
sailing
under
belligerent
convoy.

(*b*) Neutral vessels, with their cargoes, taking the protection of belligerent convoy are by the British Courts regarded as endowed with the belligerent character.

The British practice was ably vindicated by Story, J., in his dissenting judgment in the Supreme Court in the "Nereide" in 1815. "The belligerent convoy is bound," he said, "to resist all visitations by enemy ships, whether neutral to the convoyed ships or not. This obligation is distinctly known to the party taking its protection. If, therefore, he choose to continue under the convoy, he shows an intention to avail himself of its protection under all the chances and hazards of war. The abandonment of such intention cannot be otherwise evidenced than by the overt act of quitting convoy. And it is impossible to conceive that the mere secret wishes or private declarations of a party could prevail over his own deliberate act of continuing under convoy, unless courts of prize would surrender themselves to the most stale excuses and imbecile artifices. It would be in vain to administer justice in such courts, if mere statements of intention would outweigh the legal effect of the acts of the parties. Besides, the injury to the friendly belligerent is equally great, whatever might be the special objects of the neutral. The right of search is effectually prevented by the presence of superior force, or exercised only after the perils and injuries of victorious warfare. And it is this very evasion of the right of search that constitutes the ground of condemnation in ordinary cases. The neutral, in effect, declares that he will not submit to search until the enemy convoy is conquered, and then only because he cannot avoid it."

Story, J.
in the
"Nereide,"
9 Cranch
444.

The Dano-

American contemporary diplomatists did not, however,

share the opinion of the great American judge, and during American controversy, 1810—30.
the twenty years between 1810 and 1830, the Government
of the United States continued to contest the legitimacy of
the action of the belligerent Danes in condemning in the
earlier year American neutral vessels which had accepted the
convoy of the hostile British while trading with the Baltic.
Ultimately the Danish Government admitted the hardship
of the peculiar case of the individual American sufferers
by paying an indemnity, but with express reservation of the
question of legal right. This special settlement seems to
have been equitable enough, as the American shipowners
would appear to have sought the protection of the British
not against the Danes but against the French, and to have
been condemned under a Danish ordinance with the fact
of the issue of which they were unacquainted; but the
general principle enunciated by the Danes seems sufficiently
well founded. "Upon the whole," says the American
Woolsey, commenting on the ground of the Danish claim,
"the intention to screen the vessels behind the enemy's guns
is so obvious that the act must be pronounced to be a Woolsey, Introduction, § 211.
decided departure from the line of neutrality, and one which
may justly entail confiscation on the offending party."

(c) Neutral property laden on board an armed bellige- (c) Neutral goods laden on board an armed belligerent vessel.
rent merchantman is, according to the view of the British
Courts, fairly assimilated in character to similar property
enjoying the protection of belligerent convoy.

The "Fanny," a British vessel furnished with a letter of
marque and mounting sixteen guns, was on April 17, 1814,
when on her return voyage from Rio to Liverpool with a
cargo consisting in part of Portuguese and in part of British
property, captured by the U. S. privateer "General Armstrong." Being subsequently recaptured by H.M.S. "Sceptre,"
the owners of the Portuguese portion of the cargo resisted
the demand for salvage made by the recaptors, on the ground
that their property, being neutral, would have been in no
danger in the American prize court. Sir W. Scott, however,

was of opinion that the property would have run a very
considerable risk of condemnation, and that the Portuguese
owners would have had no very good ground of complaint
had it been actually so condemned, and accordingly decreed
salvage. The neutral owner who put his goods on a belligerent ship of force, which must be defended against the enemy,
betrayed, said Sir W. Scott, an intention to resist visitation
and search, which he could not do by putting them on board
a mere merchant vessel, and, so far as he did this, he adhered
to the belligerent, withdrew himself from the protection of
neutrality, resorted to another mode of defence, and was to
be considered *pro hac* as an enemy.

The "Fanny," 1 Dods. 443.

The legal authorities of the United States adopted a
different view.

Divergent practice of the United States.

The "Nereide," a British ship mounting ten guns, having
become separated from her convoy on a voyage from London
to Buenos Ayres, was on December 19, 1813, after a smart
fight, captured off Madeira by the American privateer, the
"Governor Tompkins." Being taken in for adjudication to
New York, the vessel and her entire cargo were in the
District Court condemned. Manuel Pinto, a merchant of
Buenos Ayres, claimed for himself, his partners and other
persons in Buenos Ayres part of the cargo as Spanish neutral
property laden at London under charter for Buenos Ayres,
and, an appeal to the Circuit Court having resulted in a
formal affirmation of the sentence of the District Court, took
the case to the Supreme Court. The majority of the
Supreme Court led by Marshall, C. J., being satisfied that in
no respect except in the matter of lading had the claimant
any direction of the ship, ruled that Mr Pinto, as a neutral
merchant, might lawfully and innocently lade his goods on
board an armed belligerent merchantman, and was in no way
concluded from successfully asserting the neutral character
of his property by reason of the resistance to seizure offered
by the British belligerent master. The value of this judgment as a statement of international law was materially

The "Nereide," 9 Cranch 388.

lessened by the strong dissenting judgment of Justice Story, who laying down the broad principle that a neutral must submit to the belligerent right of search, and might not lawfully adopt any measures whose direct object was to withdraw his commerce from the most liberal and accurate search, without the application, on the part of the belligerent, of superior force, saw such an unneutral withdrawal in the employment of belligerent convoy, and *a fortiori* in the lading of goods on board a belligerent armed vessel. "I have," he said, "no difficulty in holding that the resistance of the ship is, in all cases, the resistance of the cargo, and that it makes no difference whether she be armed or unarmed, commissioned or uncommissioned. He who puts his property on the issue of battle must stand or fall by the event of the contest." Story, J. in the "Nereide," 9 Cranch 437.

In the subsequent case of the "Atalanta," however, the Supreme Court upheld the decision of the majority of the judges in the "Nereide." The "Atalanta," 3 Wheaton 409.

(d) The "Rule of 1756," which forbade the engaging by a neutral in time of war in a commerce with one or the other belligerent from which he was excluded before the outbreak of hostilities, finds its justification in the doctrine of incorporation. The British might well see in the admission of Dutch shipowners to the privileged trade between French home ports and the French colonies "a measure not of French counsels but of British force," and decline to admit the legitimacy of a proceeding whereby in effect the Dutch merchantmen reinforced the conquered French trading and provisioning fleet, and "aided and adhered to" the enemy by carrying on that commerce without which the French islands would have of necessity fallen to the British as prize of war. The "extension" which the Rule received in 1793, however, is incapable of such defence, and belongs to the long chapter of belligerent encroachments of the Revolutionary period. (d) Neutral vessels engaged in breach of the Rule of 1756. [Obsolete.] The "Immanuel," 2 C. Rob. 197. The "Nancy," 3 C. Rob. 82. The "Phoenix," 3 C. Rob. 186. The "Minerva," Ibid. 229. Sir W. Scott in the "Immanuel," 2 C. Rob. 200.

The outbreak of war operates :—
(i) To put an end to ordinary public intercourse between hostile Governments.
(ii) To put an end to all non-hostile intercourse between subjects of hostile Governments :

The "Rapid," 8 Cranch 155.

Sir J. Nicholl in Potts v. Bell, 8 D. and E. 554.
Potts v. Bell, 8 D. and E. 543.
Antoine v. Morshead, 1 Marsh. 558.
Anthon v. Fisher, Dougl. 649 n.
The "Hoop," 1 C. Rob. 196.
Esposito v. Bowden, 4 E. and B. 963 ; 7 E. and B. 763.
The "Rapid," 8 Cranch 155.

CHAPTER II.

LEGAL EFFECTS OF THE OUTBREAK OF WAR.

§ 44. The first general legal effect of the outbreak of war is (i) the cessation of ordinary public intercourse between the hostile Governments.

The cessation of diplomatic intercourse does not in itself constitute an act of war, but is the natural accompaniment of its outbreak, and most commonly precedes it. During the continuance of war communication between hostile Governments is carried on either through the intermediary of a neutral Government, or by specially protected agents.

§ 45. (ii) The outbreak of war further legally operates to put an end to all non-hostile intercourse between individual subjects of hostile states.

There cannot be a war of arms and a peace of commerce. Though active hostilities are forbidden to subjects not being formally authorised for the purpose, all subjects of one belligerent are in law enemies of all subjects of the hostile belligerent, and the belligerent rulers may fairly claim a right to hold prohibited by the outbreak of hostilities an intercourse which is calculated alike to embarrass their military operations and to prolong the period of the struggle.

All intercourse, correspondence and business dealing between subjects of hostile states is, accordingly, held to be absolutely interdicted by the fact of war, except in so far as they arise from necessity or by special licence of the Powers.

(a) *All, trading with the enemy is, in general, illegal in a subject of a belligerent state.*

"There is no principle of law more recognised than this," said Sir W. Scott in the "Charlotta," "that during the existence of hostilities between the Crown of Great Britain and other countries, it is unlawful for British subjects to carry on a commercial intercourse with the inhabitants of those countries. The consent of the Crown to such a course of trade must necessarily be interposed in some way or other."

This principle is adopted with equal clearness in the United States.

After the declaration of war between Great Britain and the United States in 1812, Mr Harrison, an American subject, who had a long time before that declaration purchased in England and deposited on Indian Island, a small islet near the boundary line between Nova Scotia and the United States, a quantity of British goods, chartered the "Rapid," a Boston cod-fishing vessel, and despatched her to bring away these goods. On her return she was captured by the U. S. privateer "Jefferson," and condemned for trading with the enemy's country. The Supreme Court on appeal upheld the condemnation. "The universal sense of nations," said Johnson, J., "has acknowledged the demoralising effects that would result from the admission of individual intercourse. The whole nation are embarked in one common bottom, and must be reconciled to submit to one common fate. Every individual of the one nation must acknowledge every individual of the other nation as his own enemy—because the enemy of his country."

All commercial partnerships existing between subjects of opposing belligerents are *ipso facto* dissolved by the outbreak of war, and no new partnerships may be formed between such persons during the course of war, even although expressly designed to come into operation only after the return of peace.

(a) Trading with the enemy is illegal in a subject.

The "Hoop," 1 C. Rob. 196.
The "Odin," 1 C. Rob. 248.
Potts v. Bell, 8 D. and E. 548.
Sir W. Scott in the "Charlotta," 1 Dods. 390.

The "Rapid," 8 Cranch 155.

Johnson, J. in the "Rapid," 8 Cranch 161.
Effect of war on partnerships,
Clifford, J. in Hanger v. Abbott, 6 Wallace 532.
The "William Bagaley," 5 Wall. 377.
Griswold v. Waddington, 15 Johnson 57.
Willes, J. in Esposito v. Bowden, 7 E. and B. 785.

The State of
Georgia v.
Brailsford,
3 Dall. 1.
Ex parte
Boussmaker,
13 Ves. Jr.
71.
New York
Insurance
Co. v.
Statham, 93
U. S. K. 24.
Furiado v.
Rogers, 3 B.
and P. 191.
Scholefield
v. Eichel-
berger, 7
Peters 586.
Case of
Three
Spanish
Sailors,
2 Black.
1324.
Willison v.
Patteson, 7
Taunt. 439.
Story, J. in
Brown v.
United
States,
8 Cranch
136.
(b) Inter-
course
with the
enemy in-
consistent
with
actual
hostility
is in a
subject
illegal.
Johnson, J.
in the
" Rapid," 8
Cranch 155.
R. v.
Hensey,
1 Burr. 642.
R. v. Stone,
6 D. and E.
527.
Justructions
for U. S.
Armies in
the Field,
Art. 98.
Geffcken's
Heffter, 11.
§ 123 n.
(c) Inter-
course
illegal in
a subject
is illegal
in the
subject of
an ally.

No business contract entered into before the war between such persons can be enforced during its continuance. Private debts already contracted at the time of the rupture are suspended as to payment. Executory contracts whose terms do not require fulfilment during the war are similarly suspended, but executory contracts whose terms do require such fulfilment are altogether avoided.

No contract entered into during the war between subjects of opposing belligerents can, in general, be enforced. " No principle of national or municipal law is better settled than that all contracts with an enemy, made during war, are utterly void. This principle has grown hoary under the reverend respect of centuries, and cannot now be shaken without uprooting the very foundations of national law."

(b) *Intercourse with subjects of a hostile Power, whatever its description, is, if inconsistent with actual hostility, in a subject illegal.*

"Negotiation or contract has no necessary connection with the offence. Intercourse inconsistent with actual hostility is the offence against which the operation of the rule is directed."

The supply to the enemy of any information capable of assisting him in his belligerent operations is obviously in a subject directly treasonable, and, similarly, the affording to him of any indirect aid in his struggle otherwise than by such information is highly punishable. Thus the German banker Güterbock, who subscribed to a French war loan in 1871, was dealt with as a traitor.

(c) *The intercourse which is illegal in the subject of one belligerent state is illegal also in the subject of an ally.*

"It is a declared principle of the Law of Nations, founded on very clear and just grounds, that one of the belligerents may seize, and inflict the penalty of forfeiture on, the property of a subject of a co-ally, engaged in a trade with the common enemy, and thereby affording him aid and comfort, whilst the other ally was carrying on a severe and vigorous warfare."

(d) *In but two cases is an exceptional relaxation of the strict rule of non-intercourse universally admitted, namely* (1) *where the transaction is the result of sheer necessity, and* (2) *where it is entered into in pursuance of express permission given by a single-handed belligerent Government to its subject.* The case of necessity is simple enough.

In *Antoine v. Morshead* in 1815 the Court of Common Pleas permitted the French indorsee of a bill of exchange made by a British subject interned at Verdun to recover on the bill, Gibbs, L.C.J., remarking that, if the strict doctrine of the absolute illegality of all communication with hostile subjects set up by the defence were carried to the extent contended for, many British subjects must have perished in France.

Amongst *commercia belli* permissible on this principle many states include contracts of ransom entered into by the commanders of prizes with their captors, and allow the captor to sue directly upon the ransom bill. The English Courts after some hesitation refused to distinguish such contracts from other contracts unenforceable directly as being made with alien enemies during war, and the entering into such contracts by British subjects was in 1781 expressly forbidden by statute. But now under the Naval Prize Act 1864, the Queen in Council may allow at pleasure the ransoming of their property by British owners, and the jurisdiction over such contracts is assigned to the Court of Admiralty.

Further, it is well agreed, that intercourse with hostile individuals may legally take place under special licence, provided, however, that in the case of the issue of a licence by a belligerent engaged in other than a single-handed struggle his ally concur.

"Since the world has grown more commercial," said Sir William Scott, "a practice has crept in of admitting particular relaxations; and if one state only is at war, no injury is

The " Nayade," 4 C. Rob. 251.

The " Neptunus," 6 C. Rob. 403.

Kent, *Int.* Law (ed. Abdy), p. 208.

(d) A contract during war is valid if entered into (i) under stress of necessity,

Antoine v. Morshead, 1 Marsh. 562.

Abdy's Kent, 206.

Ricord v. Bettenham, 3 Burr. 1734; 1 Black. 563. Anthon v. Fisher, Dougl. 649 n. Stat. 22 Geo. 3, c. 25.

Stat. 27 and 28 Vict. c. 25, s. 45.

or (ii) under special licence.

Usparicha v. Noble, 13 East 322.

committed to any other state. It is of no importance to other nations, how much a single belligerent chooses to weaken and dilute his own rights. But it is otherwise when allied nations are pursuing a common cause against a common enemy. Between them it must be taken as an implied, if not an express contract, that one state shall not do anything to defeat the general object. If one state admits its subjects to carry on an uninterrupted trade with the enemy, the consequence may be that it will supply that aid and comfort to the enemy, especially if it is an enemy depending, like Holland, very materially on the resources of foreign commerce, which may be very injurious to the prosecution of the common cause, and the interests of its ally. It should seem, that it is not enough, therefore, to say that the *one* state has allowed this practice to its own subjects; it should appear to be at least desirable that it could be shown, that either the practice is of such a nature, as can in no manner interfere with the common operation, or that it has the allowance of the confederate state."

In every case the terms of a special licence must be strictly construed.

§ 46. (iii) **The outbreak of war operates to abrogate or otherwise in a lesser degree affect the mutual treaty engagements of the hostile Governments.**

The effect of the outbreak of war on treaties previously existing between the belligerents depends upon the character of the treaty.

Treaties of alliance are naturally extinguished by the outbreak of hostilities between the parties. But "where treaties contemplate a permanent arrangement of territorial and other national rights, or which, in their terms, are meant to provide for the event of an intervening war, it would be against every principle of just interpretation to hold them extinguished by the event of war. ....Treaties stipulating for permanent rights and general arrangements, and professing to aim at perpetuity, and to deal with the case of war as well as of peace, do not cease on the occurrence of war, but are at most only suspended while it lasts; and unless they are waived by the parties, or new and repugnant stipulations are made, they revive in their operation at the return of peace." Washington, J. in S. P. G. v New Haven, 8 Wheat. 494.

Treaties providing for the event of war are, of course, called into exercise by its outbreak.

When third Powers are parties to a treaty formerly entered into by the belligerents, the terms of those treaties are in general unaffected in respect of the rights of those third Powers, though as between the belligerents they may be temporarily suspended or even entirely extinguished. (iv) To expose to belligerent assault hostile persons and property in certain situations.

§ 47. (iv) The outbreak of war legally operates to expose to hostile assault belligerent persons and property found in certain situations. (a) Hostile persons and

The legal liabilities of belligerent persons and property vary with their local position. The belligerent may on the outbreak of war discover the person and property of the subject of a hostile state in any one of three situations. He may find him or it within his own, within a neutral or within a hostile jurisdiction. His belligerent rights in his or its regard vary accordingly. property found by a belligerent within his territory on the outbreak of war. (1) Hostile persons are commonly permitted to remain

§ 48. (a) All subjects of a hostile state found by the modern belligerent on the outbreak of hostilities within his jurisdiction, whether ashore or under his flag on the high seas or in waters where no other Power exercises control, are, with their property, granted a fairly certain and comprehensive protection from unfriendly interference. during good behaviour: if ordered to depart they are entitled to a reason-able time for pre-paration.

(1) *The foreign resident, who is rendered hostile by the outbreak of war, is commonly permitted to remain during good behaviour; if required to depart, he is held entitled to a reasonable allowance of time within which to withdraw with his property.* The "Sarah Starr," Blatch. Pr. Ca. 650. The "General Pinckney," Ibid. 668. 3 Wharton, Dig. 250.

(i) The citizens of a belligerent state found within the territory of an enemy at the outbreak of war were under the war-practice of antiquity exposed without distinction of History of practice.

class to the full exercise of hostile force alike in person and property. And so late as the early years of the present century the Turks, like many other semi-civilised and barbarian peoples, were still accustomed on the outbreak of war to seize as hostages the persons, and to confiscate the property, of all resident subjects of the hostile Power, including even the members of the hostile resident Legation.

Magna Charta, c. 30, 27 Edw. 3, st. 2, c. 17. 4 Hen. 5, c. 5.

(ii) But with certain civilised Powers, notably with Great Britain, it became at a very early date usual to permit the merchant-stranger a limited period within which to withdraw himself and his on the outbreak of hostilities between his native state and the land of his sojourn. This practice soon obtained very general recognition, but in the 18th century still required the confirmation of treaties in certain quarters[1].

(iii) In the middle of the eighteenth century a yet more extensive tolerance, displayed in a few earlier instances, began to be generally shown, and citizens of hostile Powers were allowed to remain during the continuance of war, subject to the obligation of lending no assistance to their native Government[2]. In 1803 on the rupture with England after the Peace of Amiens, Napoleon issued an Arrêté,

Vattel, iii. 4, §§ 63, 64.

[1] A limited period varying from three months to two years from the outbreak of hostilities was agreed to be allowed to citizens of hostile Powers within which to prepare for and take their departure by the following, amongst other, treaties:—Great Britain and Portugal 1654; Great Britain and Spain 1667; Great Britain and Holland 1667; Great Britain and France 1697 and 1713; Great Britain and Spain 1713; Great Britain and France 1744; The Empire and Algiers 1748; Hamburg and Algiers 1751; Denmark and Morocco 1753; Great Britain and Morocco 1763; Great Britain and Russia 1766; Denmark and Morocco 1767; France and United States 1778; Russia and Denmark 1782; Holland and United States 1782; Sweden and United States 1783; Russia and the Porte 1783; Prussia and United States 1785; Austria and Russia 1785; Spain and Algiers 1786; Russia and France 1787; Russia and Portugal 1787; Russia and Two Sicilies 1787; Spain and United States 1795; Great Britain and Russia 1798; Portugal and Russia 1798; France and United States 1800; Sweden and Russia 1801.

[2] This practice was made the subject of treaty stipulation by Great Britain and France in 1786 and by Great Britain and the United States in 1795. Martens, *Recueil*, ii. 681, vi. 380; Chalmers, i. 519.

whereby all Englishmen between 18 and 60 years of age found at the moment on French soil were made prisoners of war, the persons so arrested being detained until the fall of the tyrant in 1814. But this edict is unique in its kind amongst civilised powers of the present century. The widest toleration is now universally accorded to the person of the citizen of the hostile State. A distinction may indeed be drawn between an active national agent such as a military man or responsible public minister and a mere private individual. An active agent of the hostile Power coming during the course of war within belligerent jurisdiction without the protection of a flag of truce or safe-conduct may be seized, and made prisoner of war. Marshal Belleisle, for example, chancing, when travelling as French plenipotentiary to the Court of Berlin in 1744, to cross an outlying strip of Hanoverian hostile territory, was promptly arrested, and sent a prisoner to London. But even a military or naval officer or any other minister, official or civil servant of a hostile Government will by the modern civilised belligerent be permitted on the outbreak of war a reasonable time within which to withdraw with his private effects. In strict law, perhaps, such a person might be fairly detained; and accordingly the French Government in the early days of the Franco-Prussian struggle refused to allow the departure from French soil of German subjects who were not past the age of active military service. "No rule of international law," wrote the Duc de Gramont to Mr Washburne, on July 23, 1870, "obliges a belligerent to allow to depart from his territory subjects of the enemy who, from the day of their return to their own country, will be enrolled in the ranks to take part in the hostilities." The decision of the Government of the Duc de Gramont did not, however, escape adverse comment, and represents a harsh and unpopular practice. The ordinary citizen of a belligerent found at the outbreak of war on hostile soil is at any rate commonly granted the option to retain during the

Browning, *England and Napoleon in 1803,* pp. 272—295.

Hostile persons, being public servants, are commonly permitted to withdraw on the outbreak of war, but may be detained.

Wash-burne's *Recollections,* I. p. 44.

struggle on condition of good behaviour the position of a
domiciled subject. Thus during the Crimean War citizens of
Russia were permitted to continue their residence in Great
Britain and France, and the like treatment was accorded in
1870 to French subjects resident in Germany. The right to
expel the resident subject of the hostile power does, nevertheless, undoubtedly still remains in the belligerent, to be
exercised should necessity so require.

On July 21, 1870, all the Consuls of the North German
Confederation resident in France were, with a number of
German newspaper correspondents, ordered to leave French
soil, and on August 28 the adoption of a new policy with
regard to resident Prussians brought about the issue of an
Arrêté of the Governor of Paris which ordered every person,
belonging to any of the states at war with France and not
being a naturalised French subject, to quit within three
days, on pain of punishment by court-martial, Paris and the
department of the Seine, either by retiring altogether from
French territory or by withdrawing beyond the Loire. An
immense number of German subjects were by these measures
driven out of France under circumstances of great hardship,
and obtained no compensation in respect of their losses on
the return of peace.

(2) *The legal position of hostile property found by a
belligerent within his jurisdiction on the outbreak of war
varies with its character as state-owned or privately owned,
and as real or personal.*

(i) State-owned real property so found may be seized
and administered for the benefit of the belligerent local
Government until the return of peace, the intermediate
revenues being applied to the uses of that Government,
while state-owned personal property, whether consisting of
movables ashore on hostile soil or of vessels or chattels afloat
within hostile territorial waters, are immediately confiscable.

(ii) Private property is held entitled to more considerate
treatment. The grant to the private citizen of a hostile

Wash-
burne's
*Recollec-
tions*, I.
p. 83.
Rolin Jac-
quemyns,
*La Guerre
Actuelle*,
pp. 33—36.

Hozier, *The
Franco-
Prussian
War*, I.
p. 336.

(2) Hostile
property.

(i) State-
owned
property
is seques-
trated or
confis-
cated.

(ii) The
private
property

state of permission to remain naturally involves the right to of the hostile resident is respected: retain possession of all his property, whether real or personal, subject only to the ordinary obligations incumbent upon the the private personal property domiciled stranger. With regard to the personal property of the non-resident hostile private citizen found within the of the non-resident hostile private citizen state at the outbreak of war the best founded doctrine of international law seems indeed to be that laid down by the Supreme Court in 1814 in the famous case of *Brown v. the United States.* The case arose on the claim of one Armitz Brown, a resident citizen of the United States, to certain timber originally British but sold during the war to the claimant, it being then water-borne in a creek at New Bedford, where it was seized as British hostile property. The Supreme Court allowed the appeal of the claimant from the sentence of condemnation passed in the District Court is confiscable, though not *ipso facto* confiscated: and upheld in the Circuit Court, on the ground that, although the power to confiscate hostile property in the situation of the property claimed did internationally belong to the Government of the United States, that power was Brown v. United States, 8 Cranch 110. vested in the legislature, and the legislature had not declared its will to confiscate such property. Said Marshall, C. J., Marshall, C. J. in Brown v. United States, 8 Cranch 123—125. "That war gives to the sovereign full right to take the persons and confiscate the property of the enemy wherever found is conceded. The mitigations of this rigid rule, which the humane and wise policy of modern times has introduced into practice, will more or less affect the exercise of this right, but cannot impair the right itself....It may be considered as the opinion of all who have written on the *jus belli*, that war gives the right to confiscate, but does not itself confiscate the property of the enemy; and their rules go to the exercise of this right[1]."

[1] Story, J., while agreeing with the majority of the Court on the general principle, dissented from the judgment admitting the claim of Mr Brown on the two distinct grounds that the claim was based on a contract made with an alien enemy during war, and that the Executive was already sufficiently empowered by law to effect a seizure without awaiting any further legislative authorisation. 8 Cranch 129.

his real
property
is re-
spected.

To confiscate the real property of the non-resident citizen
of a hostile Power would, however, be to act contrary to
modern civilised practice, although the transmission *flagrante
bello* of revenues therefrom to a proprietor resident on
hostile soil would fall within the rule shortly to be stated,
which prohibits intercourse between subjects of hostile
Powers during war.

Hostile
property
coming
into port
after de-
claration
of war
is con-
fiscable.
Cussy,
*Phases
et Causes
Célèbres*, II.
12, §§ 4—8.

Hostile property, whether national or private, coming
within the territorial jurisdiction of a belligerent after the
outbreak of war is, in general, confiscable. A claim for
exemption has been in some quarters set up and occasionally
admitted on behalf of vessels driven in by stress of weather
or entering a hostile port in ignorance of the outbreak of
war, and in some few recent instances the privilege has been
extended by belligerents to hostile vessels sailing or laden
for their ports before the declaration of war, but this practice
represents only a special and by no means widely approved

The
"Johanna
Emilie,"
Spinks, 14.

mitigation of strict war-right. In general such vessels are
unhesitatingly seized and condemned.

(iii) Pri-
vate
hostile
property
in the
form of
debts is in
practice
respected.
Martens,
*Causes
Célèbres*, II.
p. 97.

(iii) Private property in the form of debts, public or
private, are endowed by practice with a peculiar sanctity.

A belligerent state cannot be fairly called upon to pay
dividends on public stock to hostile bondholders during time
of war, but no Government has had recourse by way of
reprisals or as an act of war to the confiscation of the funds
of hostile creditors since the famous incident of the Silesian
Loan.

The case
of the
Silesian
Loan.

Frederick the Great of Prussia, having obtained at
Breslau in 1742 the confirmation of his Silesian conquests,
took over under the treaty of cession all liabilities in respect
of a debt contracted in 1735 by the deceased Emperor
Charles VI. with certain Dutch and British capitalists on
the security of the revenues of Silesia. War having broken
out in 1744 between Great Britain and France, the British
courts condemned under circumstances of great hardship as
being engaged in contraband trade the property of certain

Prussian neutral shipowners. Remonstrances being found vain, Frederick at length by way of reprisals confiscated the funds of the British Silesian creditors. The report of the Prussian legal Commission[1] which recommended this step has, however, obtained an unenviable reputation as a repertory of bad law. The sequestration was withdrawn under treaty of compromise signed at Westminster in Jan. 1756, and no Government has since shown any inclination to follow the evil example of the Prussian king.

Between the confiscation of the goods of a foreigner and the confiscation of debts due to him in respect of the sale of those goods there seems no distinction in principle, and more than one American judge has asserted the extension in strict law of the doctrine of *Brown v. the United States* to the case of private debts. "On a review of the authorities," said Story, J., "I am entirely satisfied that, by the rigor of the law of nations and of the common law, the sovereign of a nation may lawfully confiscate the debts of his enemy during war, or by way of reprisal."

Marshall, J. C. in Brown v. United States, 8 Cranch 124.

Ware v. Hylton, 3 Dall. 199.

Story, J. in Brown v. United States, 8 Cranch 143.

Practice has, however, drawn a distinction, which reason fails to suggest[2]. The goods of the non-resident foreigner may be condemned under the doctrine of *Brown v. the United States*: the collecting by a belligerent of a debt due from a subject to the citizen of a hostile Power is by recent authority strictly condemned.

Wolff v. Oxholm, 6 M. and S. 92.

Furtado v. Rogers, 3 B. and P. 201.

Ware v. Hylton, 3 Dall. 254.

In 1807, war having broken out between Great Britain and Denmark, the Danish Government by ordinance seques-

---

[1] The famous "Exposition des Motifs" of 1752. Martens, *Causes Célèbres*, ii. p. 106.

[2] By Art. 10 of the Treaty of London of Nov. 19, 1794, it was agreed by the United States and Great Britain that "neither debts due from individuals of the one nation to the individuals of the other, nor shares, nor monies which they might have in the public funds or private banks, shall, even in any event of war or national differences, be sequestrated or confiscated; *it being unjust and unpolitic that debts and engagements contracted and made by individuals having confidence in each other, and in their respective Governments, shall ever be destroyed or impaired by national authority on account of national differences and discontents.*"

trated all ships, goods, money or monies worth, of or belonging to British subjects within Danish dominions, and ordered the payment into the Danish treasury of all debts due in Denmark to such British subjects. One Oxholm, a Danish born subject resident in Denmark, being indebted to the British firm of Wolff and Dorville in a considerable sum, paid the amount to the Danish treasury commissioners. In 1814 Oxholm, having come to England, was arrested and held to bail in respect of the debt. Lord Ellenborough, C. J., held that the payment under the Danish ordinance into the Danish exchequer furnished no defence to the action of the British creditors, the ordinance not being conformable to the usage of nations. The right of confiscating debts contended for by the Danish defendant on the authority of citations from Vattel was, he said, not recognised by Grotius and was impugned by Puffendorf and others, such confiscation was not general at any period of time and no instance of it, except the ordinance in question, was to be found for more than a century.

The judgment of Lord Ellenborough is at variance with high American authority, and his sweeping dicta lack historic support, but the tenor of the decision is in accordance with the current of modern thought.

The action of the Confederate Government in 1861 in confiscating private debts due to Northerners affords the only instance of such a proceeding in recent times, and that instance evoked a strong protest from the Government of Great Britain.

The received doctrine with regard to such debts is that they are suspended as to payment by the fact of the outbreak of war, but that payment may be enforced after the return of peace.

§ 49. (β) **The persons and property of subjects of a belligerent Power found within the territorial jurisdiction of a neutral Power, including such persons and property under a neutral flag on the high seas, are legally inviolable at the hands of a hostile belligerent.**

Marginal notes: Wolff v. Oxholm, 6 M. and S. 92. Ware v. Hylton, 3 Dall. 199. Brown v. United States, 8 Cranch 110. Parl. Papers, N. America, No. 1, 1862, p. 108. Ex parte Boussmaker, 13 Ves. Jr. 71. Hanger v. Abbott, 6 Wall. 532. (β) Hostile persons and property found by a belligerent within the territorial jurisdiction of a neutral Power or under the neutral flag on the high seas.

It is now clear law that every overt act of hostility must cease with the passage of the combatant within the protection of the boundary line of the territorial jurisdiction of a neutral Power. As between the belligerents the question of the legitimacy of an attack made within neutral limits cannot be litigated, but such an attack imports an offence against the sovereignty of the neutral ruler, which it is for him to resent by intervening to secure the restoration of the captured property and proper indemnity for the insult offered to himself. Thus the "Chesapeake," an American steamer seized on the high seas by a party of Confederate passengers, having been recaptured by U. S. gunboats, when lying abandoned in the Nova Scotian harbour of Sambro, the United States Government, on complaint of Great Britain, delivered up the vessel to the Halifax authorities, and offered a full apology for the violation of British sovereignty involved in the action of the gunboats. And a similar confession of wrongdoing was made in respect of the cutting out of the "Florida" by the "Wachusett" from the neutral Brazilian harbour of Bahia.

It is equally clear law that the neutral flag on the high seas protects all persons thereunder from belligerent attack, unless the vessel have rendered herself liable to capture by unneutral conduct, as by engaging in the hostile belligerent transport service, by contraband trading or blockade running. The unhesitating consensus of civilised opinion supported the British Government in its demand for the restoration to liberty of the Confederate agents, Slidell and Mason and their secretaries, seized by the commander of the U. S. man-of-war, "San Jacinto," upon the British neutral mail steamer, the "Trent," in Old Bahama Channel.

And by Art. 2 of the Declaration of Paris, "The neutral flag covers enemy's goods, with the exception of contraband of war," the vast majority of civilised Powers thus at length uniting, after centuries of dispute and of varying practice, in the common recognition of the principle "Free ships,

Margin notes:

Sanctity of neutral territory.

The "Anna," 5 C. Rob. 373. The "Perle," Snow, 398. The "Purissima Conception," 6 C. Rob. 45. The "Anne," 3 Wheat. 435. The "Santissima Trinidad," 7 Wheat. 349. The "Eliza Ann," 1 Dods. 244.

U. S. Dipl. Corresp. 1864, Pt. II. p. 474.

Sanctity of the neutral flag on the high seas.

Parl. Papers, North America, No. 5, 1862.

"Free Ships, Free Goods."

Ward, Treatise on Maritime Law. Jenkinson, Discourse.

free goods," a principle which has moreover the strong approval of the United States, whose Government declined for special reasons to sign the Declaration of Paris.

§ **50.** (γ) **The persons and property of subjects of a belligerent Power found within their own territorial jurisdiction, including such persons and property under their own flag on the high seas, or in places where no recognised Government exercises control, are exposed to the exercise by the hostile Power of belligerent force, subject to the limitation that only that amount of force may be legally applied which is necessary to secure the objects of the war.**

The restraints imposed by the Laws of War upon the action of a belligerent in respect of his enemy on hostile soil, and under the hostile flag on the high seas, connect themselves mainly with the clear distinction drawn by modern war practice between the public armed forces of a belligerent state and its private individuals.

" The citizen or native of a hostile country is an enemy, as one of the constituents of the hostile state or nation, and as such is subjected to the hardships of the war. Nevertheless, as civilization has advanced during the last centuries, so has likewise steadily advanced, especially in war on land, the distinction between the private individual belonging to a hostile country and the hostile country itself, with its men in arms."

1. *Members of the public armed forces of a hostile state, being combatants armed and offering resistance to attack, are exposed under the laws of war to direct destruction alike in life and limb, and, on surrender, to the treatment of prisoners of war.*

The public armed forces of a state may be composed of combatants, being persons entitled to exercise, and in turn exposed to the exercise of, the fullest measure of lawful belligerent force, and non-combatants, being individuals, who, without actually enlisting in the ranks of the army, have joined themselves thereto in some useful capacity.

3 Wharton, *Dig.* § 342.

(γ) Hostile persons and property found by a belligerent within their own territorial jurisdiction or under their own flag on the high seas may be exposed to that amount of belligerent force which is necessary to secure the objects of war.

Instructions for the government of U. S. Armies in the Field, Arts. 21, 22.

1. Combatant members of public armed forces are exposed to necessary destruction of life and limb.

Distinction of combatants and non-combatants.

Projected Declaration of Brussels, 1874, Art. 11.

The combatant is commonly distinguished from the non-combatant by his possession of a formal national authorisation to levy war. It is, in fact, clear law that a combatant to be lawful must be formally authorised by a recognised Government, or be a member of a *levée en masse* rising on the approach of an invader.

"By a due consideration of the law of nations," said Iredell, J., in *Talbot v. Janson*, "whatever opinions may have prevailed formerly to the contrary, no hostilities of any kind, except in necessary self-defence, can lawfully be practised by one individual of a nation against an individual of any other nation at enmity with it, but in virtue of some public authority."

A private person assailed by hostile force may defend himself and his, but no such person may safely make an attack. The individual, who, not being a member of a *levée en masse* rising to resist an invader, engages without formal authorisation in active belligerent operations by land, is not entitled on capture to the treatment of the prisoner of war.

"Men, or squads of men, who commit hostilities, whether by fighting, or inroads for destruction or plunder, or by raids of any kind, without commission, without being part and portion of the organised hostile army, and without sharing continuously in the war, but who do so with intermitting returns to their homes and vocations, or with the occasional assumption of the semblance of peaceful pursuits, divesting themselves of the character or appearance of soldiers—such men, or squads of men, are not public enemies, and therefore, if captured, are not entitled to the privileges of prisoners of war, but shall be treated summarily as highway robbers or pirates."

The uncommissioned merchant master who attempts to make prize does so at his own risk. If captured, he will find it hard to repel a charge of piracy at the hands of the assailed belligerent or neutral: if successful, his efforts will,

A combatant to be lawful must be formally authorised by a recognised Government or be a member of a *levée en masse* rising on the approach of an invader.

The "Curlew," Stewart, 312. Iredell, J. in Talbot v. Janson, 3 Dall. 160.

Instructions for the government of U. S. Armies in the Field, Art. 82.

Captures by uncommissioned vessels.

Story, J. in
Brown v.
United
States,
8 Cranch
131, and the
"Nereide,"
9 Cranch
449.
The
"Amiable
Isabella," 6
Wheaton 66.

The com-
mission of
the com-
batant
must be
express
but need
not be in-
dividual.

Grenander,
pp. 25, 26.

Possession
of commis-
sion less
important
than ap-
pearance
and con-
duct of the
soldier.
Rolin-Jac-
quemyns,
La Guerre
Actuelle,
p. 25.

indeed, according to Anglo-American practice, operate to divest the property of the original hostile owner, but will not result in any advantage to himself, the prize being condemned to his Government. He may in addition subject himself to penalties under his own municipal law.

The commission of the combatant must ordinarily be express, but need not be individual.

The German commanders in 1870 required that each Frenchman found in arms should, in order to claim the treatment of a prisoner of war, be able to justify his claim to be regarded as a soldier by establishing that, by an order emanating from lawful authority and addressed to him in person, he was called to the flag and borne on the lists of a corps militarily organised by the French Government. If this requirement went to demand the carrying by each private of a regular commission signed by a French Government agent, it exceeded the demands of international law. If it fell short of this, the exact extent of the test proposed is by no means clear.

The characteristics which a belligerent may well require in hostile would-be combatants are responsibility and a loyal setting out of combatant intention. Looking to this last end, the possession of a direct Government commission is practically of less importance in the constitution of the lawful combatant than the appearance and conduct of the soldier.

This principle may be easily traced in the regulations adopted by the delegates at the Conference of Brussels, 1874.

"The laws, rights and duties of war are applicable not only to the army, but likewise to militia and corps of volunteers complying with the following conditions:—

(1) That they have at their head a person responsible for his subordinates;

(2) That they wear some settled distinctive badge, recognisable at a distance;

(3) That they carry arms openly; and

"4. That, in their operations, they conform to the laws and customs of war.

"In those countries where the militia form the whole or part of the army, they shall be included under the denomination 'army' (Art. 9). The population of a non-occupied territory, who, on the approach of the enemy, of their own accord take up arms to resist the invading troops, without having had time to organise themselves in conformity with Article 9, shall be considered as belligerents, if they respect the laws and customs of war." *Proposed Declaration of Brussels, Arts. 9 and 10.*

These regulations stand in need in practice of detailed interpretation. Count Bismarck in 1870 announced to the French Government, through Mr Washburne, that only those Frenchmen who could at *rifle-shot distance* be recognised as soldiers would by the Prussians be held and treated as such. He added that the blue blouse of the Francs-tireurs was the ordinary national costume of the French peasantry, that their red arm-badges were discernible at but a short distance, and were easily removable, and threatened with punishment under military law any person who, being incapable of recognition as a soldier at all times and at the necessary distance, should kill or wound a Prussian. The Prussians might fairly demand in forces acting in small bodies the wearing of distinctive and irremovable insignia, and a French law of Aug. 20, 1870, had prescribed a uniform as one of the distinctive signs of the French *garde nationale*, "en sorte que les combattants soient reconnaisables *à portée de fusil*." A distinctive uniform is, however, not necessarily a conspicuous one. In the case of a *levée en masse* of an entire population the wearing of uniform is neither requisite in principle nor possible in fact. *The French Francs-tireurs. Washburne's Recollections, I. pp. 83, 98.*

Persons rising within an occupied district to throw off the control of an invader are war-rebels, and as such not entitled on capture to the treatment of the ordinary prisoner of war. In 1809 the heroic Prussian Schill, having risen without authorisation from his Government in a desperate attempt *Members of a levée en masse in an occupied district are war-rebels.*

to throw off the yoke of the French, was proclaimed as a brigand by Napoleon, and a price of 10,000 francs set on his head. Schill himself fell in the open field, but twelve of his subordinates, being taken by the French, were shot after a second court martial, the finding of a first court which declared them prisoners of war being quashed by the French Emperor.

The distinction of lawful and unlawful combatant being thus premised, it may be laid down as well recognised law that :—

Armed combatants may be subjected to that amount of force which is necessary to overcome their resistance. ⎰ (*a*) Lawful combatants, being armed and offering resistance to attack, may, within belligerent territory, under the belligerent flag on the high seas or in places beyond the territorial jurisdiction of any Power, be subjected to that amount of force, including death, which is necessary to overcome that resistance and compel their surrender.

Not all forcible measures or agents are deemed permissible even between actively struggling hostile combatants.

Prohibited measures of force. "The laws of war do not allow to belligerents an unlimited power as to the choice of means of injuring the enemy. According to this principle are strictly forbidden—

"(*a*) The use of poison or poisoned weapons.

"(*b*) Murder by treachery of individuals belonging to the hostile nation or army.

"(*c*) Murder of an antagonist who, having laid down his arms, or having no longer the means of defending himself, has surrendered at discretion.

"(*d*) The declaration that no quarter will be given.

"(*e*) The use of arms, projectiles, or substances which may cause unnecessary suffering, as well as the use of the projectiles prohibited by the Declaration of St Petersburg in 1868[1].

[1] Any projectile which being filled with a fulminating or inflammable substance should weigh less than 400 grammes. Hertslet, *Map of Europe*, III. 1860.

"(ƒ) Abuse of the flag of truce, the national flag, or the military insignia or uniform of the enemy, as well as the distinctive badges of the Geneva Convention."

The test of the legitimacy of forcible measures applied between combatant and combatant is, in fact, military necessity. The Laws of War admit the necessity for the application of force: they repudiate superfluous cruelty, forbidding the employment of agents, instruments or measures, whose use involves gratuitous suffering. Thus the use by one civilised belligerent against another of savage auxiliaries is strictly condemned, and on the same ground may be placed the disuse amongst signatories of the Declaration of Paris of the employment of privateers in maritime war, the abolition of this combatant arm by the parties to that treaty being the result of the notorious abuses of the system.

(β) The justification of forcible action ceases with the resistance of the enemy. *i e upon surrender.*

Certain offenders against the municipal law of the captor or against the laws of war are, indeed, on capture legally punishable at the hands of a belligerent. Thus (1) a deserter captured in arms against his native state, (2) a prisoner taken in arms in breach of parole, and (3) a spy, being "a person who secretly, in disguise or under false pretences, seeks information with the intention of communicating it to the enemy" may be put to death. Moreover "the law of war can no more wholly dispense with retaliation than can the law of nations of which it is a branch," and accordingly the member of a force which has refused to give quarter, or otherwise grossly infringed the well recognised rules of civilised warfare, may be subjected to reprisals. But "Retaliation will never be resorted to as a measure of mere revenge, but only as a means of protective retribution, and, moreover, cautiously and unavoidably." And, in general, quarter must be granted to the active combatant who demands it, and only the sternest necessity

[margin notes]
The test, of the legitimacy of belligerent measures is military necessity.

Condemnation of savage auxiliaries and privateers. Hertslet, II. 1282—1285. *Parl. Papers,* 1856, Paris Conference, Protocol, No. 22. Franklin, *Private Correspondence,* II. 330.

The justification of measures of force ceases with the capacity for resistance.

Certain special prisoners are legally punishable with death, e.g. *Instructions for U. S. Armies,* Art. 48. deserters, breakers of parole, *Instructions for U. S. Armies,* Art. 124. and spies, *Instructions for U. S. Armies,* Art. 88. *Ibid.* Art. 27. *Ibid.* Art. 61. while reprisals or necessity will justify other executions; but, in general, quarter cannot be refused.

Instructions for U. S. Armies, Art. 28.

Ibid. Art. 60.

The collection and care of wounded required by the Geneva Convention, 1864, and the Additional Articles, 1868.

Parl. Papers, Miscell. No. 2, 1874, pp. 3—7. Herslet *Map of Europe,* iii. 1621, 1853.

Legal position of the prisoner of war.

Mr Webster to Mr Ellis, Feb. 26, 1842.

3 Wharton, *Dig.* 332.

Instructions for U. S. Armies, Arts. 75—78.

will justify the execution of a combatant who has laid down his arms or is incapable of further resistance. Disabled men and men who have surrendered are no longer objects obnoxious to the exercise of legal belligerent force.

In the Convention of Geneva of 1864, adopted by all the chief Powers of civilisation, and in the less authoritative Additional Articles of 1868, special provision is made for the case of the wounded in war. These instruments enjoin and provide in detail for the collection and care of wounded and sick combatants, without distinction of nation, for the protection from injury of medical officers and other persons exclusively engaged in this humane work, together with ambulances, military hospitals and hospital ships by them employed, and for the despatch to their homes of combatants obviously disabled for future service.

The ordinary prisoner of war is protected by well-recognised general rules.

The prisoner of war is properly regarded as in no sense a criminal. He may, it is universally admitted, be subjected to such confinement as is necessary to prevent his escape, may be required to take such exercise as is deemed advisable for his health, and may be even compelled to work for the captor's benefit according to his rank and condition, provided that he be not called upon to labour on any undertaking directly bearing on the purposes of the war. But he must be supplied, where possible, with fair food, clothing, and shelter, and may not lawfully be subjected to any species of unnecessary suffering or indignity. Should he join in a conspiracy for a general escape of prisoners, he may be punished even with death, and, should he make a personal attempt to escape, he may be shot down in the course of his flight, but in the mere attempt to escape he commits no crime, and, except for crimes, he is not legally liable to any species of punishment. In no case is he compellable to enlist in the captor's force or otherwise assist in the contest against his native sovereign. His liabilities towards his captor cease with his escape, ransom, exchange or release. No captor is legally obliged to ransom or exchange prisoners. On the other hand no prisoner can be compelled to accept his release on condition of giving his parole, and in no case can the terms of a parole voluntarily given legally exceed an engagement not to serve further against the captor during the existing war, unless after exchange. A prisoner released on parole can serve his country away from the seat of war, but breach of his engagement by service in the field is capitally punishable.

Final Act of the Conference of Brussels, 1874, Art. 32.

In a word, the prisoner of war may, in general, be subjected to such forcible measures and such only as are necessary to prevent his further sharing in the war otherwise than with the captor's consent.

2. *Members of the public armed force of a hostile state, being non-combatants and offering no resistance, are exposed to destruction only where their destruction is unavoidable, but may be made prisoners of war.*

2. Non-combatant members of a public armed force are exposed to unavoidable destruction in life and limb, and may be made prisoners of war.

Non-combatants serving with the public armed forces of a belligerent are necessarily exposed to the dangers unavoidably incidental to the position they voluntarily assume. In any event they are, as being active assistants of the belligerent in the contest, liable to be made prisoners of war. In this situation are persons serving as guides, despatch-bearers, contractors, vivandiers, and perhaps, war-correspondents.

Instructions for U. S. Armies in the Field, Art. 50.

3. *All hostile persons of importance to the hostile Government or of peculiar danger to the captor may be made prisoners of war.*

Projected Declaration of Brussels, 1874, Art. 34

3. Hostile persons of importance to their Government may be made prisoners of war.

"The monarch and members of the hostile reigning family, male or female, the chief, and chief officers of the hostile Government, its diplomatic agents, and all persons who are of particular and singular use and benefit to the hostile army or its Government, are, if captured on belligerent ground, and if unprovided with a safe conduct granted by the captor's Government, prisoners of war."

Instructions for U. S. Armies, Art. 15.

Ibid. Art. 50.

4. Hostile private individuals, so long as they abstain from interfering in the contest, may be lawfully subjected to only that amount of inconvenience which the necessities of war imperiously demand. The private non-combatant is exposed to (i) incidental unavoidable personal injury, 3 Wharton, *Dig.* § 338. *Projected Declaration of Brussels,* 1874, Arts. 15, 16. Bluntschli, § 554.

Instructions for the government of U.S. Armies in the Field, Art. 19.

Ibid. Art. 18.

(ii) forced labour in the service

4. *Hostile private individuals, so long as they abstain from interfering in the contest, may be lawfully subjected to only that amount of inconvenience which the necessities of war imperiously demand.*

Non-combatant private individuals are, by modern civilised belligerents, held exempt from any personal interference at the hands of the armed forces of a hostile Power, except in so far as military operations render such interference unavoidable. To personal injury arising incidentally out of military operations in his neighbourhood the private individual is necessarily subject. Thus private individuals within bombarded places are necessarily exposed to peril of life and limb. It is clear law that only fortified and defended places are, at any rate in land warfare, liable to bombardment, and notice for the benefit of non-combatants is not uncommonly given previous to the bombardment of a fortified town, but no such notice is legally necessary. Bismarck in 1871, in answer to the remonstrance of the members of the diplomatic body resident in Paris on the bombardment of the city without previous notice, replied that such prior notice was neither required by the principles of the Law of Nations nor recognised as obligatory by military usage, and his contention, though harsh, was well grounded. Commanders, wherever admissible, inform the enemy of their intention to bombard a place, so that the non-combatants, and especially the women and children, may be removed before the bombardment commences. But it is no infraction of the common law of war to omit thus to inform the enemy. Surprise may be a necessity."

So, too, "when the commander of a besieged place expels the non-combatants, in order to lessen the number of those who consume his stock of provisions, it is lawful, though an extreme measure, to drive them back, so as to hasten on the surrender."

An invader may within hostile territory exact forced labour from the inhabitants in road-making, bridge-building, the aiding of transport, guide-service and the like. Even within an occupied district, however, he cannot forcibly enlist recruits for his forces, although he may prevent the inhabitants from rendering assistance to their natural ruler. Within such a district his position is that of *de facto* ruler governing by martial law, but he is in no sense sovereign until his occupation is transformed into completed conquest. "A territory is considered as occupied when it is actually placed under the authority of the hostile army. The occupation only extends to those territories where this authority is established and can be exercised. The authority of the legal power being suspended, and having actually passed into the hands of the occupier, he shall take every step in his power to reestablish and secure, as far as possible, public safety and social order. With this object he will maintain the laws which were in force in the country in time of peace, and will only modify, suspend, or replace them by others if necessity obliges him to do so. The functionaries and officials of every class who, at the instance of the occupier, consent to continue to perform their duties, shall be under his protection. They shall not be dismissed or be liable to summary punishment (*punis disciplinairement*) unless they fail in fulfilling the obligations they have undertaken, and shall be handed over to justice only if they violate those obligations by unfaithfulness."

In general, the private individual within hostile territory is held exempt from direct personal assault and from all forcible coercion not required by the purposes of the war, his exemption from hostile interference only ceasing with his voluntary intervention in the course of the struggle.

Maritime war-practice is less careful of the private individual. The merchant seaman or any other hostile person found under the hostile flag on the high seas may on the capture of his vessel be legally made a prisoner of war.

5. *Hostile national property within invaded territory is, if consisting of immovables, liable to sequestration, if of*

[marginal notes:]
of an invading enemy; *Instructions for U. S. Armies, Ibid.* Art. 93. *Ibid.* Arts. 90—92. Hozier, *Franco-Prussian War*, I. 351. Case of Guérin, Snow, 375.

Projected Declaration of Brussels, Arts. 1—4.

but, in general, is exempt from direct assault or coercion.

In naval warfare, however, he may be made prisoner of war.

5. Hostile national property

is exposed
to seques-
tration or
to confis-
cation.

movables and of a nature to aid in the carrying on of the war, liable to confiscation; all hostile national property under its national flag on the high seas is liable to confiscation.

State real
property
within
invaded
territory
may be
seques-
trated;

An invader may within hostile territory occupy and administer the national real property of the invaded state, sequestrating the annual profits to his own use. Such property may not, however, be lawfully wasted or destroyed, and a purchaser under the title of the occupier will take subject to the right of postliminium vested in the original proprietor.

The German Civil Commissary in Lorraine having in 1870 sold to Prussian bankers 15,000 ancient oaks standing in the French state forests in the occupied departments of the Meuse and the Meurthe, the French Government, after the cessation of the occupation, refused to recognise the validity of the transaction, and the German Government

Mohr and
Haas v.
Hatzfeld,
Snow, 377.

by declining to intervene admitted the legitimacy of this action.

certain
excep-
tions.

An invader may occupy and employ the public buildings of the invaded state. Religious, charitable and educational foundations, including, with churches and hospitals, museums and other institutions for the encouragement of science and art,

*Instructions
for U. S.
Armies,
Arts. 34, 35.*

are, however, accorded special protection. They may, it is generally admitted, be utilised for urgent public purposes, but must be preserved from wilful and wanton damage.

State
movables
are con-
fiscable, if
of a species
to aid in
the war.
1 Wharton,
Dig. § 340.
Certain
exceptions
approved
and
asserted.

Lastly, the invader may seize to his own use the movable national property of the invaded state. Archives and other public documents are granted a well recognised exemption, and a considerable volume of sentimental opinion together with a fair amount of practice dictates the special protection from hostile seizure of art objects. But, in general, public movable property within invaded territory, of whatever description, or any rate provided it be of a species calculated to aid in the carrying on of the war, is confiscable at the hands of the enemy.

Hostile
national

On the high seas all hostile public vessels with their

equipments and fittings, and all public property found thereon, are on capture prize of war.

6. *Hostile private property within hostile territory is, in general, only liable to such obligations and impositions as are necessarily incidental to the effective carrying on of the war: hostile private property under the hostile flag on the high seas is subject to belligerent confiscation.*

Private houses and buildings within invaded territory are, under modern war-practice, liable to the obligation of providing *billets* for hostile troops, and private movables in the same situation are subject to hostile *requisitions*, i.e. to demands for supplies of food, forage, transport accommodation and the like for the immediate use and support of the invading forces, while *contributions*, being money subscriptions, are regularly levied on private hostile individuals, whether for the same purpose or by way of punishment for local offences against the war rights of the invader. These several impositions are, however, by more enlightened combatants levied on the lowest scale compatible with the carrying on of effective operations, while regular arrangements are very commonly made for the ultimate repayment of the proprietors of the property so employed by the state whose forces make the levies. Military policy unites with humanity to dictate prompt payment for supplies called for by the enormous armies of modern warfare, but even with the best organised commissariat service many instances of individual hardship must arise under the operation of the requisition system.

Many individual non-combatant proprietors within invaded territory must further suffer immense loss by reason of necessary belligerent operations; and for this there is neither remedy nor redress.

Private proprietors whose property is unavoidably damaged in the course of war have, it is generally admitted, no legal claim for compensation either against the state of the invader or against the native government. The native government

property on the high seas is confiscable.

Wharton, *Dig.* § 342.

6. Hostile private property within invaded territory is exposed to certain special obligations only: hostile private property on the high seas is generally confiscable.

Private property within invaded territory is subject to (i) the billeting of troops, (ii) requisition, 3 Wharton, *Dig.* 251. (iii) contribution, Hozier, *The Seven Weeks War*, p. 31.

(iv) incidental injury.

may see fit to grant compensation to such persons, but this of charity not of right. The Germans in 1872 reimbursed in the parts of Alsace and Lorraine acquired by them the losses of individuals resulting from German bombardments. They refused, however, to extend their charity to Swiss suffering by the bombardment of Strasburg. The French, on their side, indemnified without distinction of nationality necessitous victims of the war of 1870–1, but carefully guarded against the recognition of any absolute right. The U.S. Government in 1869 rejected a claim preferred by a Miss Murphy for indemnity for the destruction of her house in Alabama by General Sherman.

A special protection is, however, under the Convention of Geneva, accorded to proprietors within invaded territory who extend assistance to the wounded. "Inhabitants of the country who may bring help to the wounded shall be respected, and shall remain free. The Generals of the belligerent Powers shall make it their care to inform the inhabitants of the appeal addressed to their humanity, and of the neutrality which will be the consequence of it. Any wounded man entertained and taken care of in a house shall be considered as a protection thereto. Any inhabitant who shall have entertained wounded men in his house shall be exempted from the quartering of troops, as well as from a part of the contributions of war, which may be imposed."

And, in general, although private property within hostile territory suffers severely at the hands of the invader, indiscriminate plunder, or wanton destruction at any rate, is with acts of wanton violence against the person of non-combatants sternly repressed; the devastation of hostile territory, except in the last resort as a measure of self-preservation against imminent destruction, is altogether forbidden; and the enormities formerly perpetrated under cover of the regularly permitted sack of stormed places have been vastly minimised by the application of strict discipline.

Property actually taken within a stormed town belongs

Bluntschli,
§ 662.
A special exemption under the Geneva Convention.
Convention of Geneva 1866, Art. 5.
In general, private property is preserved from indiscriminate plunder and devastation.
Instructions for U. S. Armies, Art. 44.
Wharton, Dig. § 349.
The case of storms.
Instructions for U. S. Armies, Art. 45.
Alexander v. Duke of Wellington, 2 Russ. and Myl. 35.
The Banda and Kirwee Booty, L. R. 1 A. and E. 109. Stat. 2 and 3 Will. 4, c. 53.
Projected Declaration of Brussels, 1874, Art. 18.

Walker evidently didnt forsee the actions of German s ldiers —

as booty to the state of the takers, and may be distributed amongst those takers under their municipal law, but "a town taken by storm should not be given up to the victorious troops for plunder."

Private property at sea not covered by the neutral flag is in general still confiscable at the hands of a hostile belligerent.

In certain particular cases private property at sea is exempted from hostile belligerent capture on special grounds. The privilege is extended by general consent to (1) vessels engaged in exploration or scientific investigation, (2) cartel-ships actually in course of employment as transports for the conveyance of exchanged prisoners, and exclusively so employed, (3) hospital ships flying the red cross flag of Geneva and being the property of officially recognised philanthropic societies, and other vessels carrying sick and wounded under the same flag, and (4) small coast fishing boats and tackle. The special exemption thus accorded is, however, conditional on the continued innocent employment of the vessel. Thus Sir W. Scott condemned the "Venus," a cartel-ship which on her return voyage from Marseilles took on board passengers and goods for Port Mahon, and the British Government in 1798 and 1801 ordered the capture of French fishing smacks as a preventive measure against their employment by Napoleon in his projected invasion of England.

And, in general, all hostile private vessels with their cargoes, being the property of belligerent proprietors, are on capture good prize of war.

Attempts have been from time to time made within recent years to secure the general recognition of the freedom from capture at sea of private property, not being contraband nor property engaged in blockade running, and two or three important Powers, including Italy and the United States, have shown a strong inclination in this direction. But the proposed new war practice has not been accorded an universal enthusiastic reception. In the war of 1866, it was

Side notes:

Hostile private property on the high seas is confiscable. Special exemption is accorded to (1) vessels engaged in scientific investigation, (2) cartel-ships, The "Daifjie," 3 C. Rob. 139. The "Venus," 4 C. Rob. 355. The "Mary," 5 C. Rob. 200. The "Rose in Bloom," 1 Dods. 60. (3) hospital ships, Additional Geneva Articles, 1868, Arts. 10 and 13. (4) coast fishing boats, The "Venus," 4 C. Rob. 355. The "Young Jacob and Johanna," 1 C. Rob. 20. Martens, Recueil, VII. 295. Supp. II. 287. but the campaign in favour of the exemption from capture of all private property at sea has not yet been brought to a successful conclusion.

Bluntschli,
§ 665.
Ortolan, II.
3, Ch. II.
Hertslet,
*Map of
Europe*, II.
1382.
3 Wharton,
§ 342.
Rolin Jae-
quemyns,
*La Guerre
Actuelle*,
pp. 47—50.
Ortolan, II.
3, c. 2.
Hostile
property
on the
high sea
cannot be
assigned *in
transitu*.
The
"Dancke-
baar
African," 1
C. Rob. 112.
The "Carl
Walter," 4
C. Rob. 207.
Sorensen v.
the Queen, 11
Moore, 141.
The "Jan
Frederick," 5
C. Rob. 128.
Story, J. in
the "Ann
Green,"
Snow, 355.
Transfers
of vessels
*flagrante
bello* or in
anticipa-
tion of war
are scruti-
nised
The "Vigi-
lantia," 1 C.
Rob. 1.
The "En-
draught,"
Ibid. 21.
The
"Bernon,"
Ibid. 101.
The
"Welvaart,"
Ibid. 122.
Sorensen v.
the Queen,
11 Moo. 119.
The
"Soglasie,"
2 Spinks,
*Ecc. and
Adm.* 101.
or abso-
lutely
refused re-
cognition.
Sir W. Scott
in the
"Sechs Ge-
schwistern,"
4 C. Rob. 100.

adopted by the three belligerent Powers, Italy, Austria and Prussia, but in 1870 Prussia was unsuccessful in inducing France to accept it, and its comparative intrinsic merits are still hotly disputed.

Hostile private property on the high sea being confiscable, it is clear law that no such property can be permitted by a belligerent to change its national character by assignment whilst *in transitu* so as to avoid belligerent condemnation.

"The cases," said Story, J., in the "Ann Green," "are, as I think, settled upon just principles, that decide that in time of war, property shall not be permitted to change character in its transit; nor shall property, consigned to become the property of the enemy on arrival, be protected by the neutrality of the shipper. Such contracts, however valid in time of peace, are considered, if made in war or in contemplation of war, as infringements of belligerent rights, and calculated to introduce the grossest frauds. In fact, if they could prevail, not a single bale of enemy's goods would ever be found upon the ocean."

Transfers of vessels in time of war or in anticipation of its outbreak are on the like ground strictly scrutinised by belligerents or even altogether refused recognition. "The rule which this country has been content to apply," said Sir W. Scott in the case of the "Sechs Geschwistern," "is that property so transferred, must be *bonâ fide* and absolutely transferred; that there must be a sale divesting the enemy of all further interest in it; and that anything tending to continue his interest vitiates a contract of this description altogether."

CHAPTER III.

SANCTIONS OF THE LAWS OF WAR.

§ 51. War being a contest of independent Governments the Laws of War are, in general, devoid of determinate sanction.

The sanctions of the Laws of War are, in the main, of necessity either merely moral or indeterminate. The one belligerent must for the observance of those laws by his opponent rely primarily on the internal forces of civilisation : should these cease to restrain, he may appeal to the great sanction of general popular opinion, or he may seek to enlist the arms of some third Power or of a Concert of Powers against the defaulter. In the last resort he can but have recourse to the method of retaliation. "A reckless enemy often leaves to his opponent no other means of securing himself against the repetition of barbarous outrage." But the use of reprisals is "one of the most bitter necessities of war." By this method alone can in the last resort a responsible independent Government be brought to reason by his enemy.

Within the territorial jurisdiction of a neutral Government it is for that Government to guard against the perpetration by a belligerent of any offences against the Laws of War, and accordingly, it is well agreed, that not only is it incumbent on a neutral ruler to forcibly interfere to protect all persons and property against the application of

The laws of war are, in general, devoid of determinate sanction.

(a) Adherence to the laws of war by governments is secured by (1) moral influences, being mainly the sanction of public opinion, (2) the fear of reprisals, *Instructions for U. S. Armies,* Art. 27. Baron Jomini at the Brussels Conference. (3) the force of third powers.

" L'Invin-
cible," 1
Wheat. 238.
The
" Estrella,"
4 Wheat.
298.
" L'Ami-
stad de
Rues," 5
Wheat. 385.

belligerent force within his borders, but it is for him also to
seize and restore all prizes coming within his ports which
have been taken in violation of his territorial jurisdiction.
Belligerent forces driven over or voluntarily crossing a neutral
frontier are now regularly interned away from the seat of
war.

(b) Ad-
herence to
the laws
of war by
indivi-
duals is
secured
by the
fear of
punish-
ment by
the natu-
ral ruler
or the
enemy.

When individuals offend against the Laws of War they
are punishable either by their own Government or by the
enemy, should they fall within his power.

The
conduct
of indi-
viduals
in making
prize
captures
is super-
vised by
prize
courts.

In one respect belligerent Governments are wont to
exercise a close supervision over the belligerent operations
of their subjects. The determination of the validity of
captures of property as prize of war is regularly assigned
to determinate prize courts.

Lord
Mansfield in
Lindo v.
Rodney,
Dougl. 592.

"The end of a prize court is, to suspend the property till
condemnation; to punish every sort of misbehaviour in the
captors; to restore instantly, velis levatis, (as the books
express it, and as I have often heard Dr Paul quote) if, upon
the most summary examination, there don't appear a sufficient ground; to condemn finally, if the goods really are
prize, against everybody, giving everybody a fair opportunity
of being heard. A captor may, and must, force every person
interested to defend, and every person interested may force
him to proceed to condemn, without delay."

Goss v.
Withers, 2
Burr. 693.

Movable property taken by a hostile belligerent is, it is
well agreed, as between the owner and the captor, divested
from its original proprietorship by actual reduction into
possession by the captor. There is no universal agreement
as to the test of such reduction, and the character of the test
is indeed unimportant provided it be reasonable and consistently applied. But there is general concurrence in the
view that, whereas the rights of the belligerent owner are
de facto lost by the fact of completed capture, the fact of

Genoa and
its depend-
encies,
2 Dods. 446.

the belligerent ownership or other cause of liability to
hostile condemnation should, at any rate in captures made
at sea where neutral and belligerent property is commonly

intermingled, be found by a regular prize court. That prize court can by the nature of the case be only the prize court of the captor; since, on the one hand, no independent belligerent will submit the legality of his conduct to the determination of third Powers, and, on the other hand, no neutral third Power can consistently with neutrality interfere between captor and captured. It has accordingly become well-recognised law that, in general, the jurisdiction of the prize court of the captor is in prize questions exclusive, and the judgment of that court on a point within its competence is conclusive against the world.

A prize court to be competent must be regularly constituted by the captor, "L'Invincible," 1 Wheat. 254. "L'Invincible," 1 Wheat. 238. The "Estrella," 4 Wheat. 298. Hughes v. Cornelius, T. Raym. 473. Lothian v. Henderson, 3 B. and P. 517. Williams v. Armroyd, 7 Cranch 423. Le Caux v. Eden, Dougl. 572.

To that court belongs not only the decision of the question of prize or no prize, but of all questions of damage, salvage and the like arising out of the conduct of the captors in bringing the captured property within the jurisdiction of the court. No suit will, in general, run in any ordinary court against a captor in respect of his conduct in taking property as prize of war.

A prize court to be competent must not only be regularly constituted by the captor, but also sit within the territory of that captor or of his ally.

sitting in the territory of the captor or his co-ally. The "Flad Oyen," 1 C. Rob. 135. The "Christopher," 2 C. Rob. 209. The "Kierlighett," 3 C. Rob. 96. Glass v. the Sloop "Betsey," 3 Dall. 6.

Said Kent, Ch. J., in *Wheelwright v. Depeyster*, where the defendant set up a claim under a sale ordered by a French agency established at St Jago de Cuba; "It appears, that, at the time of the bringing of the vessel into St Jago as a prize, and at the time of the sale, Spain was a neutral power, and that there had not been any judicial condemnation of the cargo; but only an order of this agency for a provisional sale. I need not question a provisional sale in cases of necessity, under the orders of a competent court; but I deny the legality of the power exercised at St Jago. The object of such tribunals in neutral ports is probably to facilitate the sale, and increase the profits of prizes; but the object is not to be attained by such means. *Ausis talibus istis non jura subserviunt.* Neutral ports are not intended to be auxiliary to the operations of the parties at war, and

Kent, C. J., in Wheelwright v. Depeyster, 1 John. 481.

In certain
special
cases
prize
property
may be
disposed
of before
adjudica-
tion, even
by destruc-
tion,
The
"Felicity,"
2 Dods. 381.
Jecker v.
Montgo-
mery, 13
How. 515.
but, in
general, a
prize must
be brought
in for
speedy
adjudica-
tion.
The
"Henrick
and Maria,"
4 C. Rob. 43.
The
"Comet," 5
C. Rob. 285.
Hudson v.
Guestier, 4
Cranch 293.
The
"Peacock,"
4 C. Rob.
191.
The
"Felicity,"
2 Dods. 385.
The
"Felicity,"
2 Dods. 384.
The
"Ludwig"
and the
"Nor-
waerts,"
Dalloz, III.
94.
Cf. British
Naval Prize
Act, 1864.
Condem-
nation as
prize in a
prize court
fixes the
belligerent
Govern-
ment with
responsi-
bility.
Alexander v.
Duke of
Wellington,
2 Russ. and
Myl. 35.

the law of nations has very wisely ordained that a prize court of a belligerent captor cannot exercise jurisdiction in a neutral country. All such assumed authorities are unlawful and their acts void."

In certain cases, as where the captor cannot with safety to himself spare a sufficient number of men to man the captured prize, or where the prize is too much injured to make an extended voyage, captured property may be disposed of before adjudication or even destroyed, but a captor so acting without reasonable justification renders himself liable in respect of neutral property improperly dealt with, and will in all likelihood on subsequent proceedings in a prize court be heavily mulcted in damages and costs. Destruction was, however, freely and systematically resorted to by the U. S. cruisers in the war of 1812–14 and by the Confederates in the Civil War. And in any case it is in the formal revision of the legitimacy of the proceedings of the captor and not in the actual handling of the proceeds that consists the real value of the prize tribunal. So a sentence of condemnation may, it has been held in British courts, be well passed by a competent prize court on property taken after capture into and still lying within a neutral port, although, in general, it is the clear duty of the captor to bring his prize for adjudication as speedily as possible to a port of his own country.

For a neutral vessel destroyed by a belligerent the neutral proprietor has a clear claim to full indemnity from the destroyer: for neutral property destroyed with a justifiably destroyed hostile vessel no claim can be admitted by the belligerent.

The procedure followed in the prize court is determined by the municipal law of the state.

With the sentence of condemnation, the belligerent state, which thereby becomes entitled to the distribution of the proceeds of the capture, assumes direct responsibility for the action of the captors.

"Where the responsibility of the captor ceases, that of the state begins. It is responsible to other states for the acts of the captors under its commission, the moment those acts are confirmed by the definitive sentence of the tribunals which it has appointed to determine the validity of captures in war."

Wheaton, iv. 2, § 390.

After judgment in the highest court of the captor competent to deal with prize questions, an individual complaining of injustice can only look to the intervention on his behalf of his own Government.

CHAPTER IV.

TERMINATION OF WAR.

§ 52. The state of war, in general, ceases with the signature by the belligerent Government of a definitive treaty of peace.

Hostilities may at any time during the course of war be temporarily suspended by mutual agreement of the belligerents. Such a suspension for a period agreed upon is termed an Armistice. An armistice is not a partial or temporary peace: it works no more than the temporary cessation of active military operations within certain limits.

An armistice may be general, that is, may apply to the entire opposing front of the belligerent forces, or may be local, applying to certain forces or within certain localities only. A general armistice can only be entered into by the highest authorities of the belligerents: a local armistice may be entered into by a district commanding officer for the area of his command, but subject to ratification by superior authority.

The suspension of hostilities, again, may be for a period expressly defined, or for an indefinite period to be subsequently determined by notice from one belligerent to the other. In either case the conditions of the arrangement, including alike the definition of the degree of intermediate intercourse permissible in subjects of the parties and of the operations allowable in the belligerent forces, should be clearly set out. If no express stipulation is made, each

Marginal notes:

War ceases, in general, with the signature of a definitive treaty of peace.

Hostilities may be temporarily suspended by an armistice,

Instructions for U. S. Armies, Art. 142.

general or local,

for a definite or indeterminate period.

Instructions for U. S. Armies, Arts. 141, 143.

belligerent, while refraining from military operations along his front, may execute preparatory works in the rear beyond the reach of his opponent, all intercourse between individuals belonging to the opposing states being in the meantime suspended as during the preceding time of active hostility.

An armistice binds the parties to it from the time of its agreed commencement: its operation ceases (i) with the period delimited, (ii) with its clear breach by either party or (iii) after due notice of denunciation.

Commence-
ment and
termina-
tion of ar-
mistices.

The state of war itself may entirely cease by a mere cessation of hostilities. But one undoubted instance of such a condition of things, that of the cessation of war between [Sweden and Poland, appears, however, to be on record, and the danger involved in leaving the legal relations of belligerents and neutrals in a state of doubt is sufficiently obvious to render any other like occurrence altogether improbable.

War may
come to
an end by
(1) a mere
cessation
of hostili-
ties, or

Hall, iii. 9,
§ 203.

War may further cease without any formal announcement by the completed conquest of one belligerent state by its opponent. When such a conquest has been made is a matter of fact to be determined by circumstances, but, when such conquest is clearly established, the cessation of war is consequently evident, all legitimate warfare on the part of subjects necessarily coming to an end with the independence of their state.

(2) by the
complete
conquest
of one bel-
ligerent,
but, in
general,

In common, war is terminated by the agreement of the belligerents set out in a treaty of peace.

A treaty is not definitive as between the parties until its ratification on either side. "According to the practice now prevailing," said Sir W. Scott in 1813, "a subsequent ratification is essentially necessary; and a strong confirmation of the truth of this position is, that there is hardly a modern treaty in which it is not expressly so stipulated; and therefore it is now to be presumed, that the powers of plenipotentiaries are limited by the condition of a subsequent ratification. The ratification may be a form, but it is an

war is
brought
to an end
by (3) a
treaty of
peace.
A treaty
of peace
becomes
definitive
on ratifi-
cation,

essential form ; for the instrument, in point of legal efficacy, is imperfect without it. I need not add that a ratification by one power alone is insufficient ; that, if necessary at all, it must be mutual; and that the treaty is incomplete till it has been reciprocally ratified." So the "Eliza Ann," an American vessel whose restoration was claimed by the Swedish minister on the ground of the neutrality of Sweden within whose waters she was captured, was declared good prize, though the vessel was taken so late as on August 11, 1812, peace having been signed between Great Britain and Sweden on July 18 and ratified by Great Britain on August 4th, and the ratification by Sweden was only delayed until August 17th.

As between the contracting parties, however, a treaty is actually binding from the date of its signature, unless otherwise provided in the treaty itself. Hostilities by commissioned agents of the signatories must accordingly cease from the date of that signature. So the "Thetis," an Austrian vessel, captured on March 1, 1801, twenty-nine days after the signature of the treaty of Lunéville, but eight days before the ratification of the treaty, was restored by the French Conseil des Prises. If a limited period be in the treaty assigned for the termination of hostilities in any particular area, property taken within that locality before the termination of the period by a captor *bonâ fide* ignorant of the signature of the treaty of peace is good prize.

The "Somerset," a British vessel, was taken by the American privateer "Macedonian" on March 7, 1815, after the ratification of the Anglo-American treaty of Dec. 24, 1814, which put an end to the war beginning in 1812, but within the period of thirty days allowed by the treaty for the cessation of hostilities in the part of the world where the capture was effected. On March 31 after the specified period had expired, she was retaken by H.M.S. "Erne." The British Court of Admiralty on these facts decreed restitution of the ship and cargo to the American captors.

Sir W. Scott in the "Eliza Ann," 1 Dods. 248.

The "Eliza Ann," 1 Dods. 244.

but binds as between the contracting Governments from its signature. Davis v. Concordia, 9 How. 280. The "Thetis," Snow, 389. Pistoye et Duverdy, 1. 148. If a period be allowed for the termination of hostilities captures made within that period are good, if made in ignorance,

The "Somerset," 2 Dods. 56.

So also in the case of the "Harmony," a British ship taken on March 2, 1815 by the American privateer, "James Munroe," and on the 24th of the same month after the period specified for the termination of hostilities in the particular locality rescued out of the hands of the prize crew, Lord Stowell ordered the vessel to be released from the recapture, and delivered up to the commander of the American privateer. The "Harmony" (Norman), 2 Dods. 78.

Even if unauthoritative information of the signature of the treaty reach a belligerent commander within such a special locality he is not bound thereby. or, at least, without authoritative information of the signature of the treaty of peace.

The "Swineherd," a British vessel which had been employed as a privateer, sailed from Calcutta after receipt there of information of the signature of peace at Amiens by France and Great Britain. She was captured in the Indian seas by the "Bellone," a French privateer, the commander of which had been previously informed by passing neutral vessels and by an English prize of the signature of peace, a fact with which he was further made acquainted by the showing of a Calcutta Gazette by the "Swineherd." But the capture having been made within the five months delimited by the treaty of Amiens for the cessation of hostilities in the Indian seas, and the notifications made to the captor being unofficial, the French Conseil des Prises condemned the "Swineherd" as good prize. La Bellone contre le Porcher (the "Swineherd"), Pistoye et Duverdy, 1. 149. Snow, 388.

But where the captor is in receipt of authoritative information of the signature of a treaty of peace his action in attempting to make prize is unjustifiable, even though the period for the cessation of hostilities have not actually elapsed. Thus where the "Nymph," a British vessel, was captured within the period of two months allowed by the treaty of Amiens for the cessation of hostilities within the West Indian seas by a French privateer commissioned at Guadeloupe five days after the signature of the treaty of peace had been made known under flag of truce by the English governor of Dominica to the acting governor of Guadeloupe, the But, if a capture be made, with authoritative knowledge of the signature of peace, it is indefensible.

Conseil des Prises restored the vessel, denouncing its capture as null, illegal and contrary to the law of nations, and the conduct of the persons engaged in the proceeding as an act of perfidy and disloyalty worthy only of pirates, and calculated to disgrace the honour of the French name, if permitted to go unpunished.

The "Nymph," Snow, 386.

For any injuries done by capture after the legal date for the cessation of hostilities, even though arising out of ignorance, the captor is legally responsible as a wrongdoer, and it is for his Government to save him harmless. If, however, the ignorance of the captor be invincible, he is still entitled to the privilege of a *bonâ fide* taker, although, provided the ignorance be the result of the neglect of his Government to properly notify the true state of affairs, that Government may be bound to restitution.

For captures made after the legal termination of hostilities, the captor is personally responsible.

The "Mentor," 1 C. Rob. 183.

The "John," 2 Dods. 336.

§ 53. **The terms of the treaty of peace expressly or by implication determine, with the date of the return of the state of peace, the condition of its restoration.**

The terms of the treaty must determine the conditions of the restoration of peace.

It is for the belligerents to determine in the exercise of their independence the terms on which they will agree to the restoration of the peace footing. Should no special stipulation be made the basis of the peace is that of *uti possidetis*, territory *de facto* conquered and movables captured on either side being retained by the takers. Should restitution be in any case agreed upon the property is restorable in the condition in which the signature of the treaty of peace found it.

Where no express stipulation, the principle of uti possidetis rules.

The Schooner "Sophie," 6 C. Rob. 138.

✳In any event on the signature of a treaty of peace, unless special provision be made to the contrary,

General results of the signature of a treaty of peace.

(1) Rights vested before the outbreak of war, and suspended during its course, become reenforceable;

(2) Rights acquired under lawful contracts entered into during the war become enforceable;

Ex parte Boussmaker, 13 Ves. Jr. 71.

(3) All special war rights, such as the levy or collection of requisitions or contributions within invaded territory become incapable of legal exercise;

Antoine v. Morshead, 1 Marsh. 558; 6 Taunt. 237.

(4)   All prisoners of war become entitled to their unconditional release, the time and method of such release being, however, fairly capable of regulation by agreement;

(5)   All claims for injuries arising in the course of the war, whether by capture of property or otherwise, are extinguished; and

The "Molly, 1 Dods. 395

(6)   The operation of the Law of Normal Relations is as between the belligerents and neutral Powers and their subjects completely restored.

PART IV.

INTERNATIONAL LAW OF ABNORMAL RELATIONS.

(β) NEUTRALITY.

CHAPTER I.

NEUTRALITY WITHIN THE SPHERE OF DIRECT STATE ACTION.

It is the duty of a neutral government to abstain from *any* interference in the course of the struggle of belligerents.

§ 54. It is the duty of a neutral Government to abstain from ~~anything but~~ direct interference in the course of a war.

Neutrality, it is now well agreed, does not consist in the mere, impartial treatment of opposing belligerents, but in the entire abstinence from any assistance of either party in his warfare. Neutrality thus defined is, however, a modern growth. Antiquity and the Middle Ages knew nothing of such a conception, which was opposed alike to the mediaeval theory of the World Empire and to the mediaeval notion of the duty of a member of the World Church. Grotius himself did no more than declare it to be the duty of third parties not to hinder the cause of justice and, in "a dubious cause" to behave alike to both belligerents. With his immediate successors the utmost requirement of neutrality was the observance of strict impartiality. Vattel advanced a stage further by laying it down that a neutral state ought to furnish ~~no~~ assistance to either belligerent except under special treaty. But he and his followers admitted the right

The genesis of the conception of neutrality.

De Jure Belli ac Pacis, III. 17, 3, 1.

Vattel, III. 7, § 104.

of any neutral Power to aid a belligerent under the terms of a treaty contracted before the outbreak of war, and even advised that it was obligatory upon every state to assist any other in carrying on a just warfare. The supply of limited succours under a general treaty of alliance entered into before any appearance of war constituted, they held, no departure from the principles of strict neutrality, the auxiliary forces thus furnished being alone assailable by the belligerent opposed to them. *Vattel, III. 6, § 83. Martens, Précis, VIII. 6, § 304. Vattel, III. 6, §§ 99—101*

At a later time a distinction was set up between Perfect Neutrality, consisting in absolute abstention from all interference in the struggle of hostile belligerents, and Imperfect Neutrality, being the position of third parties granting impartial assistance to opposing belligerents, or affording limited aid to the one or the other belligerent under a previous treaty stipulation. ' *"Perfect" and "imperfect". neutrality. Wheaton, IV. 3, §§ 414—415. Heffter, II. § 144.*

In 1788 Count Bernstorff contended that the supply by Denmark to Russia under treaties of 1768, 1769 and 1773 of a contingent of troops and men-of-war to aid in a Russo-Swedish war could furnish no ground of complaint to Sweden, and was quite compatible with the maintenance of perfect neutrality. Great Britain, Prussia and Holland, however, interfered to compel the recall of the Danish auxiliaries, and opinion subsequently solidified against the Danish contention. *The case of the Danish auxiliaries, 1788. Martens, Causes Célèbres, III. 506.*

It has now become well settled law that it is the duty of a neutral Government to abstain absolutely from any interference in the contest of belligerent neighbours. Prussia in 1870 in asking of Great Britain a "benevolent neutrality" asked for a deviation from the duties of a neutral Power. Any direct interference in the course of a war on the part of the Government of a third Power is, in fact, a departure from neutral duty. *"Benevolent" neutrality. Revue de Droit Int. 1870, p. 614. A neutral Government fails in its duty by the grant to a belligerent of:*

§ 55. (a) A neutral Government fails in its duty by the grant to a belligerent of direct military or naval assistance, even though that assistance be limited in extent and accorded under treaty contracted previous to the outbreak of war. *(a) Direct military or naval assistance.*

W.   11

The day of limited assistance is now entirely over. A belligerent assailed by auxiliary forces despatched by a third Power to the aid of his opponent might indeed conceivably prefer on grounds of policy not to call out the exertion of greater force by a declaration of war against the interfering sovereign, but undoubtedly the despatch of such auxiliaries constitutes the most flagrant possible departure from neutral duty, and may well be treated as in itself an act of war.

§ 56. (β) **A neutral Government fails in its duty by the grant of permission to a belligerent to raise troops or generally to enlist military or naval recruits within its borders.**

In days gone by it was very usual for petty rulers possessed of subjects of martial instinct to permit under treaty particular foreign sovereigns to enlist forces within their territories. Thus in 1656 Great Britain entered into an alliance with Sweden in virtue of which it became lawful for either contracting party to raise soldiers or sailors by beat of drum, or to hire vessels of war or transports, within the dominions of the other. And the French were accustomed for centuries to raise regiments of Swiss foot under capitulations with the Swiss Cantons, the last capitulation continuing in force until so late as 1859. But this proceeding is now altogether condemned. In 1876 the Czar of Russia permitted the enrolment within Russian territory for the Servian service of large numbers of Russian volunteers, including many Russian officers. The violation of neutral duty herein involved was evident, and has since been generally admitted.

§ 57. (γ) **A neutral Government fails in its duty by furnishing to a belligerent vessels of war, arms, or any other species of war material.**

In 1825 the Swedish Government, having occasion to dispose of some condemned vessels of its fleet, sold a vessel of the line and two frigates to a Stockholm trading firm. The vessels were immediately resold to an English house, which, it transpired in the sequel, probably held an agency for the insurgent Mexican Government.   The Spanish Government having complained of the transaction, the Swedish ministers, whilst defending their action as absolutely within their legal right, resiled from their contract at considerable pecuniary loss.

So in 1864 the British Government, in view of the American Civil War, stopped sales of unserviceable vessels, and actually paid the sum of £100,000 by way of compensation for the detention in British ports and the prevention of the sale of a flotilla of vessels, which had been collected for the Chinese service, and subsequently left on the hands of the British commander of the expedition.

In 1870, however, during the course of the Franco-Prussian war, the United States Government authorities disposed of large quantities of surplus cannon, small arms and ammunition to French agents, the purchases being shipped directly upon French transports from the State arsenals.   And a similar neglect of neutral duty characterised the conduct of General Sheridan in 1865, he having, whilst commanding the American forces in Texas, directly assisted Escobedo and the Liberals of Mexico against the French and Austrian party by placing arms for their use in convenient places on the American side of the Rio Grande.   On complaint, indeed, made by the French Minister, Mr Seward directed the General to preserve a strict neutrality, but this injunction was not carried out.   "During the winter and spring of 1866 we continued covertly supplying arms and ammunition to the Liberals—sending as many as 30,000 muskets from Baton Rouge Arsenal alone."

The character and the motive of these several proceedings are fairly evident.

§ 58.   (δ) A neutral Government fails in its duty by the grant to a belligerent of pecuniary assistance, whether by way of gift or loan.

The command of gold constituting in these days of

Side notes:

Martens, *Causes Célèbres*, v. p. 229.

The case of the Chinese flotilla, 1864.

Bernard, *Neutrality of Great Britain*, 357—8.

The case of the American arms, 1870.

3 Wharton, *Dig.* § 512. *Revue de Droit Int.* 1874, pp. 87, 462.

The case of Sheridan and the Mexican Liberals.

Personal Memoirs of P. H. Sheridan, II. pp. 216, 224.

(δ) Pecuniary assistance. Bluntschli, § 768.

intimate trading relations the readiest way to the command
of the sinews of war, the supply to a belligerent of the
command of money can only be regarded as a direct sub-
vention to him in his war. No neutral Power can, therefore,
consistently with its neutral duty, either give or lend such
money to a belligerent neighbour. So the purchase by the
neutral of a belligerent conquest before the termination of
the war can only be regarded as an unfriendly act towards
the hostile belligerent, and, in any case, such purchase will
be subject to the verdict of the struggle.

CHAPTER II.

NEUTRALITY WITHIN THE SPHERE OF STATE
PREVENTION.

§ 59. A neutral Government becomes, in general, responsible as for a failure in international duty by omission to prevent the use of its territory in furtherance of belligerent operations.

A neutral Government is in general responsible in respect of the unneutral employment of its territories and territorial waters.

National jurisdiction being within national jurisdiction exclusive, it follows that all sovereigns must be, in general, held responsible for proceedings within their borders which have an international operation. For *every* improper act, preventable or unpreventable, of a private subject a Government cannot fairly be held responsible, but it is well agreed that, to preserve his neutrality unchallenged, the neutral ruler must not merely refrain from any direct personal interference in the course of the struggle carried on by his neighbours, but he must further (1) maintain peace within the bounds of his territorial jurisdiction and (2) exercise reasonable diligence to restrain within those bounds all unneutral conduct of a certain order. The definition of the conduct the non-restraint of which in the individual citizen or in the foreigner can be held to involve the Government in liability is a matter of international convention. Neutral Governments are accustomed to regulate the dealings of their subjects with belligerents by Foreign Enlistment Acts or other municipal edicts. These municipal regulations cannot be accepted as a complete definition of

The sphere of Foreign Enlistment Acts. Stat. 59 Geo. 3, c. 69. Stat 33 and 34 Vict., c. 90. U. S. Foreign Enlistment Acts, 1794, 1797, 1800, 1817 and 1818. Code Pénal, Arts. 84 and 85. *Papers relating to the Treaty of Washington,* II. I.

the extent of international obligation, since national policy may dictate an excess of precautionary measures, and in practice they are by no means uniform. As to the extent of international obligation, however, certain main rules are clearly recognised.

It is the international duty of a neutral Government to:
(a) Refuse passage across its territory to belligerent troops.
Wharton, *Dig.* § 397.

Vattel, III. 7, §§ 119—135. 3 C. Rob. 353.

§ 60. (*a*) **It is the duty of a neutral ruler to refuse the right of passage across his territory to belligerent troops.**

Practice has solidified in this respect. In the time of Vattel it was held that a neutral sovereign might in virtue of a treaty made before the war grant a passage to the armed troops of one belligerent to the exclusion of another, and that, although, in default of treaty stipulation, passage must be refused or accorded to hostile belligerents without distinction, passage might not be refused when it was attended with no inconvenience, or must be deemed absolutely necessary. Opinion adverse to this view grew, however, rapidly in strength, and it is now well agreed that no neutral ruler may, compatibly with neutrality, permit his territory to be made a route to the attack by a belligerent of his enemy.

Papers relating to the Treaty of Washington, II. 103, 108. *Revue de Droit Int.* 1870, p. 640.

The Swiss Federal Council in 1859 and 1870 not only ordered the disarming and interning away from the seat of war of all belligerents crossing the Swiss frontier, but prohibited the passage across Swiss territory from the soil of one to that of the other belligerent of any person capable of bearing arms.

The Belgian Government and the German wounded. Bluntschli, § 777 ter.

The Belgian Government went so far as to forbid the passage over Belgian railways after Sedan of German wounded. The delegates at the Conference of Brussels seem to have deemed this last action unduly severe, and finally agreed to the declaration that, "The neutral State may authorise the transport across its territory of the wounded and sick belonging to the belligerent armies, provided that the trains which convey them do not carry either the *personnel* or *matériel* of war. In this case the neutral State is bound to take the measures necessary for the safety and control of the operation." The difficulty of getting hostile

Proposed Declaration of the Conference of Brussels, Art. 55.

belligerents to agree to the passage of the sick and wounded of one of their number across neutral territory was, however, fully appreciated by the delegates. *Parl. Papers, Miscell. No. 1, 1875. p. 25.*

During the sitting of the Conference on August 3, 1874, the delegate of the Netherlands raised the question whether a neutral Government is under any obligation to either of the belligerents with regard to prisoners of war who may escape into neutral territory. The opinion of the military delegates was that, if a belligerent is unable to take care of his prisoners, it is not the duty of the neutral Government to do so for him. *The neutral Government and escaped prisoners of war.* *Ibid. p. 17.*

It was in this spirit that the British Government dealt with the case of the "Emily St Pierre." *The case of the "Emily St Pierre," 1862.*

The "Emily St Pierre," a British blockade runner, being captured off Charlestown in March, 1862, and despatched to Philadelphia in charge of a prize-crew, her captain, cook and steward, who had been left on board, rose on their captors, and took their ship with great difficulty to Liverpool. To the demand of Mr Adams for the restitution of the vessel, Earl Russell returned a clear refusal, pointing out that, although a failure in the attempt at rescue would have *ipso facto* rendered the vessel confiscable by the Prize Court of the captors, there was no obligation whatever upon a neutral country to aid in enforcing the belligerent right of capture. The correspondence was brought to a close by the discovery that in the early days of the century an identical claim to that preferred by the United States had been advanced by Great Britain against the United States Government, and by it rejected on the ground now taken by Earl Russell. *Mountague Bernard. Neutrality of Great Britain, 325. Snow, 361.*

It seems to be well agreed that prisoners despatched by a belligerent across neutral territory, or set ashore in a neutral port, may be released from custody and their escort disarmed. Prisoners in confinement on board belligerent vessels admitted to the courtesies of a neutral port must, however, be left by the neutral sovereign in the custody of the captor. Accordingly, when in 1856 the "Sitka," a Russian vessel *Prisoners of war in neutral harbours. Parl. Papers, Miscell. No. 1, 1875. p. 25. The case of the "Sitka," 1856.*

captured by a British man-of-war, put into San Francisco in charge of a prize crew, and an application was made to the local court for a writ of *habeas corpus* to test the legality of the confinement of certain prisoners on board, the Att.-General of the United States approved, as at once lawful and highly discreet, the conduct of the British commander in leaving the port with his prisoners in disregard of the writ.

The right of the neutral Government to admit belligerent men-of-war to the shelter of its territorial waters, subject to such regulations as it may think proper to ordain for the protection of its neutral sovereignty against violation, is universally admitted, and such vessels naturally retain in time of war as in time of peace their exterritorial privileges.

In but one recorded instance does any attempt ever seem to have been made by a neutral ruler to disarm a belligerent vessel of war entering his port, and that by the insignificant Power of Lübeck in 1848.

A belligerent man-of-war may, in fact, innocently make use of neutral territorial waters, and the fact that a belligerent has passed through a neutral territorial water zone to effect a capture in no way vitiates a capture subsequently made, provided the capture be made on the high seas or in belligerent waters.

§ 61. (*b*) **It is the duty of a neutral Government to prevent the exercise within its territorial jurisdiction of any act of belligerency, whether act of armed force or mere visit.**

With the passage of a combatant within the lines of the jurisdiction of a neutral Power every act of overt hostility by or against him becomes illegitimate, as constituting a violation of the sovereignty of the neutral ruler. As between belligerent and belligerent an act of hostility within neutral bounds cannot, indeed, be litigated, but it is alike the right and the duty of the neutral Government to prevent any such act within its bounds, and to secure redress should wrong be done. " When a violation of neutral territory takes place, that country alone, whose tranquillity has been disturbed,

---

Marginal notes (left column):

The "Sitka," *Opinions of U. S. Att. Generals,* VII. 122. Distinction between admission within land boundaries and within territorial waters. Wharton, *Dig.* § 394. Improper attempt of Senate of Lübeck to disarm a belligerent man-of-war. Geffcken's *Heffter,* II. § 147, note 10. The "Twee Gebroeders" (Northolt), 3 C. Rob. 351. (*b*) Prevent any act of belligerency within its borders, and The "Santissima Trinidad," 7 Wheat. 349. The "Etrusco," 3 C. Rob. 162 n. The "Purissima Conception," 6 C. Rob. 47. The "Anne," 3 Wheat. 435. secure redress in respect of belligerent acts there committed.

possesses the right of demanding reparation for the injury which she has sustained." As between the assailed belligerent and the neutral Government, passive inaction on the part of that Government were a dereliction of neutral duty.

Sir W. Scott in the "Eliza Ann," 1 Dods. 249.

Neutral Governments are now keenly alive alike to their rights and to their duties in this regard.

In April, 1863, the Confederate cruiser, "Alabama," captured and destroyed Northern vessels within Brazilian waters off the island of Fernando de Noronha. The United States representative promptly complained, and, it having appeared on investigation "that the captain of the 'Alabama' went several times to the island of Fernando de Noronha, accompanied by some of his men; that he communicated with the commanding officer of the island; and he went ashore several times, in order to supply the steamer with the articles needed, and to land the crews of the captured vessels," while the commander of the island did not even protest against these extraordinary proceedings, the negligent official was dismissed from his post, and the "Alabama" ordered to quit Brazilian waters within twenty-four hours.

The case of the "Alabama" at Fernando de Noronha, 1863,

U. S. Dipl. Corresp. 1863, p. 1168.

So, when the "Florida" was cut out by the U. S. war-steamer "Wachusett" from the Brazilian harbour of Bahia, the Brazilian Government at once demanded the restoration of the vessel, and fitting reparation for the violation of neutral sovereignty, and the United States Government admitted the justice of the claim, and disavowed and apologised for the action of their officials, the restoration of the "Florida" being only prevented by her sinking in Hampton Roads.

of the "Florida" at Bahia, 1864,

Case of Great Britain, pp. 75 et seqq.

On complaint by the neutral Government, whether directly to the Government of the captors or by claim preferred in the captor's prize court, prizes made in violation of neutral territorial rights are, in fact, now unhesitatingly restored.

On December 7, 1863, the "Chesapeake," an American

and the "Chesa-

peake" at
Sambro,
1863. passenger steamer plying between New York and Portland,
Maine, was, when on the high seas about 21 miles east of
Cape Cod, seized by a party of her passengers, who took
possession of her in the name of the Confederate States. In
the course of the melée the second engineer was shot and
thrown overboard, and other officers of the ship were wounded.
The captain, the rest of the passengers and the majority of
the crew were put into a pilot-boat off Partridge Island and
landed at St John's, New Brunswick. The "Chesapeake"

U. S. Dipl.
Corresp.
1864, i.
p. 497. herself ultimately came to anchor in the Nova Scotian
harbour of Sambro. Here she was discovered by two U. S.
gunboats, the commanders of which proceeded at once to
take possession of her, she being at the time in possession of
five of the members of her original crew, her Southern

U. S. Dipl.
Corresp.
1864, i. pp.
476 et seqq.;
521 et seqq. captors having abandoned her on the approach of the
gunboats. Three prisoners were made on the steamer and
upon a British schooner lying alongside.

The flagrant violation of the British neutral territorial
jurisdiction involved in the proceedings of the American
officers being promptly represented to their Government,
Mr Seward by direction of the President informed Lord
Lyons that the U. S. Government had not authorised and did
not propose to justify any exercise whatever of authority by
its agents within the waters or on the soil of Nova Scotia,
and that, if such authority had been assumed, the Government would at once express its profound regret and was
ready in that case to make amends which should be entirely

U. S. Dipl.
Corresp.
1864, ii. pp.
405, 462. satisfactory. The "Chesapeake" was subsequently brought
by the commander of one of the U. S. gunboats to Halifax,
and delivered up to the Colonial Authorities, by whom she
was restored to her original owners, Mr Seward fulfilling his

U. S. Dipl.
Corresp.
1864, i. pp.
508, 559; ii.
p. 474. promise by offering a full and complete apology for the insult
offered to the British flag, an apology which was at once
accepted by Earl Russell.

In certain
cases the
neutral ⚹ In certain cases a neutral Government may and ought to
forcibly vindicate its violated jurisdiction by directly inter-

fering to annul the effects of the acts of belligerent wrong-doers. Government may itself restore.

It is well settled law that, if prize property be brought *infra praesidia* of a neutral power, that power has a right to inquire whether its own neutrality has been violated by its capture, and, if so, to restore the prize to its original owners. The "Estrella," 4 Wheat. 298.

"The general rule," said Washington, J., in the *Brig "Alerta"* v. *Blas Moran* in 1815, "is undeniable, that the trial of captures made on the high seas, *jure belli*, by a duly commissioned vessel of war, whether from an enemy or a neutral, belongs exclusively to the courts of that nation to which the captor belongs. To this rule there are exceptions, which are as firmly established as the rule itself. If the capture be made within the territorial limits of a neutral country into which the prize is brought, or by a privateer which had been illegally equipped in such neutral country, the prize courts of such neutral country not only possess the power, but it is their duty to restore the property, so illegally captured, to the owner. This is necessary to the vindication of their own neutrality." Washington, J. in the Brig "Alerta" v. Blas Moran, 9 Cranch 364.
The "Fanny," 9 Wheat. 658.

The right of the neutral power so to restore is not lost by reason of the transfer of the property to a *bonâ fide* purchaser before it is brought *infra praesidia* by the tortious possessor under an illegal capture. The right, however, is lost if the captured vessel has in the interval been duly commissioned as a vessel of war by a responsible Government. Moreover the jurisdiction of the neutral Government extends only to the restitution of the specific property captured with costs and expenses of the suit, and does not reach to the infliction of vindictive damages or to compensation for plunderings, as in the case of ordinary maritime torts. The Schooner Exchange v. McFaddon.
"La Amistad de Rues," 5 Wheat. 385.
The limit of neutral responsibility: the right to neutral protection is forfeited by a belligerent guilty of aggression or having recourse to force within a neutral territorial jurisdiction.

The obligation incumbent on the neutral Government to defend against belligerent hostile attack within his jurisdiction, or to obtain redress therefor, ceases towards a complainant when he himself was the aggressor, or, being assailed, attempted to defend himself by forcible resistance.

The British ship "Anne" was, in March, 1815, whilst in Spanish waters captured by the U. S. privateer "Ultor."

It being admitted in the Supreme Court that the captured ship first commenced hostilities, Story, J., ruled that she thereby forfeited the neutral protection, and the capture was no injury for which any redress could be rightfully sought from the neutral sovereign.

The "Anne," 3 Wheat. 435.

So in the case of the "General Armstrong," an American vessel destroyed in the Portuguese harbour of Fayal in 1814 after a struggle with an English squadron, the President of the French Republic in 1851, as arbitrator between Portugal and the United States, ruled that the American commander, not having applied at the beginning for the intervention of the local sovereign, and having had recourse to arms to repel an unjust aggression, of which he pretended to be the object, had failed to respect the neutrality of the territory of the foreign sovereign, and released that sovereign from the obligation, in which he was, to afford him protection by any other means than that of a pacific intervention.

The "General Armstrong," 2 Whart. Dig. 604.

A novel point with regard to the exercise of belligerent acts in the vicinity of neutral territorial boundaries was raised in 1863.

The Confederate steamer "Margaret and Jessie," a successful blockade runner, was on May 31, 1863, chased by the United States war-steamer "Rhode Island" into the British waters of the island of Eleuthera in the Bahamas, and there sunk by a shot within a few hundred yards of the shore, many balls fired by the "Rhode Island" actually striking the land. Complaint being promptly made by Lord Lyons, Mr Seward gave the assurance that, if it should appear on investigation that any act of hostility or power was committed within the marine jurisdiction of Great Britain, the act would be disavowed, and redress at once given. An American Court of Inquiry held for the purpose of investigating the case found that the commander of the "Rhode Island" was desirous and anxious to avoid any violation

The case of the "Margaret and Jessic," 1863.

U. S. Dipl. Corresp. 1864, i. pp. 779 et seqq.; ii. pp. 413 et seqq.

of the British territorial jurisdiction whilst chasing the "Margaret and Jessie," and that no violation of that territorial jurisdiction did in fact take place. The proceedings of the Court having been communicated to the British Government, the British chargé d'affaires at Washington was instructed to inform Mr Seward that his Government was satisfied that, upon the evidence adduced, the Court of Inquiry was justified in its finding. " But the undersigned must nevertheless observe," wrote Mr Burnley, "that although it is shown that the ' Rhode Island ' never fired at a less distance than four miles from the shore, the evidence as to the distance from land of the ' Margaret and Jessie,' when the last shot or shots were fired, is much less distinct; and Her Majesty's Government are unable to consider that it was proved conclusively before the court of inquiry that at the time when these last shots were fired the ' Margaret and Jessie ' may not have been within three miles from the shore. The undersigned has further the honour to inform Mr Seward that he is instructed by his Government to call the attention of the United States Government to a matter of very considerable importance arising out of this case, namely, the bearing on the territorial limits of three miles beyond the sea-shore which the more powerful artillery now constructed may involve. The Parrott gun which was used on board the ' Rhode Island ' is stated by Commander Trenchard in his evidence before the court of inquiry, (page 7 of the proceedings) to carry a distance of five miles; and he also expresses an opinion, although not so positively, that the range of the Dahlgren 30-pounder rifle-gun was as great as that of the Parrott. In the present instance shot fired from the ' Rhode Island ' appear to have reached the shore, notwithstanding that that vessel did not approach within four miles of the land; and it is obvious that the use of weapons of this description, when fired at that distance toward the shore, is calculated not only to infringe neutral jurisdiction by falling within neutral waters, but also seriously

U. S. Dipl. Corresp. 1864, ii. p. 639.

A weak spot in existing international practice.

to endanger life and property on neutral territory itself. The undersigned is accordingly directed by Her Majesty's Government to express to the United States Government their hope that the United States Government will concur with them in opinion that vessels should not fire towards a neutral shore at a less distance than that which would insure shot not falling in neutral waters or on neutral territory." Mr Seward, in reply, announced that the British proposition would be brought to the attention of other maritime powers, in order that, if any change were made, it should be general. In this lame fashion the incident terminated. It suggests, however, considerations of the highest importance. It is evident that, if persons and property actually on neutral shores are to be protected from risk of injury by belligerent operations, either the zone of neutral territorial waters must be extended by common consent, or a further outside belt must be delimited from within which no belligerent vessel must be permitted to fire.

Mr Burnley to Mr Seward, Sept. 10, 1864. *U. S. Dipl. Corresp.* 1864, II. p. 704.

(c) Prevent the use of its territories or waters by a belligerent as the base of belligerent operations.
§ 62. *(c)* **It is the duty of a neutral Government to exercise reasonable diligence to prevent the use of its territory or territorial waters by a belligerent as the base of belligerent operations.**

Neutral territory or neutral waters may become a belligerent " base of operations" in very various ways.

Wharton, *Dig.* § 398. What is a " base of operations"?
The general principle was laid down by Sir W. Scott in the case of the "Twee Gebroeders" (Alberts), one of four Dutch vessels which were captured on July 14th, 1799, in the Western Ems by boats-crews despatched from H.M.S. "L'Espiegle," then lying in Prussian neutral waters in the Eastern Ems.

"It is said," remarked Sir W. Scott, "that the ship was, in all respects, observant of the peace of the neutral territory; that nothing was done by her, which could affect the right of territory, or from which any inconvenience could arise to the country within whose limits she was lying; inasmuch as the hostile force which she employed was applied to the

captured vessel *lying out* of the territory. But that is a
doctrine that goes a great deal too far; I am of opinion,
that no use of a neutral territory for the purposes of war is
to be permitted; I do not say *remote* uses, such as procuring
provisions and refreshments, and acts of that nature, which
the law of nations universally tolerates; but that no
proximate acts of war are in any manner to be allowed
to originate on neutral ground." Sir W. Scott in the "Twee Gebroeders" (Alberts), 3 C. Rob. 164.

No neutral territory or territorial water must be permitted to become a regular place of belligerent resort for
the preparation of hostile measures.

In 1805 Sir W. Scott condemned the practice frequently
adopted by belligerents of hovering outside neutral waters
for the purpose of making captures, and in 1863 the British
Government thought "that a more unneutral use of a port
could not be well conceived than lying in it for the vessels
of another neutral state, as they entered and left it, and, on
their passing the limit of three miles, boarding and visiting
them, and then returning to the port." " Hovering " belligerents. The "Anna," 5 C. Rob. 385 e. Lord Lyons to Mr Seward, May 4, 1863, U. S. Dipl. Corresp. 1863, p. 523.

§ 63. (*d*) **It is the duty of a neutral Government to prevent
the furnishing within and the exit from its territorial jurisdiction
of a hostile expedition directed against a Power with which it is
at peace.** (*d*) Prevent the departure from its territories or waters of a hostile expedition there organised.

It is clearly the duty of a neutral Government to prevent
the departure from its borders of an organised body of armed
men obviously collected for the purpose of an attack upon a
foreign State. In this spirit the British Government, in
1828–9, forcibly interfered to prevent the landing at Terceira
of the expedition prepared on British soil by Count Sal-
danha, although the interference took place so totally at the
wrong moment that it involved a violation of the territorial
jurisdiction of Portugal. Wharton, Dig. 395 a. The Terceira affair, 1828—9. Snow, 421.

Not every body of men leaving neutral soil with the
probable intent to take part in foreign warfare is, however,
a hostile expedition, and as such the rightful subject of
interference on the part of the neutral ruler. In 1870 3 Wharton, Dig. 551.

a party of 1200 . Frenchmen left New York to join the armies of France in her contest with Prussia, and the vessels which carried them carried also a large consignment of arms and ammunition for the use of the French

forces, but, these men being in no way organised, the neutrality of the United States was, it is well agreed, in no way infringed by their departure from an American port.

(e) Pre-
vent the
enlistment
of forces
or the
commi-
sioning of
armed
vessels
within its
territorial
jurisdic-
tion.
§ **64.** (e) **It is the duty of a neutral Government to prevent the enlistment of forces or the commissioning of armed vessels within its territorial jurisdiction for the service of a belligerent.**

"The right of raising troops being one of the rights of sovereignty, and consequently appertaining exclusively to the nation itself, no foreign power or person can levy men within its territory without its consent ; and he who does may be rightfully and severely punished."

Wharton,
Dig. § 395.
Mr Jeffer-
son to Mr
Morris, Aug.
16, 1793.
The right of raising forces being, as thus stated by Jefferson, a peculiar and exclusive function of the territorial sovereign, a neutral Government may well be held responsible not only in respect of the direct permission of, but of omission to guard against, the assumption by a belligerent of this special privilege. The right of the neutral Government in this regard was vindicated and its duty established by the United States against France in 1793 and against Great Britain in 1855, the recall of M. Genêt, the French minister to the American Government, having been in the former year demanded in consequence of his persistence in the issue of commissions to French privateers within the jurisdiction of the United States, whilst in the latter year Mr Crampton, the British minister, was dismissed from Washington as the result of his complicity in certain proceedings for the obtaining of recruits within the United States for the British army.

§ **65.** (f) It is (probably) the duty of a neutral Government to "use due diligence to prevent the fitting out, arming, or equipping within its jurisdiction, of any vessel which it has reasonable ground to believe is intended to cruise or to carry on war against a power with which it is at peace; and also to use like diligence to prevent the departure from its jurisdiction of any vessel intended to cruise or carry on war as above, such vessel having been specially adapted, in whole or in part, within such jurisdiction to warlike use."

Provided a fair interpretation be accorded to the phrase "due diligence" it is probable that Rule I. of the Treaty of Washington, 1871, represents good law.

The counsel of the United States contended before the Geneva Tribunal that that diligence alone could be held to be "due" which was "commensurate with the emergency, or with the magnitude of the results of negligence," and to this view the majority of the Arbitrators appear to have leaned. The view urged by the British representatives would appear to be more, reasonable. "Due diligence on the part of a sovereign Government signifies that measure of care which the Government is under an international obligation to use for a given purpose. This measure, where it has not been defined by international usage or agreement, is to be deduced from the nature of the obligation itself, and from those considerations of justice, equity, and general expediency on which the law of nations is founded." Due diligence is, in fact, that amount of diligence which may be *fairly* and *reasonably* looked for, and its extent must be determined by application to the special circumstance of the case of considerations based on positive conventional duty and practical convenience.

In practice states have, seemingly, found it hitherto impossible to agree upon a precise and uniform definition of the legitimate attitude of a neutral Government towards a vessel calculated for warlike use prepared by individuals within and issuing from its territorial jurisdiction, under circumstances rendering it possible that it may come into the hands of one or other of the belligerents. Such a vessel can, in fact, be, with some show of reason, regarded in two distinct lights. "The case of a vessel which is despatched

W.   12

Sidenotes:
armed belligerent cruisers.

Rule 1. of the Treaty of Washington, 1871. What is "due diligence" in prevention on the part of a neutral Government? "Due diligence" as defined at Geneva by the United States and *Papers relating to the Treaty of Washington*, I. 65. *Revue de Droit Int.* 1874, p. 567. the British counsel. *Case of Great Britain*, Part III. p. 24. "Due diligence" a matter of circumstances. The proper attitude of a neutral Government towards subjects dealing in armed vessels is not capable of simple definition.

An armed vessel may be regarded as merely contraband,

from a neutral port to or for the use of a belligerent, after having been prepared within the neutral territory for warlike use, is one which may be regarded from different points of view, and may fall within the operation of different principles. The ship herself may be regarded merely as an implement or engine of war, sold or manufactured to order

or its despatch may be viewed as a hostile expedition.

within neutral territory, and afterwards transported therefrom, and the whole transaction as falling within the scope of the principles applicable to the sale, manufacture, shipment, and transportation of articles contraband of war; or, on the other hand, the preparation and despatch of the ship may be viewed as being really and in effect the preparation and commencement of a hostile expedition."

Papers relating to the Treaty of Washington, 1. p. 239.

Great . commercial nations have as neutrals shown a marked disposition to treat, where possible, as purely commercial transactions the dealings of their subjects even in

Attitude of the United States as neutrals:

armed vessels, and to relegate them to the domain of mere contraband trading. Such was the attitude of the United States during the greater portion of the present century.

In *Moodie v. the ship "Alfred,"* where a vessel built at New York expressly with a view to employment as a privateer, should then existing disagreements between Great Britain and the United States terminate in war, was sent to Charleston and there sold to a French citizen, who took her to a French island, where she was completely armed, equipped and furnished with a belligerent commission, the Supreme Court adopted without hesitation the view that it was no violation of the neutrality laws of the United States to sell to a foreigner a vessel built in United States territory, though suited to be a privateer and having some

Moodie v. the ship "Alfred," 3 Dall. 307.

equipments calculated for warlike use, but frequently employed on merchant ships.

The "Santissima Trinidad," 7 Wheat. 283.

To the same effect was the judgment delivered in the "Santissima Trinidad" in 1822.

Coming on in the form of an appeal from a sentence delivered by the District Court of Virginia and affirmed by the Circuit Court, which ordered the restitution to the original Spanish owners of certain property taken on the high seas from two Spanish ships, the "Santissima Trinidad" and the "St Ander," by two armed vessels, the "Independencia del Sud" and the "Altravida," flying the flag of Rio de la Plata, and subsequently brought within the United States, the case turned on the question whether the proceedings of the capturing vessels involved a violation of American Neutrality laws sufficient to ground a decree of restitution.

The facts of the early career of the "Independencia del Sud" were stated by Story, J., in delivering the opinion of the Supreme Court.

"She was originally built and equipped at Baltimore, as a privateer, during the late war with Great Britain, and was then rigged as a schooner, and called the 'Mammoth,' and cruised against the enemy. After the peace she was rigged as a brig, and sold by her original owners. In January, 1816, she was loaded with a cargo of munitions of war, by her new owners (who are inhabitants of Baltimore), and being armed with twelve guns, constituting a part of her original armament, she was despatched from that port, under the command of the claimant, on a voyage, ostensibly to the North-west Coast, but in reality to Buenos Ayres. By the written instructions given to the supercargo on this voyage, he was authorised to sell the vessel to the Government of Buenos Ayres, if he could obtain a suitable price. She duly arrived at Buenos Ayres, having exercised no act of hostility, but sailed under the protection of the American flag during the voyage. At Buenos Ayres the vessel was sold to Captain Chaytor and two other persons; and soon afterwards she assumed the flag and character of a public ship, and was understood by the crew to have been sold to the Government of Buenos Ayres; and Captain Chaytor made known these facts to the crew, and asserted that he had become a citizen of Buenos Ayres; and had received a commission to command the vessel as a national ship; and invited the crew to enlist in the service; and the greater part of them accordingly enlisted. From this period, which was in May, 1816, the public functionaries of our own and Story, J. in the "Santissima Trinidad," 7 Wheat. 334. other foreign Governments at that port considered the vessel as a public ship of war, and such was her avowed character and reputation."

The Court was satisfied on the evidence that, as a matter of fact, the force of the "Independencia" was illegally augmented by the enlistment of men during a prolonged stay under cover of repairing at Baltimore at the end of 1816, and that the "Altravida," which was employed as a tender to the "Independencia," was illegally fitted out in American waters, and on this ground affirmed the decree of the Circuit Court for restitution. But on the question of the original outfit of the "Independencia" the decision of the Court was unreservedly with the captors.

"The question," said Story, J., "as to the original illegal armament and outfit of the 'Independencia' may be dismissed in a few words. It is apparent that, though equipped as a vessel of war, she was sent to Buenos Ayres on a commercial adventure, contraband, indeed, but in no shape violating our laws or our national neutrality. If captured by a Spanish ship of war during the voyage, she would have been justly condemned as good prize, for being engaged in a traffic prohibited by the law of nations. But there is nothing in our laws, or in the laws of nations, that forbids our citizens from sending armed vessels, as well as munitions of war, to foreign ports for sale. It is a commercial adventure which no nation is bound to prohibit, and which only exposes the persons engaged in it to the penalty of confiscation. Supposing, therefore, the voyage to have been for commercial purposes, and the sale at Buenos Ayres to have been a *bonâ fide* sale, (and there is nothing in Story, J. in the "Santissima Trinidad," 7 Wheat. 340. the evidence before us to contradict it,) there is no pretence to say that the original outfit on the voyage was illegal, or

that a capture made after the sale was, for that cause alone,
invalid."

The American Courts distinguished between the *animus* *belligerandi* and the *animus* *vendendi*, and held that the obligations of American neutrality were complied with by the restraint of the *animus* *belligerandi* only, it being therefore in no way incumbent upon the United States Government to interfere with the departure of an armed vessel from American waters for sale abroad.

As belligerents the United States were disposed to demand the application by neutral Governments of a stricter doctrine, and to distinguish broadly between trade in vessels of war and ordinary contraband dealing. "While the subjects or citizens of either country," asserted the U. S. counsel at Geneva, "have been left by law free to manufacture or sell muskets or gunpowder, or to export them at their own risk, even if known to be for the use of a belligerent, the legislatures, the executives, and the judiciaries of both Great Britain and the United States have joined the civilized world in saying that a vessel of war, *intended for the use of a belligerent*, is not an article in which the individual subject or citizen of a neutral state may deal, subject to the liability to capture as contraband by the other belligerent. Such a vessel has been and is regarded as organised war."

It may be that the phrase *intended for the use of a belligerent* is the flying bridge between the earlier and later American doctrine, but, however construed, the language of the U. S. counsel at Geneva marks a distinct advance upon the judgments of Justice Story and his contemporaries.

What is a vessel *intended for the use of a belligerent*? It is clear that the preventive duty of a neutral Government must be limited to proceedings taking place within its territorial jurisdiction. If it be the duty of a neutral Government to interfere with the dealing on the part of its subjects in vessels of war *intended for the use of a belligerent*,

Marginal notes:

distinction between the *animus vendendi* and the *animus belligerandi*.
U. S. v. Quincy, 6 Pet. 445.
The "Meteor," 3 Wharton, Dig. 561.

Attitude of the United States as belligerents:
an armed vessel is organised war.
Papers relating to the Treaty of Washington, 1. 81.

Difficulty of fixing international liability by reference to individual intent.

the act of dealing and the intended use must be *both* present in combination within the neutral territorial jurisdiction, and must be moreover *there ascertainable*, since no Government could fairly be held internationally responsible in respect of omission to deal with an offence, the proof of the commission of which was not within its power. Now it may be, and probably is, good law that it is the duty of a neutral Government to prevent the departure from its port of a vessel fit for warlike use, which has been prepared within its territorial jurisdiction, when it is clearly the intention of the persons having control of her to employ her in the

Case of the "Pampero." service of a belligerent Power. So the "Pampero," a vessel manifestly intended for warlike use, built on the Clyde under contract for sale to a citizen of the Confederate States, was seized in 1863 by the British Government, and impounded until the end of the war, and the same Government deemed it advisable to seize, and ultimately to buy at

The "El Tousson" and the "El Monassir." *Papers relating to the Treaty of Washington*, I. 261—265. a considerable cost, the "El Tousson" and the "El Monassir," two iron-clad rams built by Messrs Laird and Co. at Birkenhead, there being reasonable grounds for the belief that their real destination was the Confederate service. But even in this last case the British Government experienced the difficulty which must be met in every prosecution which involves proof of the *intent* of the supposed culprit. The real intent of builder or purchaser is capable of easy concealment, and only becomes apparent when the vessel is beyond the jurisdiction of the sovereign in whose territory she was built or purchased. Thus when

Case of the "Florida." *Papers relating to the Treaty of Washington*, I. pp. 133—143, 274—307. Walker, *Science of Int. Law*, P. 474. the "Florida" quitted her Liverpool builder's yard, she sailed from port as the merchant steamer "Oreto," unarmed and without warlike stores of any kind, with a cargo of spirits, wines and groceries, ostensibly for Palermo and Jamaica. Had she received her subsequent equipment on the high seas, instead of in British waters at Green Cay in the Bahamas, the Arbitrators at Geneva must have acquitted Great Britain of all international responsibility in her regard.   A favourable decision was actually found in the case of the "Georgia."

These and other considerations seem to point to the practical conclusion that no definition of international responsibility in respect of the building or sale of vessels fit for warlike use can be perfectly satisfactory, which involves the necessity of proof of the actual belligerent intent of builder or owner.

This fact was recognised by the framers of the British Foreign Enlistment Act, 1870.

By virtue of section 8 any person, who, within Her Majesty's dominions, without the license of Her Majesty, with intent or knowledge or having reasonable cause to believe that it shall or will be employed in the military or naval service of any foreign state at war with any friendly state, (1) builds or agrees to build, or causes to be built, (2) issues or delivers any commission for, (3) equips, (4) despatches, or causes or allows to be despatched, any ship, is declared an offender against British Neutrality obligations, and rendered punishable by fine, imprisonment and forfeiture.   And "where any ship is built by order of or on behalf of any foreign state at war with a friendly state, or is delivered to or to the order of such foreign state, or any person who to the knowledge of the person building is an agent of such foreign state, or is paid for by such foreign state or such agent, and is employed in the military or naval service of such foreign state, such ship shall, until the contrary is proved, be deemed to have been built with a view to being so employed, and the burden shall lie on the builder of such ship of proving that he did not know that the ship was intended to be so employed in the military or naval service of such foreign state."

The terms of mere municipal law cannot indeed fairly be applied as a test of international law, but these clauses of the British Act do suggest the growth of a quickened sense of neutral national responsibility, and a consequent

3 Wharton,
Dig. 652.

tightening of the bonds of national control, a suggestion
which the subsequent judicial interpretation of the statute
has in no whit weakened.

The Prussian ship "Lord Brougham," having been
captured by a French vessel as prize of war, was driven by
stress of weather into the Downs, where she anchored on Nov.
24, 1870. After she had lain there two days, the French
Consul at Folkestone engaged an English steam-tug, the
"Gauntlet," to tow her to Dunkirk Roads. The Judge of the
Admiralty Court dismissed a suit against the tug by the Crown
under the Foreign Enlistment Act, 1870, and condemned
the prosecutors in costs, but on appeal, the Judicial Committee reversed the decree, holding that the express engage-

The
"Gauntlet,"
8 Moore, P.
C. C., N. S.,
428; L. R.,
4 P. C. 184.

ment of the owners of the tug to tow a prize vessel with her
prize crew and prisoners into French waters was despatching
a ship within the meaning of Section 8 of the Statute.

The like stringency a few years earlier would have
obviated the necessity for, or at least materially altered the
verdict of, the Geneva Arbitration Tribunal.

(g) Prevent
the ob-
taining by
belligerent
vessels
within its
jurisdic-
tion of
any aug-
mentation
of their
combatant
force.

§ 66. (g) **It is the duty of a neutral Government to prevent
the obtaining within its territorial jurisdiction by belligerent
vessels of any augmentation of their combatant force.**

The grant of mere port hospitalities by a neutral to
belligerent vessels can constitute no fair cause of complaint
for the hostile Power, provided these hospitalities be
accorded without distinction to all the belligerents. A
belligerent vessel may thus be fairly permitted within

Bellige-
rent
vessels
may be
accorded
reason-
able port
hospitali-
ties,

neutral waters to take on board a reasonable supply of fresh
provisions or coal, or to undergo necessary repairs.

But what supply is reasonable, and what repairs are
necessary?

Neutral Powers have in recent years guarded the grant
of port hospitalities to belligerents by most carefully drawn
regulations. Thus the French Government in 1861 laid
down the rule that no belligerent war-vessel could be
permitted to remain in a French port for more than twenty-

four hours, except in the case of stress of weather, injuries, or the exhaustion of provisions necessary for the safety of her voyage, and save that twenty-four hours must elapse between the sailings of hostile vessels. Similar regulations were then, and have been since, adopted by most of the great civilised Powers. These regulations have, however, themselves raised new difficulties. Thus the Confederate steamer " Nashville " was practically blockaded in the British waters of Southampton by the U. S. ship of war, "Tuscarora," by virtue of the British regulation requiring twenty-four hours to elapse between the hours of departure of hostile belligerent war-vessels, the U. S. commander keeping steam constantly up and leaving port on any sign of movement on the part of the " Nashville," only to return within twenty-four hours to repeat the same tactics.

Port hospitality to be legitimate must not extend to the increase of combatant force. The mere replacement of the original warlike equipment, after repair of the vessel, is not an augmentation of force, but any fresh addition to the combatant strength of the vessel, whether in the shape of guns, munitions of war, or men, is an "augmentation of force," and as such illegal.

In the supply of men, as in the grant of permission to repair, the just test of legitimacy would appear to be that adopted by France during the American Civil War, viz., the navigability of the vessel as distinct from her fighting power. Mr Dayton, the American representative at Paris, declared in argument with M. Drouyn de l'Huys, the French minister, that "sailors for an enemy's ship of war were contraband, as much so as soldiers for its armies." The French authorities decided, however, not to prohibit a considerable accession to the crew of the " Florida," whilst in the port of Brest, inasmuch as such accession was, in consequence of the paying off of many of her crew, necessary, as they thought, to her navigation.

It is equally a violation of the neutrality of the territorial

French Declaration of June 10, 1861. *Papers relating to the Treaty of Washington*, I. pp. 218—9. Instructions to the Lords Commissioners of the Admiralty, Jan. 31, 1862. *Papers relating to the Treaty of Washington*, I. 226. *Case of Great Britain, App.* II. pp. 83 et seqq.

but must receive no addition to combatant force. Moodie v. the ship " Phoebe Anne." 3 Dall. 319.

Distinction between navigability and fighting power. *U. S. Dipl. Corresp.* 1863, pp. 696, 715, 723. Mr Dayton to Mr Seward, Oct. 8, 1863, *U. S. Dipl. Corresp.* 1863, p. 715.

sovereign whether the persons enlisted by a belligerent cruiser in a neutral port be native citizens of the country, domiciled foreigners or even citizens of the enlisting Power. The American Foreign Enlistment Act of June, 1794, distinguished in favour of subjects of the enlisting state transiently within the United States, but the exception did not subsequently secure much approval.

Neutral Governments now very generally forbid the entry or at all events the sale of belligerent prizes within their ports. In strictness, however, it is in no way incumbent upon a neutral Government to forbid the purchase in its port of either a prize or of a belligerent vessel of war. The validity of the transfer need not, nevertheless, be admitted by the hostile belligerent Government.

"The neutral and belligerent," said Earl Russell in April, 1863, writing with respect to the sale of the Confederate steamer "Sumter" to a British subject at Gibraltar, "have distinct rights in the matter: the neutral has a right to acquire such property offered to him for purchase, but the belligerent may, in the particular circumstances of the case, not recognise the transfer of such property as being that of his enemy, only parted with to the neutral in order to protect it from capture on the high seas. The prize court of the belligerent, whose property so circumstanced is brought before it, decides whether the transfer is fair or fraudulent."

§ 67. It is not the duty of a neutral Government to restrain the purely commercial speculations of its subjects.

"The law of nations has never declared that a neutral state is bound to impede or diminish its own trade by municipal restrictions."

(a) *It is not the duty of a neutral Government to prevent contraband trading on the part of its subjects with any belligerent.*

"Our citizens," wrote Mr Jefferson in 1793, "have been always free to make, vend and export arms. It is the constant occupation and livelihood of some of them. To suppress their calling, the only means perhaps of their subsistence, because a war exists in foreign and distant countries, in which we have no concern, would scarcely be expected. It would be hard in principle and impossible in practice. The law of nations, therefore, respecting the rights of those at peace, does not require from them such an internal derangement in their occupations. It is satisfied with the external penalty pronounced in the President's proclamation, that of confiscation of such portion of these arms as shall fall into the hands of any of the belligerent powers on their way to the ports of their enemies. To this penalty our citizens are warned that they will be abandoned, and that even private contraventions may work no inequality between the parties at war; the benefit of them will be left equally free and open to all."

"We do not know," said Parsons, C. J., in *Richardson v. the Marine Insurance Company*, "of any rule established by the law of nations that the neutral shipper of goods contraband of war is an offender against his own sovereign, and liable to be punished by the municipal laws of his own country. When a neutral sovereign is notified of a declaration of war, he may, and usually does, notify his subjects of it, with orders to decline all contraband trade with the nations at war, declaring that, if they are taken in it, he cannot protect them, but not announcing the trade as a violation of his own laws. Should their sovereign offer to protect them, his conduct would be incompatible with his neutrality. And as, on the one hand, he cannot complain of the confiscation of his subjects' goods, so, on the other, the power at war *does not impute to him these practices of his subjects*."

These declarations clearly set out the practice which has hitherto commended itself to neutral Powers. Some few jurists have of late proposed to transfer the obligation to deal with contraband traders from the injuriously affected belligerent to the neutral sovereign, but the suggestion has

99: Snow, 443.
Seton v. Low, 1 John. 1.
Ex parte Chavasse,
L. J., N. S. Bankruptcy, 1.

Mr Jefferson to Mr Hammond, May 15, 1793.
Randolph, *Corresp. of Thomas Jefferson*, III. p. 234.

Richardson v. Marine Insurance Co., 6 Mass. 112.

Parsons, C. J., in Richardson v. Marine Insurance Co. Snow, 500.

Proposed transference of the duty of repression to neutral Govern-

ments hardly likely to be favourably entertained.
U. S. Dipl. Corresp. 1863, 1138.
R. Kleen, *De la Contrebande de la Guerre,* p. 43.
Revue de Droit Int. 1893.
M. Bar in the *Revue de Droit Int.* 1894, p. 401.
(*b*) Blockade running.
Papers relating to the Treaty of Washington, I. 247.

as yet secured but cool support, and is hardly likely to be welcome to the neutral Governments of great commercial communities, which would thereby be involved in responsibility for any failure in a duty, which the most costly, perfect and irritating system of police surveillance could not enable them effectively to fulfil.

(*b*) *It is not the duty of a neutral Government to prevent blockade-running on the part of its subjects.*

"The right of blockade is a belligerent right, and the enforcement of it belongs to the belligerent and not to neutral Powers."

The United States Government complained bitterly of the inaction of the British Government in respect of the extraordinary number of British vessels which engaged from British ports in running the blockade of the Southern ports, but Earl Russell resolutely declined to interfere. "It would be an unheard of measure," he wrote, "to prohibit merchants from sending ships to sea destined to the Southern ports. Should such ships attempt to violate the blockade capture and condemnation are the proper penalty of such attempts; no authority can be found for any other."

Earl Russell to Mr Adams, March 27, 1862.

So when the owners of the British ship "Helen" set up in answer to the claim of her master for wages the illegality of the agreement upon which suit was raised, it being an agreement for running the blockade of one of the

The "Helen," L. R. 1 A. and E. 1.

Southern ports, Dr Lushington overruled the plea, with the clear declaration, that principle, authority, and usage united in calling upon him to reject "the new doctrine that, to carry on trade with a blockaded port, is, or ought to be, a municipal offence by the law of nations." "It has never been," he said, "a part of admitted common usage that such voyages shall be deemed illegal by the neutral state, still less that the neutral state should be bound to prevent them; the belligerent has not a shadow of right to require more than universal usage has given him, and has no pretence to say to the neutral: 'You shall help me to enforce my belligerent

Dr Lushington in the "Helen."

right by curtailing your own freedom of commerce, and making that illegal by your own law which was not so before.'"

(c) *It is not the duty of a neutral Government to prevent its subjects from entering into public contracts with a belligerent.* The individual subject of the neutral state who engages in certain undertakings specially helpful to a belligerent subjects himself to punishment at the hands of the hostile belligerent, but it is no part of the duty of the neutral Government to interfere with his operations, so long as they are merely commercial.

"The laws of the United States," said President Pierce in 1854, "do not forbid their citizens to sell to either of the belligerent Powers articles contraband of war, or to take munitions of war or soldiers on board their private ships for transportation; and although in so doing the individual citizen exposes his property to some of the hazards of war, his acts do not involve any breach of national neutrality, nor of themselves implicate the Government. Thus, during the progress of the present war in Europe, our citizens have without national responsibility therefor sold gunpowder and arms to all buyers, regardless of the destination of these articles. Our merchantmen have been, and still continue to be, largely employed by Great Britain and France in transporting troops, provisions and munitions of war, to the principal seat of military operations, and in bringing home the sick and wounded soldiers; but such use of our mercantile marine is not interdicted either by the international or by our municipal law, and, therefore, does not compromise our neutral relations with Russia."

(d) *It is not the duty of a neutral Government to prevent the advancing of loans by its subjects to a belligerent.* In 1823 the British Law-officers, Christopher Robinson, Gifford and Copley, on consultation by Canning, expressed the view that subscriptions for the use of one of two belligerent states by individual subjects of a nation profess-

(c) Contracting for the belligerent service.
The "Atalanta," 6 C. Rob. 440.
The "Orozembo," *Ibid.* 430.
The "Rapid," Edwards, 228.

Message of President Pierce to Congress, December, 1854.

(d) Taking up of belligerent loans.
3 Wharton, *Dig.* 507.
The British law-officers on belligerent loans, 1823.

ing strict neutrality were inconsistent with that neutrality and
contrary to the law of nations, but that the other belligerent
would not have a right to consider such subscriptions as
constituting an act of hostility on the part of the Government, although they might afford just ground of complaint,
if carried to any considerable extent. With respect to loans,
if entered into merely with commercial views, they thought
that, according to the opinions of writers on the law of
nations and the practice which had prevailed, they would not
be an infringement of neutrality; but if, under colour of a
loan, a gratuitous contribution were afforded without interest,

Halleck, 1.
24, § 15 n.

or with merely nominal interest, the transaction would fall
under the same condemnation as the direct subscription.

   In *De Wütz v. Hendricks* it was declared to be contrary
to the law of nations for persons residing in Great Britain to
enter into engagements to raise money by way of loan for
the purpose of supporting subjects of a foreign state in arms
against a Government in alliance with Great Britain, and

De Wütz v.
Hendricks,
9 Moore,
586.

decided that a British court of justice must refuse assistance
to persons raising such loans. But the principle that no

Mr
Webster
asserts the
legality of
loans to
bellige-
rents by
indivi-
duals,
1842.

neutral Government is bound to interfere to prevent loans
by its subjects to foreign belligerents was clearly laid down by
Mr Webster in 1842. "As to advances and loans," he wrote,
"made by individuals to the Government of Texas or its
citizens, the Mexican Government hardly needs to be
informed that there is nothing unlawful in this, so long

Hall, IV. 3,
§ 216.

as Texas is at peace with the United States, and that these
are things which no Government undertakes to restrain."

Loans in
1854,
1862 and
1870.

   The Prussian Government in 1854 rejected the complaints
advanced by France against the floating of a Russian loan in
Berlin and Amsterdam.

   In 1862 it became known that it was proposed to raise a
large sum of money in Great Britain for the Confederate
Government on the security of cotton, which was to be
furnished at a price yielding enormous returns to the stock-
holders. It was noticed that, on the one hand, the cotton

could only reach the hands of purchasers by breach of the Southern blockade; on the other hand, the money raised was to be expended in the purchase of vessels and war-material. The attention of Earl Russell being called to the proceedings of the Confederate agents, he declined to interfere. "It is not contrary to law," he wrote to Mr Adams, "for Her Majesty's subjects to lend money, on securities or otherwise, to the persons administering the government of the Confederate States, nor to sell to that Government ordinary munitions of war." *U. S. Dipl. Corresp. 1863, 15, 648—653. Earl Russell to Mr Adams, March 9, 1863. U. S. Dipl. Corresp. 1863, 144.*

In 1870 the French Morgan loan was largely subscribed for in the British market.

The advance of money upon interest is in fact but a special form of ordinary trade.

§ 68. It is not the duty of a neutral Government to prevent its subjects from engaging abroad in the service of a belligerent.

It is not the duty of a neutral Government to prohibit the enlistment of its subjects in a belligerent service abroad. 3 Wharton, Dig. § 392.

The preventive responsibilities of the neutral Government are limited, broadly, to acts taking their rise within its territorial jurisdiction. While it is clearly the duty of a neutral Government to exercise reasonable diligence to prevent within its territorial jurisdiction the enlistment of men for a belligerent military or naval service, that duty in no way extends to such enlistment taking place beyond that jurisdiction. True a neutral Government may, and many Governments do, denounce municipal penalties against subjects enlisting in a belligerent public service abroad, but, except where specially bound by a treaty stipulation, no Government is internationally bound to interfere with the proceedings of its subjects beyond the limits of its territorial jurisdiction. The individual subject of the neutral Power who enlists in a belligerent public service deposits his neutral character, and subjects himself at the hands of the hostile belligerent to the treatment meted out to the subject of a belligerent Power, but otherwise he is not, in general punishable.

33 and 34 Vict. c. 90, s. 4. Schmauss, 1. 171, 906; ɪɪ. 1470.

U. S. v. Skinner, 2 Wheeler, C. C. 232. Stoughton v. Taylor, 2 Paine, 655.

CHAPTER III.

Subjects of a neutral state, who abstain from unneutral conduct, are exempt from interference on the score of the war.

§ **69. Subjects of a neutral State, who abstain from any interference in the course of the war, are entitled to continue as in time of peace, and unaffected in person or property by the operations of the contest, intercourse with any belligerent.**

Within the limits of the territorial jurisdiction of a neutral sovereign all persons, whatever their conduct, and all property, whatever its quality, must be held exempt from all direct belligerent interference. In respect of injury arising or threatened by such persons or such property a belligerent can only have recourse to the neutral ruler.

The sphere of individual action. Within neutral territorial jurisdiction the exemption of person and property is complete:

The "Immanuel," 2 C Rob. 197. De Wolf v. New York Fire Insurance Co. 20 John. 228. Ludlow v. Bowne, 1 John. 11.

The international obligation of this ruler in the way of prevention is, however, limited by considerations already stated. There remains a field of individual freedom of action limited within neutral territorial limits by the dictates of policy expressed in the terms of neutral municipal law, without those limits by general international practice.

Alike within and without the limits of neutral territorial jurisdiction it is clear law that all neutral individuals are entitled to continue after the outbreak of war, without interference in its regard, their ordinary peaceful avocations, such avocations being unconnected with the course of the contest, and the same exemption extends in general to neutral property, it being of an innoxious character or not purposed to be employed in a belligerent service.

Within the limits of neutral territorial jurisdiction the exemption is naturally complete. Without those limits the law is not less clear.

On the one hand, the neutral individual found upon belligerent soil cannot be legally compelled against his will to take part in war on behalf of a belligerent Government. "No state," wrote Lord Lyons in 1861, à propos of the attempt of the Confederate Government to enforce service in its armies on the part of resident foreigners, "can justly frame laws to compel aliens resident within its territories to serve against their will in armies ranged against each other in a civil war, and, a fortiori, in the absence of any such law they cannot enforce the service."

On the other hand, so long as he maintains an attitude of strict non-interference, the freedom of locomotion of the neutral subject must be left unimpaired except under stress of imperious military necessity. The resident alien shares, in fact, the lot of the belligerent non-combatants amongst whom he resides.

All property of innocent quality to which by reason of its origin or of the condition of its owners may be ascribed a bonâ fide neutral character is legally exempt from belligerent interference, even though it be found under the belligerent flag on the high seas.

(i) All non-contraband neutral property found on board a belligerent merchantman on the high seas or in belligerent territorial waters, it not being destined to a blockaded port, is exempt from seizure at the hands of the hostile belligerent. "Neutral goods, with the exception of contraband of war, are not liable to capture under an enemy's flag.",

(ii) All neutral property found by a belligerent on his own soil is entitled to the same treatment as in time of peace.

(iii) All neutral property found on hostile belligerent soil is liable to the treatment which befalls in similar case the property of the ordinary private subject of the hostile belligerent, that is to say, it is not confiscable, but is

Marginal notes: without the neutral jurisdiction it is equally clear. (1) No neutral individual is compellable to take personal part in war, Lord Lyons to H. M.'s Consuls in the Southern States, Nov. 12, 1861, U. S. Dipl. Corresp. 1864, I. p. 857. and, taking no part, he is entitled to exemption from belligerent interference. (2) Innocent neutral property is exempt from belligerent interference under the belligerent merchant flag on the high seas, Declaration of Paris, 1856, Art. 3. or on belligerent soil.

The right of Angary. *Daily News Correspondence of the War between Germany and France,* pp. 406—410.

Subjects of a neutral state guilty of unneutral conduct which does not call for the interference of their Government forfeit their neutral character beyond the limits of neutral territorial protection.

The "Immanuel," 2 C. Rob. 186. The "Anna Catharina," 4 C. Rob. 107. The "Rendsborg," *Ibid.* 121.

obnoxious to the mere accidents of war, and is liable to the exercise of the belligerent rights of requisition, contribution and the billeting of troops. On December 25, 1870, six English colliers lying in the Seine off Duclair were sunk by the Prussians to prevent the operations of French gunboats. Count Bismarck at once admitted the claim of the owners for full compensation in respect of this exercise of what is known as the belligerent right of Angary, and only justified the Prussian action on the ground of strict military necessity.

§ 70. Subjects of a neutral state, who interfere in the course of a war, if dispunishable by their neutral Government, may, beyond the limits of neutral national protection, be dealt with by the assailed belligerent as having deposited their neutral and assumed a hostile character.

In respect of their unneutral conduct on neutral soil or within neutral territorial waters neutral individuals are punishable by the neutral sovereign, and by him only. Neutral individuals accordingly, who engage in proceedings which do not call for the exercise of the preventive powers of their neutral ruler, however injurious may be the effect of their acts upon the cause of one or the other belligerent, escape all legal liability in respect of those acts, so long as they remain within the neutral territorial jurisdiction or under the neutral flag of war. But a neutral individual, who, beyond the area of neutral national protection, by person or property directly assists any belligerent in his warfare, thereby exposes himself to hostile treatment at the hands of the opposing belligerent.

(*a*) Neutral individuals who enlist in a belligerent public service or otherwise assist a belligerent thereby deposit their neutral character.

§ 71. (*a*) A belligerent may treat as hostile any individual who, beyond the bounds of neutral territorial jurisdiction, enlists in the public military or naval service of the hostile Power, or, otherwise than by such actual enlistment, actively in person assists that Power in its warfare.

The position of a neutral individual enlisting in a belligerent service beyond the neutral jurisdiction may be thus defined.

(1) The neutral individual commits no international
offence. The Executive Directory in October 1798 decreed
the punishment of death against all neutrals taking commissions from or serving on board the vessels of an enemy of
France, but this bloodthirsty edict was speedily recalled, and
the Directory has found no imitators. The foreign volunteer
is, it is universally admitted, internationally a lawful
combatant.

*Martens,
Recueil,* vi.
775.

(2) A neutral state may under its municipal law impose
penalties on subjects enlisting in a belligerent service
abroad, as on those who so enlist at home, but it is under no
international obligation so to do.

Stat. 33 and
34 Vict. c. 90,
s. 4.

(3) A belligerent state is free to accept the services of
neutral individuals voluntarily tendered within its jurisdiction.

The United States Government in 1862–3 vindicated its
right to enlist, and frankly admitted its practice of enlisting,
on United States soil foreign volunteers for the United
States army and navy. The British Government in appearing to require a contrary practice asked, as Mr Adams well
said, " more than has ever been suggested under any theory
of international law, and directly the opposite of what it has
been heretofore in the habit of practising itself."

Mr Adams
to Earl
Russell,
Apr. 25,
1863.
*U. S. Dipl.
Corresp.*
1863, p. 234.

" The United States," wrote Mr Seward, " do not deny,
but, on the contrary, they avow that voluntary immigration
is a cardinal element of their prosperity. They invite and
encourage it, but only by lawful means. The army and
the navy, as well as the occupations of civil life, whether in
time of peace or war, are open always to immigrants, as they
are to all other classes of competent persons who may desire
to volunteer on their arrival within the country, or at any
time afterwards, but not until they have arrived on our
shores and identified themselves with the masses who are
subject to our jurisdiction and laws."

*U. S. Dipl.
Corresp.*
1863, p. 16.

(4) The assailed belligerent may treat the foreign
volunteer as having deposited his neutral character.

13—2

The neutral individual, in fine, who, beyond the bounds of neutral territorial jurisdiction, enlists in a belligerent public service, or, otherwise than by such actual enlistment, actively in person assists a belligerent in his warfare, thereby assumes in respect of the opposing belligerent the international liabilities of a subject of the assisted Power in like case.

(b) Neutral property embarked in a belligerent public service assumes the belligerent character.

#§ 72. (b) **A belligerent may treat as hostile any property which is embarked by its neutral owner in the public service of the opposing belligerent.**

The best illustrations of unneutral service are commonly afforded by the operations of neutral masters and shipowners.

The "Commercen," 1 Wheat. 392.

#(1) A neutral vessel advisedly employed by its owner in the conveyance of belligerent public despatches is confiscable at the hands of the opposing belligerent.

(1) Neutral vessels conveying belligerent public despatches.

Within the description of public despatches fall "all official communications of official persons on the public affairs of the Government."

The "Atalanta," 6 C. Rob. 440.
The "Constantin," and the "Susan," 6 C. Rob. 461 n.
The "Hope," 6 C. Rob. 463 n.

The willing transport of such documents on behalf of a belligerent is clear cause of hostile condemnation of the vessel and in certain cases of the cargo.

The "Atalanta," a Bremen ship with a cargo of coffee and sugar from Batavia, was captured on July 14, 1807, by a British privateer. On search being made amongst luggage on board, there was found in the chest belonging to one of the supercargoes a packet addressed to the Minister of Marine at Paris by the French Commandant of the Isle de France, where the vessel had been unnecessarily delayed. Circumstances pointing to the falsehood of the denial by the master and supercargoes of knowledge of the character of the transaction in which the vessel was thus employed, Sir W. Scott condemned both ship and cargo. "It is a service," said he, "which in whatever degree it exists, can only be considered in one character, as an act of the most noxious and hostile nature."

What is a "public despatch"?

Sir W. Scott in the "Caroline," 6 C. Rob. 465.

The conveyance of such despatches is good ground of confiscation.

The "Atalanta," 6 C. Rob. 440.

The con-

To establish the offence against the vessel it is sufficient

to show guilty knowledge on the part of her master, who is naturally the agent of the owner. To involve the cargo evidence must be further forthcoming to connect its proprietors with the transaction, the master not being necessarily an agent in its regard.

veyance to involve condemnation must be advised.
The "Susan," 6 C. Rob. 461 n.

Not every advised transportation of belligerent public despatches is, however, good cause of condemnation. A belligerent is entitled to keep up innocent communications with neutral countries, and neutral vessels employed in conveying despatches between a belligerent Government and its public agents in such neutral countries are entitled to a presumption in favour of the innocence of the transaction in which they are engaged.

The "Hope," Ibid. 463 n.
A belligerent is entitled to maintain innocent communication with neutral states,

The "Caroline" (Doah) being taken on April 1, 1808, on her voyage from New York to Bordeaux with despatches from the French Minister and the French Consul in the United States to their own Government, Sir W. Scott decreed restitution. This was not, he said, a case of despatches coming from any part of the enemy's territory, whose commerce and communications of every kind the other belligerent had a right to intercept. These despatches were from persons who were, in a peculiar manner, the favourite objects of the protection of the law of nations, ambassadors resident in a neutral country for the purpose of preserving the relations of amity between that state and their own Government. The neutral country has a right to preserve its relations with the enemy, and you are not at liberty to conclude, that any communication between them can partake in any degree of the nature of hostility against you."

The "Caroline," 6 C. Rob. 461.
The "Madison," Edwards, 224.
The "Rapid," Ibid. 228.

Sir W. Scott in the "Caroline," 6 C. Rob. 466.

The carrier of a noxious public despatch received on board at a neutral port, and addressed to a neutral or open belligerent port, may thus be fairly held entitled to a presumption in favour of his ignorance of the nature of the packet so taken.

and the carrier of a despatch received at a neutral port is entitled to a favourable presumption.

So in the case of the "Rapid," an American vessel

captured whilst carrying from New York a despatch addressed to the Dutch Colonial Minister at the Hague, but under cover to a commercial house at Tonningen, the port of discharge of the ship, Sir W. Scott admitted the denial by the American master of all knowledge of the character of the incriminating papers, and decreed restitution.

(2) *A neutral vessel employed as a belligerent transport is confiscable at the hands of the hostile belligerent.*

For the ascription of the character of a belligerent transport it is sufficient that the vessel be in fact "hired by Government to do such acts as shall be imposed upon them in the military service of the state," the mere form of hiring and the fact that she was or was not employed in the *immediate active* service of the belligerent being of comparatively little moment.

Thus the "Friendship," an American neutral vessel captured in 1807 whilst on a voyage from Baltimore and Annapolis to Bordeaux, was condemned by Sir W. Scott as a French transport, although the terms of the charter party under which her passengers were conveyed were not forthcoming and a few bales of merchandise were likewise carried, it being proved that, with the exception of a single American subject and five French merchants, the passengers, ninety in number, were French military officers and mariners shipped by the French Minister Plenipotentiary in the United States at the expense of the French Government, and travelling as members of a French disciplined force.

So, too, the mere number of persons carried is in no way decisive of the character of the employment.

The "Orozembo," an American neutral vessel, having discharged a cargo at Rotterdam, proceeded thence in ballast immediately to Lisbon, under a charter party with a merchant at Lisbon "to proceed in ballast to Macao and there take a cargo for America." At Lisbon, she was, under the direction of the charterer, fitted up for the reception of three Dutch

The "Rapid," Edwards, 228.

(2) Neutral vessels employed as belligerent transports.
The "Carolina," 4 C. Rob. 256.
The "Friendship," 6 C. Rob. 420.
The "Orozembo," *Ibid.* 430.
The "Carlo Alberto," Martens, *Causes Célèbres,* v. 535.
The "Commercen," 1 Wheat. 382.
What is a "transport"?
Sir W. Scott in the "Friendship," 6 C. Rob. 425.
Form of hiring, and manner of employment, inconclusive :
The "Friendship," 6 C. Rob. 420.
so, too, number of persons carried.
The "Orozembo," 6 C. Rob. 430.

military officers of distinction and two persons in civil departments in the Government of the Dutch possession of Batavia, who had come from Holland to take their passage to Batavia under the appointment of the Government of Holland. There were twelve other passengers, namely, a lady and a party of servants. The vessel being taken on her outward voyage from Lisbon by a British cruiser, Sir W. Scott condemned her on the broad general ground of unneutral employment in the Dutch transport service. "To send out a veteran general of France to take the command of the forces at Batavia might be a much more noxious act than the conveyance of a whole regiment."

Sir W. Scott in the "Orozembo," 6 C. Rob. 434.

In February 1864 the Confederate Government issued certain regulations to carry into effect an act previously passed "to impose regulations upon the foreign commerce of the Confederate States, to provide for the public defence," in virtue of which the owners of all vessels sailing with cargoes from Southern ports were required to give up one half the tonnage of their vessels at a fixed freight for the use of the Confederate Government both on the outward and homeward voyage, and were required to enter into a bond for the speedy return of the vessels so engaged to Confederate ports with cargoes of a particular character.

The affair of the Confederate regulated trade.

U. S. Dipl. Corresp. 1863, p. 608.

Mr Adams intimated to Earl Russell that this proceeding, taken in all its parts, must be regarded as placing British subjects and British ships engaged in the affected trade in the category of allies and servants of the insurgents, and that persons in this position must be held enemies to the United States, and treated accordingly. Earl Russell protested against this conclusion, but, in view of the strict and comprehensive character of the Confederate regulations, the action of the U. S. Government would seem to have been reasonably well grounded.

U. S. Dipl. Corresp. 1864, p. 634.

U. S. Dipl. Corresp. 1864, II. p. 183.

If a neutral vessel be in fact employed as a belligerent transport, the innocent intent of its owner or master will not purge the service of its unneutral character, and even the

The innocence of the master

affords no defence for a vessel *de facto* employed as a belligerent transport. The "Orozembo," 6 C. Rob. 434. The "Carolina" (Nordquist), 4 C. Rob. 260.

plea of actual compulsion exercised by the belligerent will furnish no defence against confiscation by the enemy. If any loss is sustained by a neutral in yielding to the demands for unneutral service made upon him by a belligerent, he must look for reparation to the Government exercising the improper force and not to the mercy of that Government against whom he is compelled to serve.

(c) Neutral property found at sea, being contraband, is confiscable.

§ 73. (c) **A belligerent may treat as hostile property all contraband merchandise found by him on its way to his enemy under the trading flag on the high seas or within belligerent waters.**

What is contraband?

There is no universally received definition of contraband.

The Anglo-American practice. *De Jure Belli ac Pacis*, III. 1.

The "Peterhoff," 5 Wall. 28, 58. The "Jonge Margaretha," 1 C. Rob. 189. The "Edward," 4 C. Rob. 68. The "Ranger," 6 C. Rob. 125. The "Commercen," 1 Wheat. 388. The rule of "Occasional contraband." Sir W. Scott in the "Jonge Margaretha."

It is clear law that certain goods, on account of their value for the furtherance of belligerent operations, may, as *contraband*, be seized and confiscated by a belligerent when found by him at sea in course of transport to his enemy. Unfortunately, however, it is necessary to lay it down as the first principle of the existing Law of Contraband of War, that: *there is as yet no universally accepted definition of Contraband*. The Anglo-American practice rests upon a distribution of subjects of traffic suggested by Grotius. Distinguishing articles of merchandise as being (1) useful only for war, (2) of no warlike use, and (3) of ambiguous nature, Anglo-American authorities class things useful only for war as in all cases contraband, dismiss articles of no warlike use as in all cases subjects of innocent traffic, and determine in each individual case the character of articles of ambiguous use (*ancipitis usus*) as contraband or non-contraband by the special circumstances of their particular situation.

Thus provisions, being articles of ambiguous use, are not generally contraband, but may become so under circumstances arising out of the particular situation of the war. In determining their character the Courts will take into consideration such facts as whether they are native products of the country exporting them, whether they are in their natural or in a manufactured state, and whether they are intended for ordinary or for military or naval consumption, the main test in this last regard being the character of their port of destination. So in the case of the " Frau Margaretha " on July 25, 1805, Dutch cheese on a voyage from Amsterdam to Quimper was held by Sir W. Scott not to fall within the definition of contraband, whilst on the following day Dutch cheese, fit for naval stores, going on a voyage from Amsterdam to Corunna on the " Zelden Rust " was condemned as contraband on account of the proximity of its destination to the naval port of Ferrol.

The Anglo-American practice is varied in certain cases by the exercise of an asserted belligerent right of Preemption, or compulsory purchase of neutral merchandise. If the right be asserted over property of an innoxious character it constitutes undoubtedly an arbitrary extension of belligerent power at the expense of neutral owners, and in this guise is very properly condemned, but, if it consist in the substitution of purchase where confiscation would be legally justifiable, it may well be held legitimate as an actual mitigation of belligerent war right.

In 1864 the British Government found it necessary to protest against the exercise by the Government of the United States under an Act of Congress of an assumed right to appropriate to national purposes before actual condemnation in a prize court any captured neutral vessel, subject to compensation to the owners should the capture be subsequently pronounced illegal by the court.

Great Britain and the United States have not been alone in their appreciation of the belligerent value of the principle of " Occasional Contraband."

In 1885 the French Government intimated to the Governments of Great Britain and Germany that, in view of the conditions under which war was then being carried on by France with China, the Government of the Republic had determined henceforth, during that contest, to treat rice as contraband of war. Earl Granville, whilst admitting that particular consignments of rice might under the special

The "Commercen," 1 Wheat. 388.
The "Apollo," 4 C. Rob. 158.
The "Twee Juffrowen," Ibid. 242.
The "Evert," Ibid. 354.
The "Welvaart," 1 C. Rob. 195 n.
The "Neptunus," 3 C. Rob. 108.
The "Twende Brodre," 4 C. Rob. 33.
The "Frau Margaretha," 6 C. Rob. 92.
The "Zelden Rust," Ibid. 93.
The practice of preemption.
Stat. 27 and 28 Vict. c. 25, s. 38.
Gessner, Droit des Neutres, p. 132.
The "Sarah Christina," 1 C. Rob. 237.
U. S. Dipl. Corresp. 1864, II. 715.
France declares rice contraband, 1885.

circumstances of their destination be fairly treated as contra-

Parl.
Papers,
France, No.
1 (1885).
Revue de
Droit Int.
1885, p. 149.

band, deemed it necessary to protest against the doctrine that it was for the belligerent to decide what was or was not contraband of war, regardless of the well-established rights of neutrals.

An objection to the Anglo-American practice. It is perhaps not altogether surprising that a war-practice seemingly so elastic as is that of the United States and Great Britain should be regarded with marked disfavour by the jurists of countries which, like the Powers of the Armed Neutralities, have evinced a strong inclination to establish a final definition of contraband. The principle of "Contraband by Circumstances," it may be argued with a sufficient show of reason, covers a fair compromise between the conflicting rights of belligerent Government and neutral trader at the *moment of capture*, but no maritime practice involving confiscation as contraband of neutral merchandise found on the high seas can be strictly just, which does not rest upon circumstances actually or potentially within the knowledge of the lader at the *time of lading*. The neutral shipper in his home port cannot fairly be deemed potentially cognisant of all the circumstances, which will determine the decision of an English or American Prize Court at a subsequent period as to the classification of an article of ambiguous use as contraband or non-contraband, and, unless he be so cognisant, he cannot with any real appearance of justice be visited with condemnation.

Its defence. On the other hand, it is urged on behalf of the Anglo-American practice, that:—

(1) It is practically impossible to determine a list even of arms and war material for all time, since the progress of scientific discovery must from time to time render obsolete old, and bring into the field new, warlike agents. "It is the *usus bellici* which determine an article to be contraband, and as articles come into use as implements of war, which were before innocent, there is truth in the remark, that as the means of war vary and shift from time to time, the law

shifts with them; not, indeed, by the change of principles, but by a change in the application of them to new cases, and in order to meet the varying uses of war." Kent, *Int. Law* (ed. Abdy), c. 9, p. 359.

(2) The injurious character of traffic can only be fairly measured by its special circumstances. The supply of coal to a belligerent may, for example, at one time have no bearing on the course of war: at another it may be more injurious to the cause of the enemy than would be the furnishing of actual arms.

On the whole, it seems clear that the laying down of a permanent definition of contraband at once universally accepted, completely comprehensive and universally applicable is, if practicable, a consummation to be desired. Its practicability has, however, as yet to be proved[1]. A permanent definition of contraband desirable, if possible.

Subject to the definition of contraband it is clear law that the supply of contraband of war to a belligerent is an offence against the opposing belligerent, which may be visited with punishment by the confiscation of the incriminated goods. In Anglo-American practice the penalty is extended to non-contraband property of the same owner found in association with the contraband articles, and in certain cases to the vessel, even though the property of a distinct owner. The penalty of contraband trading is belligerent confiscation.

The "Staadt Embden," 1 C. Rob. 26. The "Ringende Jacob," *Ibid.* 90. The "Mercurius," *Ibid.* 288 n. The "Jonge Tobias," *Ibid.* 329. The "Neutralitet," 3 C. Rob. 295. The "Franklin," *Ibid.* 217. The "Peterhoff," 5 Wall. 28.

"According to the modern law of nations, for there has been some relaxation in practice from the strictness of the ancient rules, the carriage of contraband goods to the enemy subjects them, if captured *in delicto*, to the penalty of confiscation; but the vessel and the remaining cargo, if they do not belong to the owner of the contraband goods, are not subject to the same penalty. The penalty is applied to the latter, only when there has been some actual cooperation, on

---

[1] Perhaps the most satisfactory definition hitherto suggested is that proposed by M. Kleen: "Sont réputées contrebande de guerre les munitions de guerre *proprement dites*, c'est-à-dire les objets qui, expressément faits pour la guerre et y servant dans leur état actuel immédiatement et spécialement, sont sujets à saisie, s'ils sont livrés à un ennemi." R. Kleen, *De la Contrebande de Guerre*, p. 19. Conf. M. Kleen in the *Revue de Droit International*, 1893. But see also *Revue de Droit Int.* 1894, p. 401.

their part, in a meditated fraud upon the belligerents; by covering up the voyage under false papers, and with a false destination."

§ 74. A belligerent destination is of the essence of contraband.

"The rule respecting contraband, as I have always understood it," said Sir W. Scott in the case of the "Imina," "is that the articles must be taken *in delicto*, in the actual prosecution of the voyage to an enemy's port."

This consideration is *per se* decisive of the contention advanced by Mr Seward in the case of the "Trent."

On November 8, 1861, the "Trent," a British packet employed in carrying the London mails between Havana and St Thomas, was brought to, whilst on the high seas in the Bahama Channel, by the U.S. war-steamer, "San Jacinto," Captain Wilkes, when four of her passengers, Messrs Slidell, Mason, McFarland and Eustis, the two former being envoys accredited by the Confederate States to the Courts of Paris and London, the two latter their secretaries, were, after a sufficient display of force, carried off by the American, and lodged in Fort Warren, a military prison in Boston harbour.

The immediate liberation of the prisoners and an apology for "an act of violence which was an affront to the British flag and a violation of international law" was at once demanded by Earl Russell.

Mr Seward, the American Secretary, was materially hampered by the view of the incident taken in the United States, the action of Captain Wilkes having secured not only the emphatic approval of the Secretary of the U.S. Naval Department, but the reward of the public thanks of Congress, while popular feeling in the North ran enthusiastically on the same side.

The argument adopted by the U.S. Secretary shows clear marks of the situation. Whilst repudiating in the name of the U.S. Government any original authorisation or suggestion of the proceedings of Captain Wilkes, he advanced the contention that the four prisoners might well have been legally carried off from the "Trent" in pursuance of the ordinary belligerent right of search for and capture of contraband, and grounded his consent to their immediate release on the simple technicality that the American commander, after capturing the, in his view, contraband persons, did not send the vessel herself into port for adjudication, but allowed her to proceed, and thereby prevented the judicial examination of the legality of the capture which should properly have taken place.

Mr Seward to Lord Lyons, Dec. 26, 1861.

The contention is effectually disposed of by two distinct considerations.

(1) There was absolutely no authority for the treatment of *persons*, or at any rate of free civilians, as contraband of war.

(1) Non-military persons are not contraband.

The carriage by a neutral shipowner of persons of a certain class, viz. persons in the military or naval service of a belligerent, had been generally recognised as an act of un-neutral service, and as such justifying the condemnation in the prize court of the belligerent of the property employed by the neutral in the transaction, and in one or two treaties *soldiers* by a loose usage of language had been referred to as contraband of war.

The "Friendship," 6 C. Rob. 420. The "Orozembo," *Ibid.* 430. Treaty of Commerce between U.S. and the Netherlands, 1782, Art. 24. Jenkinson, *Treaties,* III. 307.

But (i) Messrs Slidell and Mason and their secretaries were not persons of this dangerous class : they were mere civil servants. As ambassadors, they might indeed have been arrested if found on belligerent soil, but there was absolutely no authority for the arrest of an ambassador under the neutral flag.

Case of Marshal Belleisle, Martens, *Causes Célèbres,* II. I.

The suggestion that they were bearers of despatches may be set aside, as no such despatches were found on board the "Trent," and no search was made for them.

The "Trent" was not a belligerent transport.

(ii) There was no special hiring of the vessel, such as would have been necessary to constitute the "Trent" a belligerent transport. The Commissioners came on board the "Trent" as ordinary passengers at ordinary fares in the

The "Friendship," 6 C. Rob. 425.

ordinary way at a neutral port, the ordinary place of call of the packet.

(2) The commissioners were destined to a neutral port.

(2) The Commissioners were not on their way to belligerent, but *bonâ fide* to neutral, territory. They came on board at a neutral port, they were sailing directly for a neutral port, and their final destination was neutral soil. And a belligerent destination is of the essence of contraband.

What, however, is the "destination" of goods? Real and assumed destination of the *vessel* distinguishable.

The "Franklin," 3 C. Rob. 217.

The "Edward," 4 C. Rob. 68. Destination of *cargo* distinguishable from destination of *ship.* The "Doctrine of Continuous Voyages."

The "Polly," 2 C. Rob. 360. The "Maria," 5 C. Rob. 365. The "William," 5 C. Rob. 385. The "Thomyris," Edwards, 17. The "Ebenezer," 6 C. Rob. 250. Its early statement.

The neutrality of the nominal port of discharge of the vessel is not, however, to be taken as conclusive as to the destination of either vessel or cargo. In 1801 in the case of the "Franklin," a Prussian ship going with a cargo of hemp and iron from Lübeck ostensibly to Lisbon, but actually, as was inferred from the place of seizure and course of the voyage, to Bilboa, Sir W. Scott after mature deliberation declared it to be a settled rule of law in the British Court of Admiralty that the carriage of contraband with a false destination would work a condemnation of the ship as well as of the cargo. So the "Edward," a Prussian ship from Bordeaux with a cargo of wines ostensibly for Embden, but taken whilst pursuing a course for Brest, was with her cargo condemned.

In the early days of the present century, under the name of the "Doctrine of Continuous Voyages," the British Courts, dealing with cases of attempted breach of regulation forbidding traffic on the part of neutrals between belligerent colonies and belligerent home ports, laid down the rule that the interposition of an intermediate port of nominal discharge between port of lading and port of final destination did not alter the illegitimate character of a voyage which was conceived of as one by the lader at the time of lading.

"The truth," said Sir W. Grant, "may not always be discernible, but when it is discovered, it is according to the truth and not according to the fiction, that we are to give to the transaction its character and denomination. If the voyage from the place of lading be not really ended, it matters not by what acts the party may have evinced his desire of making it appear to have ended. That these acts have been attended with trouble and expense cannot alter their quality or their effect. The trouble and expense may weigh as circumstances of evidence to show the purpose for which the acts were done; but if the evasive purpose be admitted or proved, we can never be bound to accept as a substitute for the observance of the law, the means, however operose, which have been employed to cover a breach of it."

In 1816 in the case of the "Commercen" Story, J., employed language suggestive of the application of the doctrine of continuous voyages to contraband trading. "It is well argued," he said, "that the doctrine of contraband cannot apply to the present case, because the destination was to a neutral country; and it is certainly true that goods *destined for the use of a neutral country* can never be deemed contraband whatever may be their character, or however well adapted to warlike purposes. But, if such goods are destined for the direct and avowed use of the enemy's army or navy, we should be glad to see an authority which countenances this exemption from forfeiture, even though the property of a neutral. Suppose, in time of war, a British fleet were lying in a neutral port, would it be lawful for a neutral to carry provisions or munitions of war thither, avowedly for the exclusive supply of such fleet? Would it not be a direct interposition in the war, and an essential aid to the enemy in his hostile preparations? In such a case the goods, even if belonging to a neutral, would have had the taint of contraband in its most offensive character, on account of their destination; and the *mere interposition of a neutral port would not protect them from forfeiture.*"

During the American Civil War the Northern Courts applied this principle of reference to the *ultimate* destination of *the goods* to deal with the numerous contraband traders, who traded with the Confederates through Matamoras on the Mexican side of the Rio Grande or by running the blockade of the Southern seaboard from various British West Indian

Marginalia: Sir W. Grant in the "William," 5 C. Rob. 396. Its suggested. Story, J., in the "Commercen," 1 Wheat. 388. and actual extension to contraband trading.

208   NEUTRALITY.   Part IV.

The "Bermuda," 3 Wall. 551.
The "Springbok," 5 Wall. 1.
The "Peterhoff," Ibid. 28.

ports, the goods being in this latter case commonly transshipped in the intermediate neutral harbour to swift steamers of light draught specially constructed for the navigation of the Southern waters. Not only were vessels captured on the voyage to the American mainland from Nassau and elsewhere in the West Indies condemned as contraband traders, but the like fate befell vessels taken on the outward voyage from England to West Indian and Mexican ports, even where the port in question was the final destination of *the ship.*

The "Stephen Hart," Blatchford, *Pr. Ca.* 387.

The "Stephen Hart," a British schooner, was captured by a Northern man-of-war on January 29, 1862, when off the coast of Florida about 25 miles from Key West, bound from London to Cardenas in Cuba with a cargo of munitions of war and army supplies.

Statement by Betts, J., of the doctrine as applied to contraband.

Betts, J., condemned both vessel and cargo. "The commerce," said he, "is in the destination and intended use of the property laden on board of the vessel, and not in the incidental, auxiliary and temporary voyage of the vessel, which may be but one of many carriers through which the property is to reach its true and original destination. If this were not the rule of the prize law, a very wide door would be open for fraud and evasion.....The law seeks out the truth, and never, in any of its branches, tolerates any such fiction as that under which it is sought to shield the vessel and her cargo in the present case. If the guilty intention, that the contraband goods should reach a port of the enemy, existed when such goods left their English port, that guilty intention cannot be obliterated by the innocent intention of stopping at a neutral port on the way. If there be, in stopping at such port, no intention of transshipping the cargo, and if it is to proceed to the enemy's country in the same vessel in which it came from England, of course there can be no purpose of lawful neutral commerce at the neutral port by the sale or use of the cargo in the market there; and the sole purpose of stopping at the neutral port must merely be to have upon the papers of the vessel an ostensible neutral terminus for the voyage. If, on the other hand, the object of stopping at the neutral port be to transship the cargo to another vessel to be transported to a port of the enemy, while the vessel in which it was brought from England does not proceed to the port of the enemy, there is equally an absence of all lawful neutral commerce at the neutral port; and the only commerce carried on in the case is that of the transportation of the contraband cargo from the English port to the port of the enemy, as was intended when it left the English port. "This court holds that, in all such cases, the transportation or *voyage of the contraband goods* is to be considered as a unit, from the port of lading to the port of delivery in the enemy's country; that if any part of such voyage or transportation be unlawful, it is unlawful throughout; and that the vessel and her cargo are subject to capture; as well before arriving at the first neutral port at which she touches after her departure from England, as on the voyage or transportation by sea from such neutral port to the port of the enemy." *Betts, J. in the "Stephen Hart," Snow, 514.*

This judgment does indeed appear to represent but a logical extension of the principle laid down by Grant and Scott, but the doctrine so administered provides the belligerent with a legal engine of immense power, and opens up a wide vista of possible unjustifiable and oppressive restriction of special branches of neutral industry and commerce. *Its effect.*

§ 75. The offence of the contraband carrier is deposited with the discharge of the noxious cargo.

The offence of the contraband carrier is deposited with the discharge of the cargo.

In order that the penalty of belligerent confiscation may attach it is essential that the contraband carrier be surprised *in delicto*, and, the offence being primarily one of the cargo, it is universally admitted that the liability of the carrier is discharged with the discharge of the noxious merchandise, and he is not legally punishable if subsequently taken. *The "Imina," 3 C. Rob. 168.*

(d) Neutral property engaged in blockade-running is confiscable at the hands of the blockading belligerent.

§ 76. (d) **A belligerent may treat as hostile all neutral property taken whilst employed in the breach of his lawfully instituted blockade.**

"It is unnecessary for me to observe," said Sir W. Scott in the case of the "Columbia," "that there is no rule of the law of nations more established than this that the breach of a blockade subjects the property so employed to confiscation. Among all the contradictory positions that have been advanced on the law of nations, this principle has never been disputed: it is to be found in all books of law, and in all treaties; every man knows it; the subjects of all states know it, as it is universally acknowledged by all governments who possess any degree of civil knowledge."

Sir William Scott in the "Columbia," 1 C. Rob. 154.

Definition of a blockade.

A blockade may be defined as the maritime investment by a belligerent of a port or other portion of coast in the possession of his enemy by which all communication by sea with the invested area is interrupted. It is a "sort of circumvallation round a place, by which all foreign connexion and correspondence is, as far as human force can effect it, to be entirely cut off."

Sir W. Scott in the "Vrouw Judith," 1 C. Rob. 151.

M'Call v. Marine Insurance Co. 8 Cranch 65.

The right of a belligerent to institute such a measure is universally recognised. The penalty incurred by its breach is equally well established.

The blockade-runner is not liable to personal punishment.

In 1864 the British Government found it necessary to complain to the Government of the United States of the personal detention of British subjects captured on vessels running the Southern blockade. In reply Mr Seward repudiated any intention on the part of the U.S. authorities to detain *bonâ fide* neutral subjects by way of punishment, but, while claiming the right to deal more strictly with American citizens, he justified the detention of even *bonâ fide* neutral individuals to secure their presence as witnesses in the necessary prize court proceedings. Whether under the head of detention as necessary witnesses or in consequence of suspicions as to their real national character many British subjects would appear to have undergone periods of im-

U. S. Dipl. Corresp. 1864, 11. 609, 621, 630.

Ibid. pp. 610, 613, 623, 698.

prisonment of considerable duration, and the remonstrances of Lord Lyons were earnest and frequent.

In general, however, it is well established law that the punishment of the blockade-runner is, at most, legally restricted to the confiscation of vessel and cargo. The offence is primarily an offence of the ship, but the cargo is commonly equally involved.

The "Adonis," 5 C. Rob. 256.

"It is true," said the Court in condemning the cargo of the "Alexander," a neutral vessel captured on April 3, 1801, on a voyage from Lisbon ostensibly to Altona, but in reality to the blockaded port of Havre, "that the owners of the cargo are not, in general cases, held to be affected by the act of the master, unless he is specially appointed their agent: but it would be impossible to maintain a blockade in cases of this nature, which is directed more against the cargo than against ships, if the Court did not draw the inference, that a ship going in fraudulently is going in the service of the cargo, with the knowledge and by the direction of the owner."

The "Alexander," 4 C. Rob. 93.

The owner of goods captured on board a blockade-runner can only escape the effects of the adverse presumption by express proof that (1) he might fairly be expected to be, and was actually in fact, ignorant of the existence of the blockade, and that (2) he had not constituted the master his agent. Goods belonging to the shipowner are in any case confiscable, under the Anglo-American practice, by virtue of the doctrine of infection.

The "Mercurius," 1 C. Rob. 84. U. S. v. Guillem, 11 How. 47. (i) A blockade to be binding must be real. Radcliff v. Mutual Ins. Co. 7 John. 48. The "Mercurius," 1 C. Rob. 83.

§ 77.   (i) A blockade to be binding must be real.

In order that a neutral may be penally affected with the consequences of blockade-running it is legally essential that there be a blockade in *fact*. A mere proclamation of blockade unsupported by the presence of an actual blockading force, *i.e.* a "paper blockade," is in no way binding upon a neutral.

The "Betsey," *Ibid.* 93. (ii) A blockade to be binding must be effective. Declaration of Paris, 1856, Art. 4.

§ 78.   (ii) A blockade to be binding must be effective.

A block-
ade to be
binding
must be
main-
tained
by an
adequate
force
3 Wharton,
Dig. 370.

1. The presence of an adequate force is an absolutely
essential condition for the existence of a valid blockade. The
Powers of the Armed Neutralities required for the validity
of a blockade that it should be maintained by vessels
"anchored and sufficiently near" to make the attempt to
enter manifestly dangerous. In the Convention with Great
Britain of 1801 Russia accepted the alternative condition
that the blockading ships be "anchored or sufficiently near."
The plenipotentiaries at Paris were content to demand merely
that the blockade be "maintained by a force sufficient really
to prevent access to the coast of the enemy."

The "Cir-
cassian,"
2 Wall. 135.

A blockade may in certain cases be effectively maintained
by land batteries, and it would seem that even the actual
physical blocking of a water channel is not illegitimate,
provided that the obstructions employed be not of a nature
calculated permanently to injure the channel as a highway

3 Wharton,
Dig. 381.
exercising
reason-
able vigi-
lance.

of commerce. Much indignation was aroused in Great
Britain and elsewhere in 1862 by the action of the Northern
Government in sinking vessels laden with stone in one of the

The
"Juffrow
Maria
Schroeder,"3
C. Rob. 147.
The
"Christina
Marga-
retha," 6 C.
Rob. 62.
Sir W. Scott
in the
"Juffrow
Maria
Schroeder."

entrances of Charleston harbour, but the protest against this
"stone blockade" addressed by Lord Lyons to Mr Seward
was confined to the point of permanency.

2. Not only must the force employed be reasonably
adequate for the purpose set out, but the actual blockaders
must exercise a reasonable vigilance in the execution of their
commission.

Permis-
sive entry
of vessels
will in-
validate a
blockade.
The
"Rolla," 6
C. Rob. 372.

A blockade of Havre and other ports of the Seine was
ordered by the British Government in February, 1798, and
nominally maintained for many months. So loose, however,
was the investment that many neutral vessels were allowed
to pass in and out without hindrance. The "Juffrow Maria

A block-
ade ceases
with its
effective
mainten-
ance.
The "Nep-
tunus," 1 C.
Rob. 171.

Schroeder," a Prussian vessel, went into Havre unmolested
in May, 1799, and quitted the port in June without seeing
any ship for forty-eight hours. She being subsequently on
June 14 taken off the North Foreland and proceeded against
for a breach of blockade, Sir W. Scott decreed restitution.

" If," said he, " the ships stationed on the spot to keep up the blockade will not use their force for that purpose, it is impossible for a court of justice to say, there was a blockade actually existing at that time, so as to bind this vessel."

The permissive entry by the blockaders of vessels not specially privileged by law will thus invalidate a blockade otherwise lawfully instituted.

A blockade, in fact, originally actually and effectually established ceases to be binding with the cessation of its effective maintenance. Mr Seward in 1861 ventured to contend that the blockade established by the Federals upon the port of Charleston and duly notified to neutral Powers must be held to be continually in effect until notice of its relinquishment should be given by the President of the United States, and that in spite of the temporary absence of blockading vessels. The contention was, however, rightly repelled by Earl Russell. The continuity of a valid blockade is not, indeed, legally interrupted by the momentary absence of the blockading vessels in consequence of a merely accidental or unavoidable circumstance, such, for example, as the pursuit for a reasonable distance of a blockade-runner or stress of weather. " The law considers an attempt to take advantage of such an accidental removal as an attempt to break the blockade, and as a mere fraud." But the withdrawal, even though temporary, of the blockading squadron for other employments, or in consequence of the approach of superior hostile force, operates to raise the blockade, so as to render a new notification necessary on its resumption.

§ 79. (iii) A blockade to be binding must be authoritatively instituted.

The " Rolla," an American vessel, being proceeded against for a violation of the blockade of Monte Video in November, 1806, it was urged, amongst other grounds of defence, by the claimants, that the blockade in question was imposed without competent authority, having originated in the unauthorised

The "Vrow Johanna," 2 C. Rob. 109.
The " Neptunus," 2 C. Rob. 114.
Mr Seward to Lord Lyons, May 27, 1861.
Bernard, *Neutrality of Great Britain*, 238
Continuity of blockade not broken by momentary accidental or unavoidable absence,
Radcliff v. United Ins. Co. 7 John. 54.
The " Frederick Molke," 1 C. Rob. 87.
The " Columbia," *Ibid.* 154.
Sir W. Scott in the " Columbia," 1 C. Rob. 136.
but a withdrawal in consequence of belligerent force raises the blockade.
The " Triheten,' 6 C. Rob. 65.
The " Hoffnung," *Ibid.* 112.
The " Nancy," 1 Acton, 57.
(iii) A blockade to be binding must be authoritatively instituted. State authority may be indirectly or

proceedings of the British Commander, Sir Home Popham, only, and without any communication from his Government. Sir W. Scott ruled that, however irregularly Sir Home Popham might have acted towards his own Government in undertaking an unauthorised expedition, the blockade could not be impeached by other Powers on the ground of insufficient authority. "On stations in Europe, where Government is almost at hand to superintend and direct the course of operations under which it may be expedient that particular hostilities should be carried on, it may be different. But in distant parts of the world it cannot be disputed, I conceive, that a commander must be held to carry with him sufficient authority to act as well against the commerce of the enemy as against the enemy himself for the more immediate purpose of reduction."

Directly or indirectly, however, a blockade must to be binding be established under State authorisation.

§ 80. (iv) To justify belligerent confiscation the fact of the existence of the blockade must have been, prior to the act of breach, actually or potentially within the knowledge of the neutral owner.

To justify the condemnation of the blockade-runner the neutral owner must, it is universally agreed, be affected with knowledge of the existence of the blockade actually infringed. Practice is not, however, uniform as to the extent of evidence which is required to establish the guilty knowledge. The approved Continental practice demands that, before seizure as a blockade-runner, a neutral vessel should in every case have been previously specially notified of the existence of the blockade and warned off by a vessel of the blockading squadron, the fact being attested by an entry upon the papers of the neutral ship.

According to the Anglo-American rule the neutral trader may be affected with knowledge of the existence of a blockade either by reason of a public notification of its establishment given by the Government of the blockading squadron to

---

The "Rolla," 6 C. Rob. 364. directly given, but must in some form be present. Sir W. Scott in the "Rolla." (iv) To justify condemnation the blockade-runner must be affected with knowledge of the existence of the blockade. Radcliff v. United Ins. Co. 7 John. 47. How may knowledge be proved? Continental practice requires an individual warning on the spot. Gessner, Droit des Neutres, p. 179. Revue de Droit Int. 1878, p. 400. The Anglo-American practice accepts (1) a diplomatic notification,

neutral Governments, *or* by a special notice given to the trader himself in some reasonably authoritative manner.

In order that a neutral subject may be held responsible under a public notification given to his Government, it is requisite that (1) a reasonable time have been permitted to elapse for the communication of the notification by the neutral Government to its subjects, and (2) the statements of the public notification be fully borne out by the facts of the actual blockade. In determining the period which can be deemed reasonably sufficient for the percolation of the notice, the Anglo-American Courts specially provide for the case of vessels sailing from their home ports before the issue of the public notification.

"A blockade may," however, "exist without a public declaration; although a declaration unsupported by fact will not be sufficient to establish it."

"It is certainly necessary," said Sir W. Scott in the case of the "Vrouw Judith" in 1799, "that a blockade should be intimated to neutral merchants in some way or other. It may be notified in a public and solemn manner, by declaration to foreign governments; and this mode would always be most desirable, although it is sometimes omitted in practice; but it may commence also *de facto*, by a blockading force giving notice on the spot to those who come from a distance and who may be ignorant of the fact." In the case of blockades commenced by naval commanders without express authorisation any notification must necessarily be, at least in the early days of the blockade, special. But even when a blockade has been *de facto* established without notification, a special warning off is not judged requisite by the Anglo-American Courts, when the vessel can otherwise be affected with knowledge of the existence of the blockade. And in the case of vessels sailing *out* of a port, when a reasonable period has elapsed after the establishment of a *de facto* blockade upon it, no special warning is deemed by these Courts necessary. A neutral

The "Neptunus," 2 C. Rob. 110. Wharton, *Dig*. 367. The "Mercurius," 1 C. Rob. 82. The "Vrouw Judith," 1 C. Rob. 152. The "Jonge Petronella," 2 C. Rob. 131. The "Calypso," *Ibid*. 298. The "Henrick & Maria," 1 C. Rob. 146. The "Franciska," 10 Moore, P. C. C. 59.

or (2) special warning. A blockade may commence *de facto* without diplomatic notification, but Sir W. Scott in the "Mercurius," 1 C. Rob. 82, Sir W. Scott in the "Vrouw Judith," 1 C. Rob. 152. in that case a special notification should ordinarily be given. The "Columbia," 1 C. Rob. 156. The "Prize Cases," 2 Black 635. The "Vrouw Judith," 1 C. Rob. 150. The existence of knowledge may

be established by
(3) proof
of public
notoriety,

The
"Tutela," 6
C. Rob. 177.
The "Franciska," 10
Moore, P.
C. C. 57.
but such
knowledge
must be
reasonably
authentic.
The "Franciska," 10
Moore,
P. C. C. 58.
The
"Adelaide,"
2 C. Rob.
111 n.

(v) To
justify
condemnation
there
must be
an overt
act of
violation
of the
blockade.
Instances
of privileged
communication
with
blockaded
areas:
1. Neutral
vessels
already
in port.

The
"Vrouw
Judith," 1
C. Rob. 150.
The "Neptunus,"
Ibid. 171.
Olivera v.
Union
Insurance
Co. 3
Wheaton,
194.
Limitation of
the privilege.

will, in fact, according to the Anglo-American practice, be deemed to be in certain cases affected with guilty knowledge by proof of the public notoriety of the existence of a blockade. "If a blockade *de facto* be good in law," said the Court in the case of the "Franciska," "without notification, and a wilful violation of a known legal blockade be punishable with confiscation—propositions which are free from doubt— the mode in which the knowledge has been acquired by the offender, if it be clearly proved to exist, cannot be of importance." To induce legal responsibility, however, knowledge acquired by public notoriety must be reasonably authentic. A public notification to one neutral Government will, after the lapse of a reasonable period, affect by public notoriety subjects of Governments not in receipt of notice.

§ 81. (v) To justify belligerent confiscation there must have been on the part of the vessel some overt act of violation of the blockade.

Certain vessels are by general international practice allowed to pass the lines of a blockading squadron. Thus

1. Neutral vessels already within a port at the time of the establishment of a hostile blockade upon it are permitted to come out within a reasonable period with cargo laden before the establishment of the blockade. But the term of stay must not be excessive, and any attempt to bring out cargo laden after, though purchased before, the institution of the blockade will induce confiscation. So, when a Prussian neutral vessel, which was in the Texel when the British on June 11, 1798 notified a blockade, proceeded, instead of withdrawing, to lade a cargo consisting of Portuguese property purchased before the notification, with which cargo she was taken when quitting port on September 7, Sir W. Scott decreed condemnation.

The rule of exemption extends to merchandise sent in before the blockade and withdrawn *bonâ fide* by its neutral proprietor on the institution of the blockade. But no neutral merchantman can set up any legal claim to enter a port after the institution of a blockade upon it, even though the entry be merely for the purpose of bringing away property purchased by a neutral merchant before the establishment of the blockade.

2. Neutral men-of-war are permitted to communicate with blockaded ports, and to maintain intercourse between their own or any other neutral Government on the one side and neutral consular or diplomatic agents in the port on the other.

The limits of neutral right in this regard were, however, well pointed out in a Circular of Vice-Admiral Milne in 1863 occasioned by the action of the British Acting Consul at Mobile in sending out a large amount of Confederate specie through the Northern blockading lines on H.M.'s ship "Vesuvius." "I deem it right to point out to the officers in command of ships under my orders that even communications by neutral ships-of-war with a blockaded port are permissive only, to be regarded as a relaxation of the more rigid rule of war which formerly obtained, and which would probably be again reverted to in a great maritime war; and, further, that ships of war so communicating are not invested with a shadow of right to embark any property with the object of passing the blockade."

3. Neutral vessels in distress are permitted to seek the shelter of a blockaded port, when recourse thither is absolutely and unavoidably necessary. The plea of distress is, however, strictly scrutinised, and "nothing less than an unavoidable necessity which admits of no compromise and cannot be resisted" will be accepted as sufficient to justify the passing of the blockading lines. So the plea of fear of danger within a blockaded port will not be lightly received in excuse for the egress of a neutral vessel.

With the exception of such specially privileged communications any attempt on the part of a neutral vessel at entrance into or egress from a blockaded port is deemed an infringement of the blockade, and as such visited with condemnation.

The "Vrouw Judith," 1 C. Rob. 151.
The "Calypso," 2 C. Rob. 298.
The "Neptunus," 1 C. Rob. 170.
The "Juffrow Maria Schroeder," 4 C. Rob. 89 n.
The "Comet," Edwards, 32.

2. Neutral men-of-war.
3 Wharton, Dig. 375, 386.
Limits of the privilege.
U. S. Dipl. Corresp. 1863, 119, 129, 446, 460.
Circular of Vice-Admiral Milne, Feb. 16, 1863.
U. S. Dipl. Corresp. 1863, p. 474.

3. Neutral vessels en relâche forcée.
The "Charlotta," Edwards, 252.
Radcliff v. Unit. Ins. Co. 7 John. 55.
The "Diana," 7 Wall. 354.
The "Hurtige Hane," 2 C. Rob. 124.
The "Fortuna," 5 C. Rob. 27.
The "Neutralitet," 6 C. Rob. 30.
The "Charlotte Christine," Ibid. 101.
The "Gute Erwartung," Ibid. 182.

To constitute an infringement of the blockade, however, the entrance or exit must be by a channel under the control of the blockading squadron, and communication may accordingly be innocently kept up with a blockaded place by land carriage or by interior unblockaded waterways.

So where goods, ordered by neutral merchants in the blockaded port of Amsterdam with an original purpose of forwarding them to London, were despatched from Amsterdam by internal canal navigation to the open neutral port of Embden, and there shipped, restitution was decreed.

The blockade is infringed whether goods be introduced within or brought out of the invested area by the incriminated vessel herself or by boats, such as lighters, acting in conjunction with her.

According to the Anglo-American practice the bare fact of sailing with intent to enter a blockaded port with knowledge of the existence of a blockade thereon is, in general, deemed an overt act of violation and as such cause of condemnation, and when a public notification has been issued to neutral Governments the onus of proof is upon the master or owner alleging the absence of guilty intent. The plea of sailing with an intent to enter contingent on discovery by inquiry *at the port* that the blockade is raised will be rejected.

This practice was pushed to its furthest limits by the American Courts in the case of the " Springbok."

The " Springbok," which left London for Nassau on December 9, 1862, was on February 3, 1863, when about 150 miles from her port of destination and on the direct route for it, captured by the Federal cruiser " Sonoma," and taken in for adjudication. Of her cargo valued at £66,000 goods to the value of £700 only were contraband of war. In the District Court of New York Justice Betts condemned both ship and cargo on the ground that the vessel was at the moment of capture laden in whole or part with contraband of war, and that the real destination of ship and cargo was not the neutral port of Nassau, but some port regularly blockaded by the forces of the United States, the blockade being intended to be broken. The Supreme Court on appeal released the vessel on the ground that her papers, which were regular and showed no sign of fraud, set out a destination for the neutral port of Nassau, and no evidence connected her owners with interest in or knowledge of the irregular destination of the cargo. The condemnation of the entire cargo was, however, affirmed. "Upon the whole case," said the Court, "we cannot doubt that the cargo was originally shipped with intent to violate the blockade; that the owners of the cargo intended that it should be trans-shipped at Nassau into some vessel more likely to succeed in running safely to a blockaded port than the Springbok: that the voyage from London to the blockaded port was, as to cargo, both in law and in the interest of the parties, one voyage; and that the liability to condemnation, if captured during any part of that voyage, attached to the cargo from the time of sailing."

This judgment which imports the declaration that non-contraband merchandise on board a neutral vessel, which is sailing on a *bonâ fide* voyage from one neutral port to another, may be condemned in respect of the *presumed* intention on the part of the owners of the merchandise that it shall ultimately be conveyed on board *another vessel* through the blockade of some *indefinite* belligerent port, has been most strongly and wellnigh universally condemned, and can probably be now unhesitatingly set aside as a mere curiosity in legal history, worthless as a precedent.

§ 82. (vi) To justify belligerent confiscation, the blockade-runner must be taken *in delicto*.

Continental authorities hold the offence of the blockade-runner to be deposited by safe escape after egress through the lines of the blockading squadron. The Anglo-American practice is more strict.

The "Welvaart van Pillaw," a Prussian vessel, escaped

Marginal notes:

Maryland Insur. Co. v. Wood, 6 Cranch 29; 7 Cranch 402. The "Neptunus," 2 C. Rob. 110. The "Posten," 1 C. Rob. 335 n. The "Spes" and the "Irene," 5 C. Rob. 76. The "Cheshire," 3 Wall. 231. The case of the "Springbok." The "Springbok," 5 Wall. t. Blatchford, Pr. Ca. 380, 434. 3 Wharton, Dig. 394. Revue de Droit Int. 1875, p. 241; 1882, p. 328. 3 Wharton, Dig. 396.

(vi) To justify condemnation the blockade-runner must be taken *in delicto*.

Divergence of Continental and Anglo-American practice. Gessner, p. 213; Heffter, II. § 156, n. 11. Bluntschli, § 836. The "Welvaart van Pillaw," 2 C. Rob. 128. The "General Hamilton," 6 C. Rob. 61. The "Wren," 6 Wall. 532.

in March through the squadron blockading the port of
Amsterdam, and was captured in the following April off
Dungeness by a British cruiser. Sir W. Scott ruled that
her successful egress constituted no defence against condemnation as a blockade-runner during the course of the
same voyage. "If the principle is sound, that a neutral
vessel is not at liberty to come out of a blockaded port with
a cargo, I know no other natural termination of the offence
but the end of the voyage....Being of opinion that the
principle is sound, I shall hold, that if a ship, that has
broken a blockade, is taken in any part of that voyage, she

The
'Welvaart
van Pillaw,"
2 C. Rob.
128.

is taken *in delicto*, and subject to confiscation." In virtue
of this practice a vessel may be dealt with as a blockade-
runner if taken either on her outward or homeward voyage,

The
'Lisette," 6
C. Rob. 387.

provided that at the time of capture the blockade infringed
be still maintained.

(c) A
belligerent
may treat
as hostile
neutral
property
withdrawn
from the
exercise of
his lawful
belligerent
rights.

§ 83. (e) **A belligerent may treat as hostile, property which
is fraudulently or forcibly withdrawn from the exercise of his
lawful belligerent rights.**

Whilst the general freedom of neutral commerce from
belligerent interference is now universally recognised, it is
equally generally admitted that a belligerent has the right
to satisfy himself by actual visit and search of the innocence
of the traffic carried on with his opponent by merchantmen
flying the neutral flag. The neutral flag, amongst signatories
of the Declaration of Paris, now protects on the high seas
even belligerent property found thereunder, provided such
property be not contraband nor destined for a blockaded
port. But a belligerent is still entitled to ascertain by visit
and search the genuineness of the neutral character assumed
by the vessel, and to guard himself against the operations of

Confisca-
tion is
incurred
by

contraband traders and blockade-runners. Any proceeding
which is calculated to obstruct him in the exercise of this
right calls for due chastisement.

1. Resist-
ance to
search.

1. Actual forcible resistance to belligerent search offered
by a neutral merchantman constitutes in itself, it is well

agreed, a cause of condemnation at the hands of the belligerent.

The Baltic Powers at the close of the 18th century set up a claim to defeat or vary the belligerent right by the presence of neutral convoy, the declaration of the convoying officer as to the innocence of the cargoes under his protection being asserted to be a sufficient substitute for actual visit and search. Great Britain, however, repelled the contention, and finally vindicated the right of search of merchantmen even under convoy, at least as exercised by *men-of-war.* "The only security known to the law of nations upon this subject," said Sir W. Scott in the "Maria," one of several merchantmen of a Swedish convoy which in 1798 resisted British search in the Channel, "independent of all special covenant, is the right of personal visitation and search to be exercised by those who have the interest in making it....The penalty for the violent contravention of this right is the confiscation of the property so withheld from visitation and search."

2. The forcible rescue or attempted rescue of neutral property *bonâ fide* taken possession of by a belligerent works a similar condemnation. So the "Dispatch," a neutral Danish ship, being rescued out of the hands of a British prize master by her Danish captain and crew, was with her cargo condemned by Sir W. Scott on the ground of the parties having "declared themselves enemies by this act of hostile opposition to lawful enquiry."

3. Concealment or destruction of papers in the presence of a belligerent vessel is by some Powers held to be *per se* good cause of condemnation of a neutral vessel: in British maritime practice it is not instantly fatal, but is deemed to generate a most unfavourable presumption, property escaping from its effects only as "by fire."

§ 84. For loss occasioned by the acts of a belligerent proceeding in the regular and *bonâ fide* exercise of his belligerent rights a neutral individual has no valid international claim to redress.

The "Maria," 1 C. Rob. 340.
The "Elsabe," 4 C. Rob. 403.
No privilege obtained, by convoy. Walker, *Science of Int. Law,* p. 310. Martens, *Recueil, Supplément.* II. 347 et seqq.
The "Maria," 1 C. Rob. 340. Martens, *Supplément,* II. 476. Sir W. Scott in the "Maria," 1 C. Rob. 362.

2. Attempted rescue. The "Dispatch," 3 C. Rob. 278.

3. Destruction of papers. Livingston v. Maryland Ins. Co. 7 Cranch 545. The "Hunter," 1 Dods. 486. The "Two Brothers," 1 C. Rob. 131. The "Rising Sun," 2 C. Rob. 104. The "Pizarro," 2 Wheat. 227. Sir W. Scott in the "Hunter."

A neutral has no legal remedy in respect of loss by the regular exercise of belligerent rights.

A belligerent cruiser which with probable causes seizes a neutral vessel and takes her in for adjudication, proceeding regularly, is not a wrong-doer, and accordingly is not liable in damages, although the vessel be released. A capture made in good faith and on reasonable grounds of suspicion can furnish no matter of valid international complaint, and a *bonae fidei* possessor under such a capture is not liable for merely accidental injuries suffered by the captured property

whilst in his possession, so long as he is guilty of no irregularity. In the case of the "Carolina," a Swedish neutral vessel which had been compulsorily engaged in the transport of French troops to Alexandria, and which was captured on leaving that port by a vessel of the British fleet, it was held that, the original seizure being justifiable, the captors were in no way responsible for the subsequent loss of the ship whilst in their possession, such loss being the

result of accident and stress of weather. So in the case of the "Maria" and the "Vrow Johanna" in 1803, when goods lawfully seized by a captor and stored by him in warehouses under order of the Court were thence stolen by burglars, it was held that the captor, having used due diligence in the keeping of the goods, was not responsible

to the owners in respect of the loss. "In all countries, under whatever system of police," remarked Sir W. Scott, " thieves break through and steal."

§ 85. For loss occasioned by wrongful proceedings on the part of a belligerent, whether by original unjustifiable seizure and detention or by misconduct subsequent upon an original justifiable capture, the neutral individual has a valid international claim to redress.

When a capture is not originally justifiable the captor is answerable for any damage happening to the prize when in his possession. Moreover a belligerent originally a *bonae fidei* possessor may by the subsequent misconduct of himself or his agent forfeit the protection of his fair title and become responsible for losses suffered by the neutral proprietor.

Thus when "Der Mohr," a neutral vessel on her voyage from Surinam to Altona, was sent to port by H. M. S. "Captor," and lost in coming through the Needles in consequence of the misconduct of the prize-master, Sir W. Scott decreed restitution in value, including freight, against the captors, although the original seizure was perfectly justifiable and the conduct of the captors themselves was altogether unexceptionable.

The "Betsey," 1 C. Rob. 93. The "Peacock," 4 C. Rob. 185. "De Fire Damer," 5 C. Rob. 357. The "William," 6 C. Rob. 316. "Der Mohr," 3 C. Rob. 129; 4 C. Rob. 314.

So, if a belligerent in good faith destroy as hostile property which is actually neutral, "the act of destruction cannot be justified to the neutral owner, by the gravest importance of such an act to the public service of the captor's own state; to the neutral it can only be justified, under any such circumstances, by a full restitution in value."

A belligerent is responsible for destruction of neutral property. The "Felicity," 2 Dods. 381.

Redress must, according to the doctrine of the British Courts in the case of the "Mentor," be primarily sought from the actual wrong-doer.

Sir W. Scott in the "Felicity," 2 Dods. 386. Redress must be sought primarily from the actual wrong-doer,

In 1783 the "Mentor," an American vessel on her voyage from Havannah to Philadelphia, was destroyed by the "Centurion" and the "Vulture," two vessels of Admiral Digby's squadron cruising off the Delaware. Hostilities between Great Britain and the United States had at the time ceased, but both parties were in complete ignorance of the fact. Subsequently a suit was raised by the American owners in the British Court of Admiralty against the commanders of the British vessels, but the action was dismissed. Ten years later a new suit was commenced in the same Court against Admiral Digby, as the superior officer in command of the station where the wrong was done, but Sir W. Scott, whilst admitting the hardship of the case, discharged Admiral Digby from the effect of the monition, and ruled that the actual wrong-doer was the only person who could in that Court be held responsible, and that if an earlier erroneous decision had been given an appeal ought to have been presented to a higher Court.

The "Mentor," 1 C. Rob. 179.

but his Govern-ment may save him harmless.

It is for the wrong-doer's Government, should it deem it proper, to save him harmless, by assuming direct responsibility.

The "Acteon," 2 Dods. 52.

§ 86.   **The measure of redress due to the injured proprietor is, in general, the measure of the deprivation suffered.**

The measure of legal redress is, in general, *restitutio in integrum.*

"The natural rule is," said Sir W. Scott in the case of the "Acteon," an American vessel which with a valuable cargo was destroyed by Captain Capel of H. M. S. "La Hogue" in May 1813, when on her voyage from Cadiz to Boston under British licence, "that, if a party be unjustly deprived of his property, he ought to be put as nearly as possible in the same state as he was before the deprivation took place; technically speaking, he is entitled to restitution, with costs and damages. This is the general rule upon the subject, but like other general rules it must be subject to modification. If, for instance, any circumstances appear which shew that the suffering party has himself furnished occasion for the capture, if he has by his own conduct in some degree contributed to the loss, then he is entitled to a somewhat less degree of compensation, to what is technically called simple restitution. This is the general rule of law applicable to cases of this description, and the modification to which it is subject. Neither does it make any difference whether the party inflicting the injury has acted from improper motive or otherwise. If the captor has been guilty of no wilful misconduct, but has acted from error and mistake only, the suffering party is still entitled to full compensation, provided, as I before observed, he has not by any conduct of his own contributed to the loss."

The "Acteon," 2 Dods. 48.

Sir W. Scott in the "Acteon," 2 Dods. 51.

INDEX.

W.   15

W.